METHODS FOR EXODUS

Methods for Exodus is a textbook on biblical methodology. The book introduces readers to six distinct methodologies that aid in the interpretation of
the book of Exodus: literary and rhetorical, genre, source and redaction, liberation, feminist, and postcolonial criticisms. Describing each methodology,
the volume also explores how the different methods relate to and complement one another. Each chapter includes a summary of the hermeneutical
presuppositions of a particular method with a summary of the impact of the
method on the interpretation of the book of Exodus. In addition, Exodus 1–2
and 19–20 are used to illustrate the application of each method to specific
texts. The book is unique in offering a broad methodological discussion with
all illustrations centered on the book of Exodus.

Thomas B. Dozeman is professor of theology at the United Theological
Seminary in Dayton. He has written extensively on the book of Exodus and
the Pentateuch in general and is the author of *God on the Mountain: A Study
of Redaction, Theology and Canon in Exodus 19–24; God at War: Power in
the Exodus Tradition; The Commentary on Numbers* in the New Interpreters
Bible; *The Commentary on Exodus* in the Eerdman's Critical Commentary
series; *Holiness and Ministry: A Biblical Theology of Ordination*, and, with
Konrad Schmid, *A Farewell to the Yahwist? The Interpretation of the Pentateuch
in Contemporary European Scholarship*.

METHODS IN BIBLICAL INTERPRETATION

The *Methods in Biblical Interpretation* (MBI) series introduces students and general readers to both older and emerging methodologies for understanding the Hebrew Scriptures and the New Testament. Newer methods brought about by the globalization of biblical studies and by concerns with the "world in front of the text" – like new historicism, feminist criticism, postcolonial/liberationist criticism, and rhetorical criticism – are well represented in the series. "Classical" methods that fall under the more traditional historical-critical banner – such as source criticism, form criticism, and redaction criticism – are also covered, though always with an understanding of how their interactions with emerging methodologies and new archaeological discoveries have affected their interpretive uses.

An MBI volume contains separate chapters from six different well-known scholars. Each scholar first elucidates the history and purposes of an interpretive method, then outlines the promise of the method in the context of a single biblical book, and finally shows the method "in action" by applying it to a specific biblical passage. The results serve as a primer for understanding different methods within the shared space of common texts, enabling real, comparative analysis for students, clergy, and anyone interested in a deeper and broader understanding of the Bible. A glossary of key terms, the translation of all ancient languages, and an annotated bibliography – arranged by method – help new, serious readers navigate the difficult but rewarding field of biblical interpretation.

Volumes in the series

Methods for Exodus, edited by Thomas B. Dozeman
Methods for the Psalms, edited by Esther Marie Menn
Methods for Matthew, edited by Mark Allan Powell
Methods for Luke, edited by Joel B. Green

Methods for Exodus

Edited by

THOMAS B. DOZEMAN
United Theological Seminary

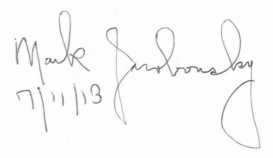

CAMBRIDGE
UNIVERSITY PRESS

CAMBRIDGE UNIVERSITY PRESS
Cambridge, New York, Melbourne, Madrid, Cape Town, Singapore,
São Paulo, Delhi, Dubai, Tokyo

Cambridge University Press
32 Avenue of the Americas, New York, NY 10013-2473, USA

www.cambridge.org
Information on this title: www.cambridge.org/9780521710015

First published 2010

Printed in the United States of America

A catalog record for this publication is available from the British Library.

Library of Congress Cataloging in Publication data

Methods for Exodus / edited by Thomas B. Dozeman.
p.   cm. – (Methods in biblical interpretation)
Includes bibliographical references and index.
ISBN 978-0-521-88367-2 (hardback) – ISBN 978-0-521-71001-5 (pbk.)
1. Bible. O.T. Exodus – Hermeneutics.   2. Bible. O.T. Exodus – Criticism, interpretation, etc.
I. Dozeman, Thomas B. II. Title. III. Series.
BS1245.52M48   2010
224′.406–dc22   2009023308

ISBN   978-0-521-88367-2 Hardback
ISBN   978-0-521-71001-5 Paperback

Contents

Contributors   *page* ix

Preface: Methods in Biblical Interpretation   xi

    Introduction   1
    Thomas B. Dozeman

1   **Literary and Rhetorical Criticism**   13
    Dennis T. Olson

2   **Genre Criticism**   55
    Kenton L. Sparks

3   **Source and Redaction Criticism**   95
    Suzanne Boorer

4   **Liberation Criticism**   131
    Jorge Pixley

5   **Feminist Criticism**   163
    Naomi Steinberg

6   **Postcolonial Biblical Criticism**   193
    Gale A. Yee

Glossary   235

Name Index   241

Scripture Index   247

Contributors

Suzanne Boorer, Senior Lecturer in Old Testament Theology, Murdoch University

Thomas B. Dozeman, Professor, Old Testament, United Theological Seminary

Dennis T. Olson, Charles T. Haley Professor of Old Testament Theology, Biblical Studies, Princeton Theological Seminary

Jorge Pixley, Seminario Teologico Bautista-Managua

Kenton L. Sparks, Professor of Biblical Studies, Eastern University

Naomi Steinberg, Associate Professor, Religious Studies, DePaul University

Gale A. Yee, Nancy W. King Professor of Biblical Studies, Episcopal Divinity School

Preface: Methods in Biblical Interpretation

BACKGROUND

From the mid-nineteenth century until the 1980s, the historical-critical method dominated the study of the Hebrew Bible and New Testament. A legacy of J. P. Gabler, Friedrich Schleiermacher, Julius Wellhausen, and their immediate intellectual heirs as well as of philologists studying nonbiblical ancient texts, the historical-critical method can best be understood as an unproblematic quest for the provenance of scripture. A product of Enlightenment thinking, it attempts to find the "true," original political and social contexts in which the Bible was created, redacted, and first heard and read.

The "linguistic turn" – or, the use-and-abuse of different critical theoretical approaches to texts – was relatively late coming in the scholarly interpretation of the Bible. When, in the 1970s, biblical scholars began experimenting with methodologies borrowed from philosophy, anthropology, and literary studies, the results were at times creative and invigorating, as theoreticians demonstrated how biblical texts could yield new ethical, political, aesthetic, and theological meanings. Sometimes, valuable older interpretations that had been effaced for many years by historical-critical concerns were recovered. Frequently, however, the results also could be painfully derivative and the authors' motivations transparent. Students' and scholars' strange vocabulary and obfuscations couldn't hide unexamined political and theological (or antitheological) commitments.

Thanks to the globalization of biblical studies and the emergence of concerns rooted in issues related to ethnicity, gender, economics, and cultural history, the quest for the Bible's meaning has intensified and proliferated. Both within the academy and within a larger, more inter-connected, religiously inquisitive world, the methodologies used to study biblical texts have multiplied and become more rigorous and sophisti-cated. Their borders may be porous, as a single scholar may work with two or more methodologies, but several schools of criticism in biblical studies are now established and growing. Interest in new historicism, feminist criticism, rhetorical criticism, postcolonial/liberationist criti-cism, and several other methodologies that focus on the "world in front of the text" consistently has provided paradigm-shifting questions as well as contingent, but compelling, answers. This is not to say that older historical-critical scholarship has simply evaporated. Most scholarship in the United States, and an even larger majority of work done in Europe, still falls comfortably under the historical-critical banner. So, the practice of "Classic" historical approaches, like source criticism, form criticism, and redaction criticism, is still widespread, though much of their findings have been altered by coming into contact with the emerging methodolo-gies as well as by new archaeological discoveries.

RATIONALE

What, then, is needed at this time is a group of short books that would introduce the best work from within these various schools of criticism to seminarians, graduate students, scholars, and interested clergy. *Methods in Biblical Interpretation* aims to fill that need.

The key to reaching the full, wider spectrum of this readership is to build these books around the most widely studied books of the Bible, using the best possible writers and scholars to explain and even advocate for a given perspective. That is, rather than long, separate introductions to methodological "schools," like Postcolonial Criticism, Rhetorical Crit-icism, Source Criticism, and so on, *Methods in Biblical Interpretation* publishes separate, shorter texts on the most popular biblical books of the canon, with chapters from six leading proponents of different schools of interpretation.

DESCRIPTION

In order to make the volumes truly introductory, comparative, *and* original, each of the chapters is divided into two parts. The first part of the chapter introduces to students the given method, a bit of its history, and its suitability and promise for the entire book under discussion. This part gestures toward various ideas and possibilities of how this particular methodological approach might interact at various points with the biblical book.

The second part of the chapter, building on the background material presented in the first, then shows the method "in action," so to speak. It achieves that by asking each contributor to focus this second part of the chapter on one of two passages from within the biblical book. The comparative and pedagogical value of this second section of each chapter allows students to view different methods' interactions with the same biblical verses.

The two-part chapters offer opportunities for scholars both to explain a methodology to students and then to demonstrate its effectiveness and cogency, that is, the chapters do not merely offer bland, shallow overviews of how a theory might work. Subjective, opinionated scholarship, especially in the second half of each chapter, is in full display. Authors, however, also have written their contributions for a student and general audience, and thus have explained and distilled theoretical insights for the uninitiated. So, lucidity and accessibility are equally manifest.

Each of the *Methods of Biblical Interpretation* volumes also contains an annotated bibliography, arranged by methodology, and placed at the end of the book. Such material, as well as a short glossary, provides students with tools to understand the application of any given theory or methodology and further investigate the history of its development.

It is not desired, nor probably even possible, to have the same methodologies included in every volume of the series. Certain biblical books lend themselves much more easily to certain forms of criticism (e.g., rhetorical criticism and Paul's letters; narrative criticism and the synoptic Gospels). Therefore, there is some flexibility on which methods will be included in a volume. The selected methods depend, of course, on the choice of

contributors and are determined by the volume editor in consultation
with Cambridge University Press. Such flexibility helps ensure that the
best people, writing the most exciting and compelling scholarship, are
contributing to germane volumes. Following these considerations, the
series aims to have half of the essays closely related to historical-critical
work and half devoted to more recently emerging methodologies.

It is hoped that these carefully structured volumes will provide students
and others with both a sense of the excitement involved in such a wide
spectrum of approaches to the Bible and a guide for fully making use of
them.

Introduction

THE GOALS OF THE BOOK

Methods for Exodus is intended to be a textbook for students on biblical methodology. We have two aims in writing this book. Our first goal is to introduce six distinct methodologies that aid in the interpretation of the book of Exodus. The six methodologies are literary and rhetorical, genre, source and redaction, liberation, feminist, and postcolonial criticisms. These methodologies are not exhaustive, but they illustrate the range of contemporary critical interpretations of the book of Exodus. The introduction of the distinct methodologies is similar to many other books on methodology that are available to students. Yet we hope to contribute to the growing literature on the subject by focusing in particular on the role of the six methodologies in the interpretation of the book of Exodus. To this end, each of the following six chapters of the volume will illustrate how a particular methodology has contributed to the interpretation of the book of Exodus. The authors will clarify the hermeneutical presuppositions of the methodology under study and the impact of the method on the interpretation of the book of Exodus as a whole. We have also selected Exodus 1–2 and 19–20 to illustrate in more detail the application of each methodology to specific texts.

Our second aim is to demonstrate the ways in which the different methods relate to each other. This goal is more innovative, since there has been a growing tendency in contemporary biblical interpretation to isolate methodologies from each other in an effort to focus on one particular way of reading over another. The volume will clarify significant differences between the six methodologies. But it will also illustrate ways

1

in which a critical reading of the book of Exodus is enriched through the use of multiple methodologies. Thus the authors will often note where methods conflict, qualify, or complement each other. Our aim is to equip readers with a range of distinct methodological tools for interpreting the book of Exodus, while also providing guidelines, where possible, on the points of contact between the divergent methodologies, indicating where they may work in consort or supplement each other.

The book of Exodus has been and continues to be a significant resource for the development of biblical methodologies in the Modern and Post-Modern periods. In the Modern period, the account of the Israelites' liberation from slavery in Egypt gave rise to a range of important historical-critical methodologies, which continue to inform the interpretation of the book, including the exploration of the genre of the ancient literature, the identification of the authors, and the investigation of the social setting out of which the narratives and laws were written. The questions of authorship, genre, and social setting are primary aims of interpretation in the methods of source, redaction, and genre criticisms. At the close of the Modern period interpreters began to supplement the questions of authorship, genre, and social setting with a more concentrated investigation of the literary character of the book of Exodus in its own right, paying particular attention to the organization and the stylistic features of the narratives and laws within the book. The new interest in the literary character of the book of Exodus fueled the development of literary and rhetorical criticism toward the end of the twentieth century, with the result that the study of plot, character, and rhetorical features of narrative and law became a firmly fixed methodology in the interpretation of the book of Exodus.

Literary and rhetorical criticism also provided transition from the Modern to the Post-Modern period. The interest in the literary study of the text, rather than authorship or composition, paved the way for a further change in the focus of interpretation, in which the social and political context of the reader become the resource for critical study. Thus, in the Post-Modern period, interpreters have moved beyond the concentration on the author or the text in order to turn a critical gaze on the role of the reader in fashioning the meaning of the book of Exodus. The result is that the Exodus has become a springboard for a series of methodologies, where the emphasis is on the dynamic role of the interpreter, whose identity, experience, and social location are recognized as formative for the creation of meaning. This shift in emphasis is important in liberation, feminist, and postcolonial criticisms, which explore the ideology of gender, race, class, and empire in the interpretation of the Exodus.

The history of interpretation in the Modern and Post-Modern periods illustrates a significant change concerning where interpreters search for meaning in the book of Exodus. The result is an array of different methodologies now available to all interpreters of the book of Exodus. In the early twentieth century, meaning was located in the authors of the literature, giving rise to the "historical-critical" methodologies of source, redaction, and genre criticisms. By the end of the century, interpreters came to recognize their own creative role in the construction of meaning, which fueled the more "ideologically" oriented methodologies of liberation, feminist, and postcolonial criticisms. The emergence of the different methodologies reflects significant social and intellectual reflection in the twentieth century over the nature of authority and where it should be located in the interpretation of religious texts. Does the authority of the book of Exodus reside in the past with the authors and their social setting? in the book itself detached from its historical context? or in the present reader who infuses the literature with his or her own lived experience which, in some cases, may have been excluded from past interpretations? The rapid pace of social change at the end of the twentieth century has resulted in a growing dichotomy between the so-called historical-critical and ideological methodologies as interpreters debated the nature and location of religious authority in the interpretation of the book of Exodus. We hope that the following chapters will clarify the important differences between the six methodologies and enable readers to become competent practitioners of each hermeneutical approach for reading the text.

We also hope to assist readers in bridging the dichotomy between historical-critical and ideological methodologies that has developed over the past decades. A careful reading of the following chapters will illustrate how interdependent the different methodologies are even though they represent a variety of hermeneutical approaches to interpretation. A comparison of the chapters will illustrate, for example, that the literary criteria which allow for the identification of distinct authors in source criticism, such as repetition and key works, are the same features that literary critics use to discern the unified structure and plot of texts; that the study of Hebrew stylistics incorporates the unique literary features which arise from the identification of a composite text in source criticism; and that the literary approach of rhetorical criticism even emerged as an extension of redaction criticism, thus intertwining the history of composition and the literary study of the present text. A similar interdependence between methods is evident in genre and postcolonial criticisms, where the quest to describe the genre of ancient historiography includes the topics of empire, colonizer, and colonized that are central to a postcolonial reading of the Exodus. Any number of other examples might also be listed such as the importance of the historical reconstruction of the social world of ancient Israel for liberation criticism, or the crucial role of the recovery of the role of women in the ancient world in feminist criticism. We will see further that the recognition of the reader's active role in creating meaning so central to feminist, liberation, and postcolonial criticisms has also transformed the study of genre criticism from a quest to describe preexisting categories, such as myth, history, or legend, to the recognition that humans create generic categories as we interpret literature. The following chapters will provide many more examples of the interdependence between the distinct methodologies, with the work in one chapter often cross-referenced to that of another. The few examples already listed underscore the importance of overcoming the growing dichotomy between the so-called historical-critical and ideological approaches to the interpretation of the Hebrew Bible. It is our hope that this volume will provide a clear understanding of the distinct methodological tools for interpreting the book of Exodus, while also encouraging readers to look for points of contact and even interdependence among the divergent methodologies.

THE BOOK OF EXODUS

The following summary is intended to provide a brief overview of the structure and thematic development of the book of Exodus as background for the more detailed studies in the following chapters. The book of Exodus is an episode in the larger story of the Pentateuch.

The background to the events in the book is the divine promise of lineage and land to the ancestors in the book of Genesis (e.g., Gen 12:1–4, 13:14–17). The book of Exodus opens by recalling the divine promise to the ancestors, when it states that the family of Jacob had grown into a great nation, fulfilling one aspect of the divine promise (Exod 1:7). But Israel's vast population in the land of Egypt, not Canaan, threatens Pharaoh, prompting oppression and even genocide. The result is a paradoxical situation at the outset of the book of Exodus. The partial fulfillment of the divine promise creates suffering, not blessing, for Israel.

The suffering of Israel in Egypt and the unfulfilled divine promise of land provide the background for probing two central themes about YHWH, the God of Israel: the character of divine power and the nature of divine presence in this world. Although the two themes are interwoven throughout the entire book, each takes prominence at different stages in the story, allowing for a loose division in the outline of the book of Exodus. The division is indicated by geography. The theme of divine power is explored, for the most part, in the setting of the land of Egypt (Exod 1:1–15:21). The theme of divine presence is developed in the setting of the wilderness, as Israel journeys with God from Egypt to the promised land of Canaan (Exod 15:22–40:38).

Exodus 1:1–15:21 narrates the conflict between YHWH and Pharaoh over the fate of Israel. It is an epic battle between kings and gods. The weapons of war are the forces of nature. YHWH summons reptiles, insects, and meteorological elements, including hail and darkness, in an initial assault on Pharaoh (Exod 7–10). When these elements fail to persuade Pharaoh to release Israel from Egyptian slavery, the personification of death itself, described as "the destroyer," descends upon the land of Egypt in the darkness of midnight, slaying all Egyptian firstborn children and animals (Exod 11–12). Even the plague of death does not dissuade Pharaoh from continuing the conflict. During the night he musters his army one last time and pursues the fleeing Israelites to the Red Sea (Exod 13), where YHWH destroys him at dawn, this time using the sea itself as a weapon (Exod 14). The hymns in Exodus 15 look back over the battlefield and confirm the power of God, praising YHWH as a warrior God, who possesses power over Pharaoh and over all the forces of nature.

Exodus 15:22–40:38 describes the ways in which YHWH is able to be present with Israel in this world as they journey toward the promised land. This story is also told on an epic scale. The forces of nature change their role from providing YHWH with weapons of war, to signaling the presence of God with Israel. God purifies polluted water for Israel (Exod 15:22–27). The miracles of water from the rock (Exod 17:1–7) and manna (Exod 16) save Israel from starvation. Advice by Jethro, Moses' father-in-law, about worship and government (Exod 18) provides transition from the initial wilderness journey to the revelation of the law and the sanctuary on Mount Sinai. Exodus 19–24 describes YHWH's descent on Mount Sinai to reveal covenantal law to the Israelites. Natural forces like thunder, lightning, darkness, and fire signal the nearness of God to Israel and the danger of divine holiness. The need for cultic safeguards results in the revelation of the blueprints for the tabernacle (Exod 25–31). Construction of the tabernacle holds promise for a divine descent from the mountain into the midst of the Israelite camp. But the process is halted, when Israel worships the golden calf (Exod 32). As a result, the story must begin anew, if it is to continue at all. God forgives Israel (Exod 34:1–10), issues new laws for covenant renewal (Exod 34:11–29), and commissions the building of the tabernacle (Exod 35–40). The book of Exodus ends with YHWH finally descending from Mount Sinai and entering the completed tabernacle on New Year's Day (Exod 40:1–2, 7), filling the sanctuary with fire and smoke (Exod 40:34–38).

Moses is the central human character in the book. His story provides a counterpart to the divine epic of war and revelation. The book of Exodus traces his development from being Israel's savior in their escape from Egypt to becoming Israel's mediator during the revelation of law on Mount Sinai. Exodus 2–5 introduce Moses, noting his lack of identity (he is both an Egyptian and an Israelite), his good intentions (he wishes to help his people Israel), and his violent nature (he kills an Egyptian). Moses' early life experience with the Midianites in the wilderness fore-shadows Israel's experience in the second half of the book of Exodus. YHWH appears to him at the mountain of God (Exod 3–4) and Moses returns to Egypt to mediate for YHWH in confronting Pharaoh (Exod 5–12). In the process Moses emerges as the liberator of Israel, leading them in their march from Egypt (Exod 13) and even through the Red Sea itself (Exod 14). The mediatorial role of Moses is developed during the revelation of the law (Exod 19–24) and in the construction of the tabernacle (Exod 25–40). Through repeated trips to the summit of the mountain Moses models the offices of priest, prophetic teacher, and scribe as he purifies Israel, teaches the people the covenant, and records divine law.

Exodus 1–2 and 19–20 represent literature from the two halves of the book of Exodus. Exodus 1–2 introduce the theme of divine power to liberate. The chapters constitute a single scene of several related episodes, including the setting of the Israelite people in Egypt (1:1–7), the fear of Pharaoh and the enslavement of the Israelites (1:8–14), the command for genocide, the resistance of the midwives, and the secret birth and adoption of Moses (1:15–2:10), Moses' initial failed attempt at liberation and consequent flight to Midian (2:11–22), and the slave status of the Israelites in Egypt (2:23–25). Exodus 19–20 explore the theme of the divine presence with Israel in the wilderness. These chapters recount the appearance of Yahweh on Mount Sinai and the revelation of the Decalogue, which progresses from the divine proposal of covenant (19:1–8), the descent and appearance of YHWH on Mount Sinai (19:9–19), and the revelation of the law (19:20–20:20). The two texts provide a rich resource for illustrating the distinctive methodologies in the interpretation of the book of Exodus.

THE OVERVIEW OF THE BOOK

The previous summary of the historical development of the different methodologies indicates a near exclusive interest in authorship and historical context at the outset of the twentieth century, which supported source, redaction, and genre criticisms. Literary and rhetorical criticism emerged in the later part of the twentieth century to evaluate more carefully the design of the present form of text, providing transition to the methodologies of liberation, feminist, and postcolonial criticisms, all of which evaluate the role of the reader in a more self-critical fashion. The organization of the volume departs from the historical development of the methodologies, beginning instead with a description of literary and rhetorical criticism. The focus on the present form of the text in literary and rhetorical criticism will provide a helpful introduction to the book of Exodus. The chapters on genre criticism and source and redaction criticism will describe the literary background, the history of composition, and the different genres of the literature in the book. The chapters on liberation, feminist, and postcolonial criticisms will explore the formative role of contemporary social and political experience as critical tools for interpreting the book of Exodus. The following is a brief synopsis of the chapters in the volume.

Dennis Olson describes the methodology of literary and rhetorical criticism. He states that the goal of the method is to interpret the final form of the biblical text. Olson characterizes the methodology as a "text-centered" literary approach to biblical interpretation that focuses on the structure, poetics, and rhetorical devices that organize narratives and laws. The focus on the literary design of the biblical text was originally intended to complement source and redaction criticism, where interpreters concentrated on the history of composition without paying sufficient attention to the final literary product. But the text-centered literary study of biblical narratives and laws quickly branched out into three broad categories: the constructive literary approach of new criticism that describes the artistic coherence of biblical texts; the oppositional reading of deconstruction that seeks to demonstrate the instability of meaning in biblical texts; and the more dialogically oriented forms of reading such as that of Mikhail Bakhtin that locate the meaning of biblical texts within the context of interpretive communities. The scope of literary and rhetorical criticism underscores how this methodology interacts both with historical-critical theories of composition and with the more reader oriented forms of interpretation.

Kenton L. Sparks reviews the historical development of genre criticism from its origin in form criticism. He notes that the emergence of form criticism in the late nineteenth century sought to describe oral myths and legends that stood behind the book of Exodus and reflected the earliest stage of Israelite social history. Form criticism assumed that the categories of myth, legend, and history had an independent existence, which required interpreters to discover the essence of each category, as for example in the question, what is history? Once the question was answered and the genre was defined, the interpreter could place the correct texts in the proper categories by answering the question, is the book of Exodus history? The problem with form criticism, according to Sparks, was that the application of the method resulted in circular debates over the correct definition of history and what literature conformed to the category. Form criticism has given way to genre criticism at the close of the twentieth century. Genre criticism represents a rejection of the assumption that categories preexist, or that there is "the" correct definition of myth, legend, or historiography. Genre criticism recognizes instead that humans create generic categories in the process of interpreting literature; it thus incorporates the dynamic role of the reader in the identification of genres. The result is that a text can fit many different generic categories at the same time, because readers create categories as they classify texts which share a common trait or traits. Sparks describes how the classification of literature arises from a comparison of texts within the Hebrew Bible, the broader ancient Near Eastern literary tradition, or even from anthropological evidence from humanity at large. He employs this dynamic method to evaluate the genre of the non-P and P literature in the book of Exodus, the stories of Moses in Exodus 1–2, as well as the character and function of law in Exodus 19–20.

Suzanne Boorer describes source and redaction criticism. She states that the aim of the method is to discern the history of the literary composition of the book of Exodus. Although source and redaction criticism are combined in our study, Boorer clarifies that they represent distinct methodologies. Source criticism unravels the biblical text to identify its earlier written components and, if possible, to discern the date and the historical context of the composition. Redaction criticism moves in the other direction; it puts the text back together describing the literary process by which the sources were combined to form the present text. Boorer traces the development of source and redaction criticism from the nineteenth century to the present, noting both the points of continuity and change in the emerging theories of the Pentateuch's composition and its literary relationship to the Former Prophets. She highlights the many rhetorical features that aid interpreters in recognizing a composite text of distinct authors. Many of these literary features are also important to literary and rhetorical criticism, even though the goals of source and redaction criticism are very different. Boorer's application of source and redaction criticism clarifies that Exodus 1–2 and 19–20 are not single-authored compositions, but a collection of writing from multiple authors, with competing interpretations of the meaning of the Exodus and the revelation of law at Mount Sinai.

Jorge Pixley introduces liberation criticism and applies the methodology to the book of Exodus. Pixley states that liberation criticism begins
with the hermeneutical insight that biblical interpretation is always influenced by the experience and social location of the reader. More specifically, liberation criticism is grounded in the experience of oppression.
Pixley traces the development of liberation criticism from the use of
scripture by the economically marginalized and poor in Latin America,
where the story of the Exodus plays a central hermeneutical role. This
starting point is so important to an understanding of liberation criticism
that Pixley is forced to confess the artificial character of introducing liberation criticism in an academically oriented book as this one, which is
detached from the remote villages or compact slums of the inner city
that has given rise to the method. Pixley clarifies the foundational role
of the Exodus for liberation criticism. He describes the presuppositions
and emerging methodology of liberation criticism, including the role of
memory, the correspondence of relations between the past story of the
Exodus and the present circumstances of interpreters – especially the
poor and marginalized, the interpretation of the Exodus as the incom-
plete project of God, in which the story models the freeing of people
from oppression, and the active role of praxis in the interpretation of
Exodus 1–2 and 19–20.

Naomi Steinberg writes that feminist biblical criticism is a form of
scholarly inquiry rooted in the awareness that sexism characterizes both
the biblical text and the institutions that claim it and interpret it – both
past and present. She traces four developments in contemporary feminist
criticism that highlight the importance of women's experiences for biblical interpretation, including the first wave of white North American feminism; race-, social class-, and ethnicity-based feminism; gender-based
feminism; and theological feminism. The overview underscores the rich
variety in contemporary feminist biblical criticism that has arisen from
the diverse social locations and political contexts of the feminist interpreters. Steinberg illustrates this diversity through a range of feminist
readings of the book of Exodus, including the recovery of the lost experience of women in ancient Israel, the nature of motherhood in the ancient
world, feminist interpretations of the women in Exodus 1–2, and the
role of impurity during the theophany in Exodus 19. Her interpretation

illustrates the broad research on gender and power that has emerged in biblical studies within the recent decades of feminist interpretation.

Gale A. Yee concludes the volume with a helpful summary of the emerging methodology of postcolonial criticism. Yee traces the rise of postcolonial criticism within the broader field of literary studies, noting in particular the work of Edward Said, Gayatri Chakravorty Spivak, and Homi Bhabba. A central concern in postcolonial criticism, according to Yee, is to foreground the unequal and exploitative relationships between an empire and its colonies both in ancient and modern times. From a postcolonial perspective, the book of Exodus can be used to inspire liberation, but it can also legitimate oppression. Yee explores the categories of imperialism and colonialism in the book of Exodus to uncover the double-sidedness of the story. She notes the factors of economic and cultural experience that may have influenced the formation of the biblical text as the Israelites lived under the colonial rule of different empires in antiquity. Yee employs the social categories of stereotyping, mimicry, and hybridity to evaluate the complex social relationships between colonizers and the colonized that linger in the book of Exodus and their continuing influence in the history of interpretation, where the Exodus-Conquest myth has been used both as a story of liberation and as a tool for colonial expansion.

BIBLIOGRAPHY

Each chapter will conclude with a selected bibliography of recommended works for further reading. The following is a limited selection of recent commentaries on the book of Exodus.

Childs, Brevard S. *The Book of Exodus: A Critical, Theological Commentary.* OTL. Philadelphia: Westminster John Knox Press, 1974.

Dozeman, Thomas B. *Exodus.* The Eerdmans Critical Commentary. Grand Rapids, MI: Wm. B. Eerdmans Press, 2009.

Fretheim, Terence E. *Exodus.* Interpretation. Louisville, KY: Westminster John Knox Press, 1991.

Houtman, C. *Exodus.* Volume 1. Historical Commentary of the Old Testament. Kampen: Kok Publishing, 1993.

———— *Exodus.* Volume 2. Historical Commentary of the Old Testament. Kampen: Kok Publishing, 1995.

———— *Exodus.* Volume 3. Historical Commentary of the Old Testament. Kampen: Kok Publishing, 2000.

Meyers, Carol. *Exodus*. New Cambridge Bible Commentary. Cambridge: Cambridge University Press, 2005.

Pixley, Jorge. *On Exodus: A Liberation Perspective*. Maryknoll, NY: Orbis Books, 1983.

Propp, William H. *Exodus 1–18*. The Anchor Yale Bible Commentaries. New Haven, CT: Yale University Press, 1999.

———— *Exodus 19–40*. The Anchor Yale Bible Commentaries. New Haven, CT: Yale University Press, 2006.

1

Literary and Rhetorical Criticism

DENNIS T. OLSON

LITERARY AND RHETORICAL CRITICISM: A BRIEF HISTORY

Since ancient times, interpreters have recognized the Bible's capacity as literature to delight, disturb, challenge, teach, move, or transform readers and hearers. The various methods under the broad umbrella of literary and rhetorical criticism seek to analyze in detail the cluster of words, literary forms, styles, tropes, and strategies embedded within biblical texts that work together to provoke such a wide range of reactions in audiences. Literary methods involve close readings of biblical texts with careful attention to their literary contours and textures. The questions that arise in literary approaches range widely from detailed attention to the meaning of individual words and sentences to the significance and shape of successively larger literary contexts in which the given text is situated. What is the effect of the Bible's use of one word rather than another in a given text? In what way is the word order of a sentence significant for its meaning? What role does a specific metaphor or motif play within a biblical text? What is the overall plot of a biblical narrative, and how does a particular scene or episode fit within it? From whose perspective is the story told? How do allusions or echoes from other texts shape interpretation? How are characters developed and to what end? Should an interpreter fill the gaps in a story or leave them open? How does one interpret biblical poetry with its play of language, line, metaphor, parallelism, emotion, and extravagance of expression as distinct from biblical narrative? In what ways are biblical laws uniquely shaped as literature and rhetoric, seeking to move or persuade their audiences?

These are a sample of the kinds of questions that literary and rhetorical criticism asks.

Methods of interpreting the Bible have always been influenced by the methods of reading and interpreting other important texts within a given culture and time. Writing within a Greek cultural context, the Jewish historian Josephus (first century C.E.) believed that Greek models of poetry with meter and rhythm could be applied in analyzing the biblical poems of Exodus 15 and Deuteronomy 32. (Josephus, *Ant.* 2.345–346, 4.302–303, 7.305). Early Christian interpreters like Origen of Alexandria (third century C.E.) borrowed the Greek method of allegory, a method used to interpret Greek classics like Homer's *The Iliad* and *The Odyssey*, and applied it to the Bible. Many early Christian scholars such as Jerome, Augustine, and Chrysostom applied their extensive training in Greek and Latin grammar, literature, and rhetoric to the Bible. Jewish medieval exegetes like Saadya Gaon of Babylonia, Moses Ibn Ezra of Spain, and Judah Halevi of Spain all studied and praised the Bible's literary and rhetorical style, use of words, and eloquence. The so-called Victorines (Hugh, Richard, and Andrew) were medieval Christian interpreters in France who studied the poetics and rhetoric of the Bible, delighting in its artfulness as literature as it contributed to the depth of the Bible's spiritual meaning. The literary methods used in the recovery of ancient Greek classical learning and rhetoric in the Renaissance of the fourteenth and fifteenth centuries were applied to a close reading, translation, and study of biblical texts in the commentaries of sixteenth-century reformers such as Martin Luther and John Calvin. Interest in and sensitivity to the literary and poetic qualities of biblical literature continued into the modern period as illustrated by studies of Hebrew poetry by Robert Lowth[1] and Johann Gottfried Herder[2] in the eighteenth century and detailed form-critical studies of Hebrew narrative by the German biblical scholar Hermann Gunkel in the nineteenth century (*Genesis*).[3] Gunkel was influenced by new discoveries in oral folklore studies and in new

[1] Robert Lowth, *De sacra poesi Hebraeorum* (Gottingen: Sumtibus, Pockwizil and Barmeiri, 1758).
[2] Johann Gottfried Herder, *The Spirit of Hebrew Poetry* (Burlington, VT: E. Smith, 1833, first published in German in 1783).
[3] Hermann Gunkel, *Genesis* (trans. Mark Biddle; Macon, GA: Mercer University Press, 1997, first published in German in 1901).

archaeological discoveries of ancient Near Eastern myths and literature from biblical times and with which biblical texts could be compared. These are but a small selection of biblical interpreters who appropriated the literary and rhetorical methods current in their various times and cultures as tools for biblical study.

Western biblical scholarship in much of the nineteenth and twentieth centuries was dominated not by literary and rhetorical methods but by the author-centered approach called historical criticism. The ultimate goal of historical critics was not focused primarily "in" the text but beyond or "behind" the biblical text. The methods of historical criticism sought to reconstruct the mind or historical situation of the authors or editors of a given text. Other historical critics were interested more in uncovering the history of the stages of composition and editing that led to the present form of the biblical text.

In response to the dominance of historical criticism in biblical studies, literary and rhetorical approaches to biblical interpretation reemerged, beginning in the late 1960s and 1970s. Such literary methods focused largely on the final form of the biblical text, taking seriously the literary shape, poetics, and detail of the biblical text as literature. Such text-centered or literary approaches focused their primary attention "in" the text itself rather than on a reconstructed human author, editor, or histori-cal events "behind" the text. The stages and development of this modern resurgence of interest in literary and rhetorical methods as applied to the Bible reflected new developments in modern literary studies in the disciplines of English and comparative literature, although often with a lag time of a decade or two before a given method in the field of literary studies came to be applied to the study of biblical texts.

The ways in which such text-centered literary studies impacted the study of the Bible may be separated into three broad categories: (1) con-structive literary approaches that sought to appreciate the literary art-fulness of texts and to discern a more coherent meaning in texts whose surface structure appears to be disunified (new criticism, structuralism); (2) deconstructive literary approaches that engaged in oppositional read-ing, unmasking deep internal contradictions and inconsistencies in texts that were often assumed to have a stable meaning (Jacques Derrida; poststructuralism); and (3) dialogical and rhetorical approaches that make modest provisional but sufficiently persuasive claims for meaning in a text as the result of a detailed reading and dialogue within the context of real-world audiences and interpretive communities (Mikhail Bakhtin; rhetorical criticism).

Alongside these three categories of "text-centered" approaches, an array of more "reader-centered" approaches also arose in literary and in biblical studies. Such reader-focused interpretations sometimes wed the methods of a "text-centered" literary or rhetorical approach with methods that emphasize the social and cultural location of readers for interpreting biblical texts (gender, class, race and ethnicity, faith traditions and communities, postcolonialist perspectives, and the like – see the chapters in this book on "Feminist Criticism," "Liberation Criticism," and "Postcolonial Criticism").

For the purposes of this introduction to literary and rhetorical criticism, we will focus on the three methods that concentrate on roughly the final or present form of the biblical text as a given interpretive community may define it. I say "roughly the final form" of the text because the Bibles we use are based on scholarly attempts to reconstruct the "best" text from a complex set of multiple versions of biblical texts in the original languages. The differences among these many versions are often relatively minor, but some are more significant. In any case, we do not have the one original version, the absolute "final form" of any biblical book. We only have versions of these books that are many centuries removed from the original authors and editors, versions that have been copied by ancient scribes and passed from community to community with some variations embedded within them in the course of transmission and copying. Most detailed literary and rhetorical criticism of the Old Testament or Hebrew Bible is based on the traditional form of the Hebrew text used by the Jewish community, the so-called Masoretic tradition, with some attention to other Hebrew textual traditions or other ancient versions (Greek, Syriac, Aramaic, Latin, and the like).

Constructive Literary Approaches

Many literary studies of biblical texts in the 1970s and 1980s shared a commitment to what might be called "constructive" literary readings of biblical texts. They often sought to highlight the artfulness, sophistication and meaningfulness of biblical literature, both prose and poetry. Literary scholars often assumed a basic unity, structure, and coherence in the text.

An important milestone in the modern reemergence of literary and rhetorical methods in biblical studies was marked by the presidential address of James Muilenburg to the Society of Biblical Literature in 1968. Muilenburg was a professor at Union Theological Seminary in New York. He argued in his address entitled "Form Criticism and Beyond" for a renewed focus on the detailed analysis of literary features in the prose and poetry of the Bible in a method that he labeled "rhetorical criticism."[4] His voice was joined by several scholars in the academic disciplines of English studies and comparative literature who became interested in studying the Bible as literature. Early examples include Northrop Frye (*The Great Code: The Bible and Literature*),[5] Robert Alter (*The Art of Biblical Narrative* and *The Art of Biblical Poetry*),[6] and Erich Auerbach (*Mimesis: The Representation of Reality in Western Literature*).[7] Influential work was also undertaken in Israel by literary scholars of the Bible such as Meir Weiss (*The Bible from Within*)[8] and Meir Sternberg (*The Poetics of Biblical Narrative*).[9] Alter, Sternberg, and Auerbach emphasized the distinctive elements of ancient biblical narratives in comparison to other ancient or modern Western literature. They argued for the importance of understanding ancient biblical narratives on their own terms rather than imposing alien categories or assumptions from modern literary studies upon the biblical texts.

The initial literary study of the Bible was influenced by an approach called new criticism that dominated several university literary departments from 1930 to 1960. New criticism assumed that a given literary text should be studied on its own terms as an autonomous piece of art or artifact. The reader should simply study and appreciate the internal literary dynamics of a poem or novel without being influenced by what the original author may have intended (the so-called Intentional Fallacy of new criticism) or by knowledge of the social or political conditions of the era

[4] James Muilenburg, "Form Criticism and Beyond," *JBL* 88 (1969), 1–18.
[5] Northrop Frye, *The Great Code: the Bible and Literature* (New York: Harcourt Brace Jovanovich, 1982).
[6] Robert Alter, *The Art of Biblical Narrative* (New York: Basic Books, 1981); *The Art of Biblical Poetry* (New York: Basic Books, 1985).
[7] Erich Auerbach, *Mimesis: The Representation of Reality in Western Literature* (Princeton, NJ: Princeton University Press, 1968).
[8] Meir Weiss, *The Bible from Within: The Method of Total Interpretation* (Jerusalem: Magnes Press, 1984).
[9] Meir Sternberg, *The Poetics of Biblical Narrative, Ideological Literature and the Drama of Reading* (Bloomington: Indiana University Press, 1987).

in which the literary work was written. In analyzing narratives, new critics studied narrative structure, selection and ordering of episodes, plot
conflicts, image patterns and repetitions, keywords, thematic emphasis,
point of view, and character development.

A new development in literary studies in the 1960s and 1970s called
structuralism found its way into biblical studies. Structuralism was
grounded in work by the Swiss linguist Ferdinand de Saussure who
argued that language and the meanings of words are produced not by a
simple one-to-one correspondence to a specific word or object as much
as by a network of relations and contrasts within a language system.[10]
For example, what the word "cat" means is known by the human mind
through a series of deductions which signify what it is not – a cat is not
an inanimate object, not a human, not a wild animal, not a dog, and
so on. Structural anthropologists such as Claude Lévi-Strauss extended
this insight into the study of symbolic structures and rituals in human
societies, setting up a series of binary oppositions that defined people
and elements of a social system as either one thing or its opposite: male/
female, hunter/farmer, outside/inside, friend/enemy, good/evil and the
like.[11]

A. J. Greimas took these insights and applied them to an analysis of
the underlying structures of narratives.[12] Stories may differ in surface
details, but the structuralists believed that humanly composed stories
shared at their deepest structure a common set of binary categories by
which reality was perceived and categorized. The assumption grew that
such binary oppositions reflected the way in which all human minds
processed reality and that such binary oppositions were universal across
different times and cultures, both ancient and modern.

Structuralism as applied to biblical texts succeeded in illuminating
some recurring oppositions within some narratives, laws, and poems of
the Bible. Structuralists strove to highlight parallels, echoes, and reflections across various scenes or narratives in the hope of demonstrating
a basic unity of purpose and meaning in texts. The results, however,
were so reductionistic that the most interesting details and complexities
of the text were eliminated from interpretation in order to detect the

[10] Ferdinand de Saussure, *Course in General Linguistics* (London: Duckworth, 1983).
[11] Claude Lévi-Strauss, *Structural Anthropology* (New York: Doubleday, 1963).
[12] A. J. Greimas, *Sémantique Structurale* (Paris: Larousse, 1966).

universally shared binary oppositions that the structuralists identified in diverse texts. More reader-oriented methods of studying biblical texts also presented a challenge to structuralist interpretations, since these methods clarified that people of diverse social locations could have fundamentally different readings of the same biblical text. The reader-oriented method-ologies raised the troubling question of whether the supposedly inherent binary oppositions in biblical texts were more the result of a specific reader's assumptions and construction of meaning in interacting with a biblical text rather than the result of universal categories of meaning. As a result, the presuppositions of structuralism came under increasing critical evaluation in the 1980s and 1990s in literary studies in general as well as in the field of biblical studies.

Deconstructive Literary Approaches

The reader-centered approaches to interpretation highlight the active and decisive role that readers take in constructing meaning from texts. In doing so, literary scholars began to question the new critic's assump-tion about the stability of literary texts with unified meaning. They also resisted structuralism's assumption of a set of universal binary opposi-tions that transcended cultural and social location. At the same time, it was recognized that readers were not just individualists. All readers are, to some extent, formed by their "interpretive communities" in which they live, work, and are educated (Stanley Fish). Indeed, most readers are influenced, in ways conscious and unconscious, by a complex interaction among diverse and overlapping interpretive communities that shape an individual's reading and assumptions and serve as formal or informal arbiters of persuasive or truthful readings.

These more reader-centered approaches will be covered in other chap-ters in this book. In this section, we take up another influential approach that remained "text-centered," focused "in" the details of the text itself, but an approach that is diametrically opposed to the more constructive literary approaches that we have examined thus far. The French literary scholar Jacques Derrida promoted this method of reading called "decon-struction" or "poststructuralism." Deconstruction involves a careful and detailed reading of a text, highlighting its internal complexity and the gaps and omissions that may be filled in with a variety of different meanings, many of which may be contradictory. Deconstruction involves teasing out and highlighting those details of a text that promote meanings and commitments that are in fundamental conflict with meanings and commitments that may appear at the surface of a text. The potential conflict in meaning demonstrates than any given text is unstable in meaning and open to a variety of interpretations that reflect the ideology of the reader. An urgent warning arising out of deconstructionist interpretations is that authoritative texts are used by the powerful to silence or oppress the less powerful. As a result justice is an overriding value of deconstructive readings. In the name of justice, Derrida resisted claims by "master readers" to have privileged knowledge of the one true meaning of a text. Moreover, he assumed that authors of texts are not in full and conscious command of what they write, often including repressed and unconscious elements that undo what they believe they are promoting even as they write. In his book, *Of Grammatology,* Derrida argues that a deconstructive reading

must always aim at a certain relationship, unperceived by the writer, between what he commands and what he does not command of the pattern of language that he uses.... [Deconstruction] attempts to make the non-seen accessible to sight.[13]

The quotation underscores the intense focus on fissures, fragments, and the multiplicities of meaning that characterize the deconstructive approach to texts. Derrida's work usually emphasized the texts of philosophers and other classical texts, but students of deconstruction extended his method to literary texts of all kinds, including the Bible. Although the influence of deconstruction in literary studies and biblical studies has waned, some of the spirit of its opposition to claims of self-evident and unified meanings of texts lingers. Interpreters acknowledge the need for humility, the provisional character of reading, self-criticism, and openness to hearing the challenging voice of the other as also representing legitimate readings of authoritative texts such as the Bible.

Introductions to the study of biblical narratives tend to exemplify one of these two different orientations, whether taking a more constructive or a more deconstructive posture in their literary analysis of biblical texts. Thus, for example, a more constructive orientation is evident in

---

[13] Jacques Derrida, *Of Grammatology* (trans. Gayatri Charkravorty Spivak; Baltimore, MD: Johns Hopkins University Press, 1976), 158.

Meir Sternberg's *The Poetics of Biblical Narrative* or J. P. Fokkelman's *Reading Biblical Narrative, An Introductory Guide*.[14] In contrast, a more deconstructive stance toward biblical texts is taken in David Gunn and Danna Nolan Fewell's *Narrative in the Hebrew Bible*.[15]

Dialogical and Rhetorical Approaches

A third orientation to the literary study of biblical texts seeks to mediate between the constructive and the deconstructive approaches of interpretation. I will briefly describe two such mediating literary approaches. The first is a "dialogical" approach founded on the work of a Russian philosopher and literary critic, Mikhail Bakhtin (1895–1975), whose influence was late in coming to Western literary studies and also to biblical studies. Bakhtin's writing ranged widely over the nature of literature, human discourse, truth, and reality. One of his central themes was that human life is a continual and "unfinalizable dialogue" that takes place in every moment of daily life. This dialogue occurs in the countless small and almost imperceptible exchanges among historically situated human beings in speech, writing, interpretation, and action, each one contributing in small ways to creating truth and reality: "Life by its very nature is dialogue."[16] Yet in real practice humans must also create "monologizations" – singular and temporary claims, coherent but provisional decisions, and unified but makeshift interpretations that contribute to the larger ongoing symphony of human voices. In this way, Bakhtin is somewhat different from the perspective of a deconstructionist like Derrida.

Bakhtin argued that certain literary works (such as Fyodor Dostoevsky's novels *Crime and Punishment* and *The Brothers Karamazov*) promoted a "dialogic" or "polyphonic" (multivoiced) approach to truth. The genius of Dostoevsky, Bakhtin argued, was that the author allowed competing voices to coexist to the end of the novel without one dominating

---

[14] M. Sternberg, *The Poetics of Biblical Narrative*; J. P. Fokkelman, *Reading Biblical Narrative, An Introductory Guide* (trans. Ineke Smit; Louisville, KY: Westminster John Knox, 1999).

[15] David Gunn and Danna Nolan Fewell, *Narrative in the Hebrew Bible* (New York: Oxford University Press, 1993).

[16] Mikhail Bakhtin, "Toward a Reworking of the Dostoevsky Book," Appendix 2 in *Problems of Dostoevsky's Poetics* (ed. and trans. Caryl Emerson; Minneapolis: University of Minnesota, 1984), 293.

or overcoming the other. In other literary works, different genres also often coexist side by side, each contributing a unique voice to a larger dialogue. Truth, for Bakhtin, happens not as an abstract proposition but as a dialogical "event" among many different people, characters who themselves are made up of multiple internalized voices that accumulate from previous dialogical encounters.[17] Bakhtin's insights have been applied in a wide range of biblical literature and genres, from the narratives of the Deuteronomistic History (Joshua–2 Kings), Jonah and Esther to the interplay of the poetic dialogues (chapter 3–41) and the framing prose tales (chapters 1–2, 42) of the book of Job.[18]

Another mediating approach is associated more closely to the "rhetorical criticism" of James Muilenburg with which the reemergence of modern literary study of the Bible began. Phyllis Trible, a student of Muilenburg, provides a thorough introduction to the rich tradition of "rhetorical criticism" and an illustration of its application to the book of Jonah in her book *Rhetorical Criticism: Context, Method, and the Book of Jonah.*[19] The study of rhetoric as a study of the "event of communication" in all its parts stretches back to the ancient Greeks (Plato, Aristotle) and Latin rhetoricians (Cicero) to the present day. Rhetoric embraces the intellectual, emotional, and aesthetic dimensions of both written texts and oral speech as essential to a full understanding of communication. Rhetoric is thus attentive to the audience or interpretive community and their expectations with the ultimate goal of moving and persuading others in a real-life context. Trible outlines the following series of practical steps which I have adapted for beginning a rhetorical analysis of a biblical text, whether prose or poetry:[20] I have adapted these steps in the following manner:

[17] The best sources for Bakhtin's discussion of "dialogics" is his book, *Problems of Dostoevsky's Poetics* and his essay, "Discourse in the Novel" in *The Dialogic Imagination: Four Essays* (ed. Michael Holquist; trans. Caryl Emerson and Michael Holquist; Austin, TX: University of Austin, 1981).

[18] For a helpful overview of the use of Bakhtin in studies of various biblical books, see Barbara Green, *Mikhail Bakhtin and Biblical Scholarship, An Introduction* (Atlanta, GA: Society of Biblical Literature, 2000). See also the essay by Carol Newsom, "Bakhtin, the Bible, and Dialogic Truth," *JR* 76 (1996): 290–306. Newsom's book, *The Book of Job: A Contest of Moral Imaginations* (New York: Oxford University Press, 2003) is a thorough application of Bakhtin's insights to a complex biblical book.

[19] Phyllis Trible, *Rhetorical Criticism: Context, Method, and the Book of Jonah* (Minneapolis: Fortress, 1994).

[20] Ibid., 101–06.

1. Determine the beginning and ending of the literary unit; delimit the literary boundaries.
2. Discern and mark the repetition of specific words, phrases and sentences (in the original language of Hebrew for the Old Testament or Hebrew Bible, when possible) and their significance in the context of the larger literary unit. Are there *inclusios*, that is, key repetitions at the beginning and ending of units or subunits? Is the repetition exact or varied? Slight variations may be very impor- ✓ tant. Use a system of underlining or color-coding for each set of repetitions in the text.
3. Discern the different types of discourse or points of view at play in the story including the narrator's voice (the often anonymous voice of the storyteller) and the spoken dialogue of specific characters within the story. Is there harmony or tension between the characters and the narrator?
4. Sketch out the design and structure of the literary text. How does the text break down into subunits? And how are the subunits related to one another? How do the parts relate to the whole? And how does the form relate to the content?
5. Trace the development of the plot, the movement from beginning to end. Where do changes happen? Where do conflicts occur? Where does the action slow down, interrupt, or speed up? Is there a building of suspense? Are there digressions in the story line? Is there resolution or closure or an open and unresolved ending? Poetic texts do not typically have an overall plot but sometimes have subunits with some plot development within them.
6. Describe the portrayal of characters and their interaction and relationship with one another. Who has power over others? Who is in the background or the foreground? Does the story provide insight into inner motivations of characters through a character's speech or actions or a narrator's comment? How are characters evaluated positively or negatively?
7. Pay attention to syntax in the original Hebrew, when possible. Note any deviations from normal word order between verbs and subjects or other clause structures.
8. Note the particles or small words in Hebrew that may function to create emphasis, connection, movement, and structure,

depending on the context. Such particles include Hebrew words like *kî* ("for," "because," very," "except"), *hinneh* ("look!" "see!") or *lākēn* ("therefore," "in return for," "assuredly").

9. Relate the diverse elements of your rhetorical analysis to fashion a comprehensive interpretation of the text. Identify elements that seem less important from those that are more important, dramatic, or central to the meaning of the whole. How does the form of the text fit with the content of the text? How does the interplay of all of these rhetorical elements render meaning?

Obviously, rhetorical criticism is as much an art as a series of mechanical steps. Interpretation, judgment, and discernment are required at every step. Moreover, a rhetorical analysis will move back and forth among these steps to adjust to new discoveries at each stage. The aim of the interpreter is to present a persuasive reading and analysis of a biblical text within a given interpretive community or context. A central feature of a persuasive reading arises from the interpreters use of the literary text at hand. Rhetorical interpretations rarely claim certainty or timelessness; they are provisional but seek to be sufficiently compelling for the given time and context. The long tradition of rhetorical interpretation is conscious that it is undertaken in real-world contexts, in which the interpreter has an immediate relationship with the intended audience, whether a professor who is grading a student paper or an academic meeting of biblical scholars or a faith community of laypeople to whom a religious leader is preaching or teaching.

We move next to sample some literary and rhetorical readings of the book of Exodus, illustrating the range of constructive, deconstructive, and dialogical/rhetorical approaches to Exodus.

LITERARY/RHETORICAL CRITICISM AND
THE BOOK OF EXODUS

Constructive Literary Readings of Exodus

The majority of literary studies of the book of Exodus have been in the category of "constructive" literary readings. A number of significant commentaries on Exodus have included attention to close literary readings of the final form of Exodus texts. Brevard Childs's 1974 commentary on Exodus included sections on "Old Testament Context" for each unit of Exodus which were largely close literary readings of the Exodus texts alongside other sections on translation, historical criticism, New Testament context, and history of exegesis.[21] Other more recent studies have likewise combined acknowledgement of the sources and redactional layers that underlie many of the texts of Exodus with more literary analyses of Exodus texts of patterns, repetitions, or structures that bind the diverse traditions of Exodus into a larger literary whole. An example is Mark Smith's *The Pilgrimage Pattern in Exodus*, which attends to the distinctive Priestly tradition of Exodus and the ways in which it provides an overall pattern of two pilgrimages to the central mountain of Sinai in the book of Exodus. Moses embarks on one pilgrimage to the mountain by himself (Exod 1–14; esp. Exod 3), and then Moses leads the whole people of Israel on a second pilgrimage to the central mountain of Sinai (Exod 16–40). At the center point of these two pilgrimages, the poetic Song of the Sea in Exodus 15 celebrates the two major events associated with these two pilgrimages: God's defeat of Pharaoh (Exod 15:1–12) and God's leading of the Israelites to God's "mountain" and sanctuary (Exod 15:13–18).[22]

Terence Fretheim's 1991 commentary on Exodus is a thoroughly literary reading of the book of Exodus.[23] He notes literary structural features that recur throughout Exodus: the rhythm of lament, deliverance, and praise, the interconnections of liturgy and narrative (e.g., Passover festival and Passover story in Exodus 11–12; the Red Sea crossing in Exodus 14 and the people's song of praise in Exodus 15) and the interconnections of law and narrative (e.g., the manna narrative and Sabbath theme in Exodus 16 reflecting the later commandment of the Sabbath in Exod 20:8–11). Fretheim also identifies motifs in early Exodus narratives that prefigure later events through repetition. For example, Pharaoh's daughter saves the baby Moses by drawing him out of the water (Exod 2:1–10), prefiguring God's rescue of the Israelites as God draws them out of the water

---

[21] Brevard Childs, *The Book of Exodus* (OTL; Philadelphia: Westminster, 1974).

[22] Mark Smith, *The Pilgrimage Pattern in Exodus* (JSOTSup 239; Sheffield: Sheffield Academic Press, 1997).

[23] Terence E. Fretheim, *Exodus* (Interpretation; Louisville, KY: John Knox Press, 1991), 6–7.

of the Red Sea (Exod 14). God's attack and near-killing of Moses and the role of the firstborn son and of blood in protecting Moses (Exod 4:24–26) prefigures the Passover. The Israelites use the blood of the lamb upon the doorposts to protect them from God's attack on all the firstborn sons of Egypt (Exod 12:21–32).

Elements in the ten plagues (Exod 7–12) prefigure elements of the Passover and crossing of the Red Sea (Exod 13–15) with repetitions of key words and images. For example, the first plague of water turning to blood (Exod 7:14–24) prefigures the blood on the doorposts at the Passover (Exod 12:13) and the death of Pharaoh and his army in the Red Sea (Exod 14:26–29). Frogs and locusts "covered" the land of Egypt (Exod 8:6; 10:5, 15) as the waters of the Red Sea "covered" Pharaoh and his army (Exod 14:28; 15:5, 10). The plagues represent "ecological or natural disasters" that are divine judgments on human injustice, demonstrating a vital interplay between human history and the larger nonhuman creational world. Fretheim concludes that "these internal linkages give to the overall narrative a certain mirroring effect; each story reflects aspects of another, which binds them together more closely and provides an internal hermeneutic."[24]

Other illustrations of constructive literary readings of Exodus texts include the final form readings of the golden calf story by R. W. L. Moberly and Herbert Chanan Brichto.[25] Moberly, for example, assumes a synchronic reading of the present form of the text as his default unless tensions in the text require otherwise. Whereas previous critical scholars often detect a disjointed narrative of various sources and redactions, Moberly reads Exodus 32–34 as a coherent narrative about the breaking of the Sinai covenant with the golden calf apostasy and a gradual process of negotiation between God and Moses that culminates in a new covenant with a new set of laws (Exod 34:10–28).

M. R. Hauge studied a series of parallelisms and cyclical structures in Exodus centered on God's movement and descent from the exalted

---

[24] Ibid., 7.
[25] R. W. L. Moberly, *At the Mountain of God, Story and Theology in Exodus 32–34* (JSOTSup 22; Sheffield: JSOT Press, 1983); and Herbert Chanan Brichto, "The Worship of the Golden Calf," in *Toward a Grammar of Biblical Poetics, Tales of the Prophets* (New York: Oxford University Press, 1992) = "Worship of the Golden Calf," *HUCA* 54 (1983): 1–44.

mountain of Sinai into the humanly-constructed tent and tabernacle at the end of Exodus 40. God's "descent" from mountain to tabernacle is paralleled by Moses' "descent" from the unique and exalted mediator of the divine in the golden calf story (Exod 32–34) to a humble co-worker in a democratized tent-building project involving all Israelites (Exod 35–40).[26]

Deconstructive Literary Readings of Exodus

We move next to an example of a deconstructive literary approach to an Exodus text. Edward Greenstein studies the narrative of the troubling tenth plague, God's killing of the Egyptian firstborn sons in Exodus 12:29–32.[27] The killing of the Egyptian firstborn cries out for an explanation. Why does God punish the innocent firstborn children of Pharaoh and all other Egyptian parents? Why are even "the firstborn of the livestock" in Egypt killed as well? Greenstein begins by observing in a deconstructive mode that "texts do not make sense by themselves"; it is readers who strive to impose coherence, consistency or "sense" on a text.[28] However,

resisting sense does not mean making no sense at all. Quite the opposite. But because sense cannot permanently stand, it can be unmade, just as it is made. Thus, a reader can fashion a meaning, then unravel it, then refashion it, and then unravel it again. In the end, not one meaning will have been made, but several. As I will try to show, this can be done without cancelling the effect of one meaning by proposing another.[29]

Greenstein proposes three different explanations for God's killing of the Egyptian firstborn that emerge in light of three different companion texts that may be linked to the narrative of the killing of the firstborn in Exodus 12:29–32.

The first companion text is Exodus 4:22–23, and it "explains" the killing of the firstborn of Egypt as "measure-for-measure justice" when God

---
[26] Martin Ravndal Hauge, "The Descent from the Mountain, Narrative Patterns in Exodus 19–40, JSOTSup 323; Sheffield: Sheffield Academic Press, 2001).
[27] Edward Greenstein, "Making *Non*-Sense of the Tenth Plague," *Masoret* (1994): 16–17.
[28] Ibid., 16.
[29] Ibid., 16.

instructs Moses about what he shall say to Pharaoh when he confronts him:

Thus says YHWH: Israel is my firstborn son. I said to you [Pharaoh], "Let my son go that he may worship me." But you refused to let him go; now I will kill your firstborn son."

The turning of "all the pools of water" in Egypt into blood in the first plague (Exod 7:19) may be understood as a measure-for-measure judgment in reaction to Pharaoh's order to throw "every boy that is born to the Hebrews" into the Nile River (Exod 1:22). But these texts do not resolve the interpretation. Retributional justice is unclear because Moses never recounts the divine instruction to Pharaoh. Moreover, the divine threat concerning firstborn in Exodus 4:23 was limited to Pharaoh's own firstborn son (Exod 4:23), yet all the Egyptian firstborn perish (Exod 12:29). Yet another problem is that "all the firstborn of the livestock" of Egypt are killed (Exod 12:29). Why kill innocent cattle if it is the injustice of human beings like Pharaoh that is being judged?

A second companion text is Exodus 13:1, concerning the dedication of the firstborn: "Consecrate to me all the firstborn; whatever is the first to open the womb among the Israelites, of human beings and animals, is mine." This act of consecration or dedication of all Israelite firstborn is a cultic act by which Israel worships God and acknowledges God's righteous rule over their lives. The consecration of the firstborn affirms God's right to take back everything that rightfully belongs to God, whether firstborn or last born. Pharaoh repeatedly resisted knowing God, worshipping God, or acknowledging God's power throughout the ten plagues (Exod 5:2). Thus, the last plague with the death of Egypt's firstborn may be explained as a cultic act in which God recalls or takes back from Pharaoh and the Egyptians what rightfully belongs to God (their firstborn) and thereby definitively declares God's power and sovereignty over Pharaoh and the gods of Egypt.

A third explanation arises from the death of the firstborn in Exodus 13:11–16. In this text, the story of the death of the Egyptian firstborn supplies the rationale or origin for Israel's practice of "redeeming" their firstborn human sons. Israelites were to consecrate their firstborn human sons by offering them as sacrifices to God. However, Exodus 13:11–16 offers a way of to redeem their sons by offering up the firstborn of animals instead as a sacrificial substitution. This redeeming of Israel's firstborn sons with animal sacrifices is done because "Yahweh killed all the firstborn in the land of Egypt, from human firstborn to the firstborn of animals" (Exod 13:15). One (animal firstborn) could stand in for the other (human firstborn).

We are left with three possible explanations or meanings of the story of the death of the Egyptian firstborn: measure-for-measure justice, a cultic act affirming God's sovereignty, and an explanation for the origin of a practice of redeeming humans with substitutionary animal sacrifices. Greenstein concludes that no one explanation can account for all of the textual data or evidence.

The text is too complex and unruly to be satisfied by a single interpretation. The process of highlighting and including certain textual "facts" necessarily marginalizes or trivializes others. Our pegboard has too many pieces in too many colors to be drawn into a single pattern.... Leaving the process of interpretation open is a responsible way to read, for it recognizes the unruliness of texts and respects the individuality of every reader to make sense, or non-sense, or sense after sense.[30]

Readers can and do make sense of texts, but they may do so with a recognition of the need to keep their sense-making open to new possibilities and new insights from other readers.

Dialogical and Rhetorical Readings of Exodus

An example of a dialogical reading is Stephen Geller's study of the manna story in Exodus 16.[31] The narrative recounts the Israelites' early experiences in the wilderness on their way out of Egypt and into the wilderness. They complain of the lack of food. God responds and grants the Israelites a daily dose of "manna," a miraculous food that appears each morning and supplies sufficient nourishment for one day but no more. Only on the sixth day of the week are the Israelites allowed to collect twice as much manna as they need for that day. This allows the Israelites to rest from their manna collection on the seventh or Sabbath day and still have

[30] Ibid., 17.
[31] Stephen Geller, "Manna and Sabbath: A Literary-Theological Reading of Exodus 16," *Interpretation* 59 (2005): 5–16.

manna to eat. Geller begins by noting the common scholarly source-critical discernment of two traditions in Exodus 16, one Priestly and the other non-Priestly (what Geller terms the "Covenantal" tradition). These two different traditions or versions of the manna story have been combined and interwoven to form one story, albeit with some tensions. The two combined traditions are linked by the shared theme of Sabbath and manna as well as a number of shared key words all containing the Hebrew consonants of *šin* (sh) and *bêt* (b): *šābat* ("to stop, cease"), *šabbātôn* ("stoppage, solemn rest"), *šabbāt* ("stop"), *yāšab* ("sit, remain"), and *šĕbîʿî* ("seventh"). In the end, however, the narrative holds together two very different perspectives on the manna and the theme of the Sabbath that is also part of the story. The non-Priestly or Covenantal form of the manna story focuses on the "testing" of Israel in terms of their ability to follow God's commands (Exod 16:4). Twice the Israelites disobey God's commands. Some Israelites saved the daily manna over from one morning to the next, violating the command not to store up manna for the next day (Exod 16:19–20). Other Israelites went out and tried to gather manna on the seventh or Sabbath day, violating the command to rest and not work on the Sabbath (Exod 16:27–29). "Loyalty to the Sabbath is loyalty to God, and disloyalty to the Sabbath is apostasy and breach of covenant."[32] Testing obedience to the covenant is the central concern.

The Priestly version of the manna-Sabbath story, Geller argues, has a quite different understanding of the manna story. First of all, the Priestly story ends with a command to place some manna in a jar that would be housed in the shrine or temple for worship as a reminder for future generations of God's gift of daily manna (Exod 16:32–36). Manna is associated with liturgy, worship, and remembrance. Geller notes that the Priestly manna story also contains important parallels with the Priestly version of the creation story in Genesis 1:1–2:4. For example, the first five days of creation in Genesis 1 are proclaimed as "good" (Gen 1:4, 10, 12, 18, 25) but only the sixth day as "*very* good" (Gen 1:31); this mirrors the progression in the Priestly manna story from manna sufficient for a day for the first five days of the week but an extraordinary double portion of manna (like the extra portion of "*very* good") on the sixth day

---

[32] Ibid., 11.

(Exod 16:22). Moreover, the high point of the Priestly creation story is the seventh day when God stops all creative work on the Sabbath and thus sets it apart as special and holy, different from all other days (Gen 2:1–3). Similarly, the high point of the Priestly manna story is the seventh day, the day when Israelites imitate God and stop all work (Exod 16:22–26). Thus, "humans who observe Sabbath become imitators of the divine action, partners in creation with God."[33] Humans are commanded to stop their routines and do nothing on the seventh day just as God had done in the creation story. By their inaction on the seventh day, humans thereby set the completed week off as a finished period of time. The whole completed week thus becomes set apart, made holy and dedicated to God as an act of worship, a continuation of God's ongoing creation of the world.

These two versions of the manna story – one Covenantal about testing loyalty and one Priestly about continuing God's creation – stand side by side in a complementary dialogue folded into one story about manna and Sabbath in Exodus 16. In this instance, Geller brings together historical-critical insights from source criticism with a sensitive literary and theological analysis done in a dialogical mode that affirms both voices of the conversation.

James Watts has applied broad rhetorical categories to describe the shape of the whole Pentateuch as influenced by a tradition of public reading of the law associated with the book of Deuteronomy (see Deut 31:9–13). Watts argues that later Priestly writers and editors borrowed the basic rhetorical pattern of "story – list of laws – divine sanctions" from the book of Deuteronomy and used this rhetorical pattern as the overall blueprint by which they shaped Genesis–Deuteronomy as a whole: stories (Gen 1–Exod 19), lists (Exod 20-Num 36), and divine sanctions (Deut).[34] Watts's proposal is more historical-critical than literary, yet he also takes up some issues in the tradition of rhetorical analysis as an aid for understanding the juxtaposition of story and lists of laws together in the same book in Exodus. He notes the persuasive intent of the "story – list of laws – divine sanctions" pattern as seeking to move and persuade the hearers to accept and obey the laws that are proclaimed.

---

[33] Ibid., 14.
[34] James Watts, *Reading Law, The Rhetorical Shaping of the Pentateuch* (Sheffield: Sheffield Academic Press, 1999).

Finally, literary/rhetorical criticism has been a central feature in the study of the so-called Song of the Sea in Exodus 15. The text is an important example of ancient Hebrew poetry. Biblical poetry has its own distinctive features and conventions that are markedly different from either narratives or laws. Nearly half of the literature of the Hebrew Bible is lyric poetry (Psalms, prophetic books, Job, Proverbs, Song of Songs, Lamentations). The essence of lyric poetry is language written out in lines. Biblical poetry is characterized by a terseness or economy of words, the interplay of word clusters with small subplots or subarguments that bump into one another and create sparks of meaning within a poem. There is voice (usually either "I" or "we") rather than full development of characters. Poetry is characterized by the aesthetic play of language in sound, rhythm, grammar, syntax, genre twists, and surprises. Poetry features emotion, extravagance, hyperbole, contextuality (e.g., laments in contexts of disaster, praise, or thanksgiving in contexts of well-being), and the use of striking metaphors and images. Parallelism of lines or phrases (A^1___, and what's more A^2___) involving doublets or triplets of either similarities or contrasts is a frequent feature of biblical poetry, although parallelism is absent from about a third of the Bible's poems.[35] The poem in Exodus 15:1 begins its song praising God's victory over Pharaoh and his army:

> I will sing to YHWH,
> For he has triumphed gloriously,
> Horse and rider he has thrown into the sea.

The last two lines of this verse are parallel: God's glorious triumph (A^1) is explained and made more specific by the next parallel line (A^2), "Horse and rider he has thrown into the sea." The poem is filled with such parallel lines that interpret one another through similarity and often subtle but important differences between the two lines.

Robert Alter analyzes the poem of Exodus 15 and detects three main sections: verses 1–6, verses 7–11, and verses 12–18.[36] Each section has an image or metaphor of a heavy stone or metal object. In verse 5, the poem describes Pharaoh's army and chariots sinking into the Red Sea: "they

---

[35] F. W. Dobbs-Allsopp, "The Psalms and Lyric Verse," in *Evolution of Rationality* (ed. F. LeRon Shults; Grand Rapids, MI: Eerdmans, 2007), 346–79.
[36] Robert Alter, *The Art of Biblical Poetry* (New York: Basic Books, 1987), 76–84.

went down into the depths *like a stone.*" In verse 10, the sea covered the enemy, and "they sank *like lead* in the mighty waters." In verse 16, the people of Canaan were paralyzed in fear as Israel and God passed by: "by the might of your arm, they became still as a stone." Finally, the Israelites arrive and settle in security near the stable mountain of God: "You brought them in and planted them on the mountain of your own possession" (v. 17). The stones and lead of fear and death earlier in the poem give way to the security of Israel safely on the mountain of God. Mark Smith also provides a detailed poetic analysis of Exodus 15, and sees the poem as a key to the structure of the whole book of Exodus and its overriding theme of pilgrimage.[37]

We next turn our attention to specific texts in Exodus 1–2 and in Exodus 19–20 and seek to illustrate how some of the variety of approaches under the broad rubric of literary and rhetorical criticism may be applied with the same biblical text.

EXODUS 1–2

How might we proceed with a close literary or rhetorical reading of the three narratives of Exodus 1–2? The steps of rhetorical criticism as outlined by Trible and presented earlier provide a helpful roadmap and starting point. I will illustrate a literary critical reading of Exodus 1–2 by focusing in particular on Exodus 2.

Step 1. Determine the beginning and end of the literary unit. Trible notes that this is a very important first step since it will affect the rest of the analysis. We have set Exodus 2 as the rough boundary of our literary unit. However, the beginning and ending requires some adjustment. Exodus 2:1 begins with the Levite woman hiding her newborn son, but the reason she must hide him is not evident in verse 1. For that, we need to know the content of the preceding verse, Exodus 1:22, in which Pharaoh issues a new command to all Egyptians that every Hebrew boy should be thrown into the Nile. That is the reason she is hiding her baby.

The preceding narrative in Exodus 1:15–21 about the midwives who save the Hebrew male babies appears to come to a provisional resolution

---

[37] Mark Smith, "The Poetics of Exodus 15 and Its Position in the Book," in *Imagery and Imagination in Biblical Literature* (CBQMS 32; eds. Lawrence Boadt and Mark Smith; Washington, DC: Catholic Biblical Association of America, 2001), 23–34.

with Exodus 1:21: "And because the midwives feared God, he gave them families." Thus, we could argue that our literary unit actually begins not with Exodus 2:1 but with Exodus 1:22 and the new threat from Pharaoh. The "Nile" [or in Hebrew simply "the river"] mentioned in Exodus 1:22 will play a role later with references to the same "river" in Exodus 2:3, 5; this is another reason why Exodus 1:22 should be linked with the narrative that follows in chapter 2 rather than the narrative that precedes it in chapter 1. Likewise, at the end of Exodus 2, verses 23–25 form a transitional interlude from chapter 2 to chapter 3 and may be set off by themselves as a separate literary unit. Thus, our unit is more precisely Exodus 1:22–2:22, subject to any future modifications as we continue our analysis. For example, it might be argued that the literary unit should be redrawn to include the midwives story of Shiprah and Puah (Exod 1:15–21) along with the story of Pharaoh's daughter (Exod 1:22–2:10) so that the primary literary unit would be Exodus 1:15–2:10 rather than Exodus 1:22–2:22. There may be reasons to argue for such a delineation. For example, they both deal with women saving young Hebrew children (the midwives and Pharaoh's daughter). For now, however, we will set the unit as Exodus 1:22–2:22 and see if that provides a fruitful and persuasive rhetorical analysis as a unit. We should remember, however, to be open to reconsider these boundaries as we go through the other steps of our analysis. Rhetorical or literary analysis is always a matter of moving back and forth among the various steps or stages, adjusting our conclusions in light of new findings along the way.

Step 2. Discern and mark the repetition of specific words, phrases, and sentences throughout the unit, using the original Hebrew when possible.

Many words and phrases are repeated within Exodus 1:22–2:22. The word "daughter" (Hebrew *bat*) occurs nine times (Exod 1:22; 2:1, 5, 7, 8, 9, 10, 16, 20). The frequent use of "daughter" in the first part of the unit (Exod 1:22–2:10) is echoed with the mention of Reuel's seven "daughters" at the end of the unit (Exod 2:16–20). There is also an *inclusio* (a repetition at the beginning and at the end of the unit) with the phrase, "she bore a son." The phrase is used in reference to the Levite mother and her son Moses at the beginning (Exod 2:2) and in reference to Moses' wife Zipporah and her son Gershom at the end (Exod 2:22).

A striking variety and density of female terms occur in the first eleven verses of the unit: "woman" (Exod 2:2), "sister" (Exod 2:4, 7), "nurse" or "nursing woman" (Exod 2:7), "girl" (Exod 2:8), and "mother" (Exod 2:8) along with the several occurrences of "daughter" noted earlier. Females are noticeably absent in the middle of the unit in Exodus 2:11–15, but women characters reappear with the references to the seven daughters of Reuel and to Zipporah in Exodus 2:16–22. One noticeable contrast is Pharaoh's command to throw all Hebrew babies "into the Nile" [literally in Hebrew "into the river"] in Exodus 1:22, and the act of Pharaoh's daughter which directly disobeys that command as she "draws out" a Hebrew baby from the river and gives Moses a name that memorializes that act of civil disobedience against her own father (Exod 2:10).

Step 3. Discern the different types of discourse or point of view (narrator's voice, character's dialogue).

One instance of irony in which one character says something without knowledge of what the narrator and the reader knows is Pharaoh's command at the beginning in Exodus 1:22: "Every boy that is born to the Hebrews you shall throw into the Nile, but you shall let every girl live." The statement suggests that Pharaoh is fixated on the threat of Hebrew boys and males, and he believes that the women pose no threat to him. But the narrator's description of what follows suggests that Hebrew women join together in alliance (Hebrew mother and sister) with the Egyptian daughter of Pharaoh to rescue the Hebrew child who will grow up to lead the Israelites out of Egypt and become an agent of God's defeat of Pharaoh and his army. Ironically, Pharaoh totally misjudged the source of the threat and power he so feared, totally overlooking the agency and commitment to life of the women in the text.

Step 4. Sketch out the design, structure, and subunits of the literary text.

As some of the repetitions and other analysis discussed here have begun to indicate, this larger unit of Exodus 1:22–2:22 contains within it three shorter narratives that stand side by side in the present form of the text:

1. the birth story and rescue of the baby Moses in Exodus 1:22–2:10,
2. Moses' slaying of the Egyptian foreman in Exodus 2:11–15a, and
3. Moses' rescue of the Midianite women and his marriage to Zipporah in Exodus 2:15b–22.

At first glance, the three stories in Exodus 1:22–2:22 may not seem to have all that much to do with one another other than the presence of

Moses as a character in all three narratives. However, a closer examination
reveals a number of similarities, contrasts, and overlapping themes that
bring these three stories into an interesting and lively dialogue. If one were
studying Exodus 1:22–2:22 in a group setting, it would be an interesting
exercise to print out the three stories in three columns and then ask the
group members first to list as many similarities as they could identify
between any two or three of the stories. Then ask them to list as many
differences as they could identify between any two or three of the stories.
The results might look something like the following:

Similarities

a. Someone is saved or protected in stories 1, 2, and 3 (Exod 2:6–10,
    11–12, 17).
b. An issue of injustice against the less powerful is at play in stories 1,
    2, and 3 (Exod 1:22; 2:11–12, 17).
c. A key question occurs at a pivotal point in stories 1, 2, and 3 (Exod
    2:7, 14, 20).
d. Hiding and secrecy is involved in stories 1, 2, and 3 (Exod 2:2–4, 12,
    15).
e. Water is a motif in stories 1 and 2 (Exod 2:3, 5, 16).
f. A new son enters into a family and the new child is given a name
    which bears a meaning in stories 1 and 3 (Exod 2:10, 22).
g. An attempted rescue is done by breaking the law in stories 1 and 2
    (Exod 1:22; 2:9–10; 12).
h. A Levite priest is a father in story 1 (Exod 2:1–2), and a Midianite
    priest is a father in story 3 (Exod 2:16).
i. Moses is an outcast or foreigner in stories 1, 2, and 3 (Exod 2:10, 14,
    19, 22).

Differences

a. In stories 1 and 3, rescue happens without overt violence (Exod
    2:9–10, 17). In story 2, rescue happens through the use of violence
    (Exod 2:11–12).
b. In stories 1 and 3, images of water are associated both with threat
    (Exod 1:22; 2:16–17) and with new life (Exod 2:5–10; 17). In stories
    1 and 3, a mother nurses her baby with mother's milk and a man
    waters a flock of livestock. In story 2, there are no images of water

or other life-giving fluids, only dry sand associated with death and killing (Exod 2:12).

c. In stories 1 and 3, Moses is accepted into a family (Exod 2:10, 22). In story 2, Moses is rejected by his family, his "kinsfolk" (Exod 2:11, 13–14).

d. In story 1, Moses is saved by women (Exod 2:2–10). In story 3, Moses saves women (Exod 2:17).

e. Moses matures from a baby (story 1) to a young adult (story 2) to a married man (story 3).

f. In stories 1 and 2, Moses is the only character who is named. In story 3, Moses, Zipporah, Reuel, and Gershom are all named characters.

g. In story 1, Moses is called a "Hebrew" by an Egyptian (Exod 2:6). In story 2, Moses is called a Hebrew by the narrator (Exod 2:11) but rejected as a Hebrew by a fellow Hebrew (Exod 2:14). In story 3, Moses is called an "Egyptian" by the Midianites (Exod 2:19).

This complex interweaving of similar and contrasting elements creates a fertile ground for reflecting on the meanings of these three texts that obviously have some kind of interconnection among them, given this density and quantity of overlap, similarities and differences.

Step 5. Trace the flow of the plot development and movement from beginning to end (change, conflict, suspense, closure).

As noted earlier, the overall narrative structure involves the maturing and growing up of Moses from a baby to a young adult to a married man. Ultimately, Moses is heading in the narrative toward being called by God to lead Israel out of their Egyptian slavery. Along the way, these narratives display the critical role that women played early in Moses' life in rescuing him from death, and Moses returns the favor at the end of the unit when Moses rescues the Midianite daughters of Reuel from the harassing shepherds.

Indeed, conflicts are important to all three subnarratives within the literary unit. Pharaoh wants all babies thrown into the river, and Moses' mother, sister and Pharaoh's daughter successfully resist and save Moses' life (Exod 1:22–2:10). Moses' act of killing the Egyptian foreman immediately puts him in conflict the very next day with his own Hebrew "kinsfolk" and with Pharaoh who "sought to kill Moses" (Exod 2:11, 14, 15). The third subnarrative features less overt violence or threat with

the conflict with the shepherds at the well into which Moses intervenes
and which he seemingly resolves (Exod 2:17), resulting in his marrying
Zipporah and joining the Midianite family.

Although each of the three subnarratives comes to some closure and
resolution of each conflict, the resolution is partial and temporary. In the
first story, the baby Moses is adopted into the household of Pharaoh so
that his life is saved. But the reader wonders when the Hebrew Moses may
be found out. In the end, Moses is not truly at home in the household of
Pharaoh, exiled from his true Hebrew family. The second story likewise
lacks final closure. Moses ends up as a fugitive on the run with a death
sentence hanging over his head (Exod 2:15). In the third narrative, Moses
ends up with the Midianites, a wandering people who live far into the
desert and who exemplify rootlessness.

*Step 6. Describe the portrayal of characters and their interaction with
one another. Are the characters evaluated as good or bad and, if so, by what
strategies?*

The story is, of course, told from an Israelite perspective. Thus, the
Egyptian Pharaoh is portrayed negatively by issuing the edict to kill all
male Hebrew babies and to let female babies live. The edict is against his
own self interests (he is killing off his future labor force for slaves). It is a
product of exaggerated xenophobia about the potential threat of foreign
Israelites within the empire of Egypt. And the edict ignores what is the
largest threat at the moment, the women of Israel and Egypt (including
his own daughter). In contrast to her father, Pharaoh's daughter emerges
as righteous, compassionate, and willing to risk her own well-being to
save a child's life by knowingly resisting her father's command.

Moses appears in a positive light in light of his actions of rescuing the
Midianite daughters from the shepherds who mistreat the women at the
well. His actions mirror the compassionate actions of Pharaoh's daughter
toward someone who is ethnically different and who is vulnerable. Moses
is received into the Midianite family, marries Zipporah and has a child,
all signs of being welcomed by the Midianites and blessed by God (see
Exod 1:21).

But how do we as readers evaluate Moses' killing of the Egyptian
foreman in Exodus 2:12? The narrator does not give any explicit nod of
approval or disapproval of the action in terms of an explicit assessment.
Did Moses save the life of the Hebrew slave that was being beaten and

thus engage in justified violence for the sake of social justice, saving a
life of an unjustly oppressed group by killing the life of those who were
oppressing Hebrew slaves? We will return to this question at the end of
our rhetorical analysis.

*Step 7. Pay attention to syntax in the original Hebrew, when possible.
Note unusual word order or other grammatical oddities.*

The second clause of Pharaoh's edict, at the very beginning of the
text, after he commands throwing all Hebrew male babies into the river
contains an example of inverted word order in Hebrew. Normally, the
Hebrew verb is the first element in sequence in a Hebrew clause. In
Exodus 1:22, however, the verb is placed last at the end of the clause.
One of several possible functions of such inverted verb placement is to
signal a sharp contrast with the preceding clause about Hebrew male
babies being drowned. Thus, literally in Hebrew, the clause would read,
". . . *but*-every daughter you-shall-let-live." The inverted word order and
the use of the noun "daughter" (*bat*) that occurs nine times in the rest of
Exodus 1:22–2:22 highlights the critical role that "daughters" will play in
helping to unravel Pharaoh's empire in the end.

A reversal of normal word order also occurs in the very last line of
Exodus 2:22 in which Moses explains why he has named his firstborn
son, "Gershom." The name contains within it the Hebrew word *gēr*
which means "alien" or "stranger." Thus, Moses' explanation literally in
Hebrew reads, "**An-alien** I-am in-a-land foreign." In this case, placing
the noun, "stranger" (*gēr*) at the very beginning of the clause instead
of the normal verb serves to emphasize the word "alien" as essential to
Moses' core identity.

Moses could have been portrayed as marrying Zipporah and naming
his child something like "Home At Last" or "Happy Days Are Here
Again" which would have offered more a sense of closure and resolution
to the narrative (as with the midwives in Exod 1:21). When Moses claims
the mantle of being "an alien in a foreign land," we as readers may
wonder which foreign land does Moses have in mind when he makes
that statement? Is it Egypt where he was raised in Pharaoh's court? Now
Pharaoh wants to kill him so he is an alien in Egypt (Exod 2:15). Is it
Midian? The Midianite daughters of Reuel refer to Moses not as one of
them but as an "Egyptian" (Exod 2:19)? Or is it Israel, his own "kinsfolk"
or "people" (Exod 2:11) who reject him as if he were a foreigner (Exod

2:14)? It may be that all three stories combine to affirm that Moses is indeed a foreigner in every land or human community in which he may try to find his home – Egypt, Midian, and even among the Israelites. Being a foreigner, an outsider, will perhaps be Moses' destiny from here on out. He is a permanent exile, not at home anywhere.

Step 8. Note the particles and small words in Hebrew that may have major functions of emphasis, connection, movement, and structure.

We will mention only one such example, the use of the conjunction *kî* when Pharaoh's daughter names "Moses" in Exodus 2:10. The particle *kî* can mean several different things, depending on the context. Here it is causal and translated "for" or "because." The Hebrew literally reads, "And-she-called his-name Moses [Hebrew *mōšeh*], and-she-said, '**Because** [Hebrew *kî*] from-the-water I-drew-him-out [Hebrew *māšâ*].'" What is interesting is that the name "Moses" is likely a genuinely Egyptian name in its origins. The name "Moses" corresponds to a frequent element in ancient Egyptian names (e.g., the historical pharaohs named Thut-mose, Ah-mose, and Amen-mose). In Exodus 2:10, an Egyptian daughter of Pharaoh is portrayed as deriving the meaning of the name "Moses" not from its true Egyptian origins but from its resemblance to a Hebrew verb, *māšâ*, which means "to draw out." Names often carry significance in the Bible, and as in this case, the significance serves a rhetorical function within the narrative. Here Pharaoh's daughter "draws out" Moses from the water while earlier Pharaoh had commanded everyone to "throw into" the water or river all Hebrew male babies.

Step 9. Seek to bring all of the elements into some correlated analysis that tries to account for how all the diverse elements of your rhetorical analysis relate to one another. How does the interplay of all these rhetorical elements render meaning?

Even with only these three very short narratives standing side by side, a good deal of complexity and density of rhetorical data is at hand, and our interpretation of the overall meaning of these stories could go in any number of directions. We can briefly sample three different possibilities, illustrating the three broad literary approaches of a constructive, deconstructive, and dialogical/rhetorical reading.

A Constructive Literary Reading of Exodus 1:22–2:22. Terence Fretheim interprets all that happens to Moses in Exodus 1:22–2:22 as part of his formation as a leader of Israel, an agent of God, and a foreshadowing of what will happen with Israel, Moses, and God in the rest of the narrative of Exodus.[38] On one level, Moses begins to embody Israel's experience in his own personal life experience in these stories. Moses enters in conflict with Pharaoh and has his life threatened, as the oppressed Israelites did (Exod 2:15). Moses is forced to flee into the wilderness (the land of Midian – Exod 2:15) and find safety there, as Israel will find safety in the wilderness after they are liberated from Egypt. Moses' core identity now is that he is "an alien in a foreign land," precisely what the Israelite slaves are in the land of Egypt. Moses has begun to embody Israel's experience in his own.

On another level, Fretheim argues, Moses' experience also antici-pates and prefigures the future actions of God against Egypt and for the Israelite. Moses "sees" Israel's oppression (Exod 2:11) just as God will "see" and respond to Israel's suffering under slavery (Exod 2:25; 3:7, 9; 4:31; 5:21). Moses "strikes" [Hebrew nākâ] the Egyptian foreman and kills him (Exod 2:12). The same verb is used later to describe God's actions in bringing the plagues of judgment against the Egyptians (Exod 7:17, 19; 9:15; 12:12, 13, 25; 29). Moses "saved" and "delivered" the Midianite daughters (Exod 2:17, 19), just as God will "save" (Exod 14:13, 30; 15:2) and "deliver" (Exod 3:8; 6:6; 12:27) Israel from the Egyptians.

On yet another level, Moses' conflict with Pharaoh and more impor-tantly with fellow Israelites (Exod 2:13) foreshadows the rebellions and conflicts that he will experience with the Israelites when leading them out of Egypt and in their journey in the wilderness (Exod 5:21; 6:9–11; 14:11–12; Num 12: 1–2; Num 16:12–14).

Thus, for Fretheim, all three stories play a positive role in preparing Moses for his role as future leader of Israel and servant of God. These events prefigure both the deliverance of God that will soon come as well as some of the challenges that lay ahead for Moses himself. In terms of whether Moses' killing of the Egyptian could be justified, Fretheim points out that the same Hebrew word, "to strike" [Hebrew nākâ] is applied both to Moses' action in killing the Egyptian foreman and to God's actions in the plagues that God will bring upon Egypt.

The use of the same verb suggests that Moses' action was not considered inappropriate by the narrator (cf. Acts 7:23–29), but it anticipates *God's*

[38] Fretheim, *Exodus*, 42–46.

rather than Israel's activity. Moses introduces another level of resistance into
the conflict with the Egyptians. This move from nonviolence to violence by
stealth (short of open revolution) may be related to the changing nature of
Egyptian oppression. Beating people to death seems to call for more active
resistance. An intensification of response *by God* will now be evident in the
plagues, climaxing in the slaying of the firstborn.[39]

Moses' slaying of the Egyptian was "appropriate" because the Egyptian
was about to kill the Hebrew slave. Moses action also prefigures God's
own striking of the Egyptians in the plague. The reference to Acts 7:23–
29 is a New Testament defense of Moses' action in that he "defended an
oppressed man" and yet was rejected by his own Hebrew brothers who did
not understand what he had done. It is part of the speech of Stephen who
compares this rejection of Moses by his fellow Hebrews to the rejection of
Jesus by the Jewish leaders of his day. Fretheim thus consistently defends
Moses, God, and the narrator as acting "appropriately" at every point,
but he cautions against using Moses' act of violence as a model for future
human activity. God will be the one who will bring retributive judgment
on Egypt in the plagues that will soon arrive.

A Deconstructive Literary Reading of Exodus 1:22–2:22. Was Moses'
act of killing the Egyptian foreman who was abusing a Hebrew slave a
righteous act? The majority of biblical interpreters over the ages, both
Jewish and Christian, have tended to view Moses' violent act positively.
For example, one ancient Jewish interpretation defended Moses' action
as done out of genuine zeal for God and only after Moses had consulted
with the angels, who had preapproved his action (*Exod. Rab. 1.29*). Many
Christian interpreters followed the lead of the New Testament texts such
as Acts 7:23–29 (see earlier) and of Hebrews 11:24–27, in which Moses
joins a roster of other biblical heroes of faith:

By faith Moses, when he was grown up, refused to be called a son of Pharaoh's
daughter, choosing to share ill-treatment with the people of God rather than
enjoy the fleeting pleasures of sin. . . . By faith he left Egypt, unafraid of the
king's anger.

Although the Hebrews text does not mention the act of Moses killing
the Egyptian, it did lead later interpreters to fill in the gaps in the story
in Exodus 2 regarding Moses' motivation and state of mind in doing

[39] Ibid., 43. See also Frederic Holmgren, "Violence: God's Will on the Edge–Exodus
2:11–25," *Currents in Theology and Mission* 16 (1989): 426.

the violent act. The Hebrew and Acts texts also pass over in silence the secrecy of Moses' act: "He looked this way and that, and seeing no one he killed the Egyptian" (Exod 2:12). Presumably Moses only planned to do this one act secretly and then return to his life in Pharaoh's palace; his act of violence was not a daring and public demonstration of "choosing to share ill-treatment with the people of God" as Hebrews construes it. Hebrews 11 also claims that Moses was "unafraid of the [Egyptian] king's anger." However, the text of Exodus 2:14–15 explicitly notes that "Moses was afraid" when he found out that knowledge of his act of violence was public and immediately "fled" when Pharaoh "sought to kill" him.

The Hebrews 11 text illustrates the ways in which readers pass over certain details when they interpret a text, achieving coherence and stability by ignoring the loose threads that do not conform. Or another interpretive strategy is to take the inevitable gaps in any text that we interpret it and fill them in with information drawn from other intertexts or our own imagination. Such strategies have been used not only to defend Moses but also to condemn his act of violence. Thus, the ancient Christian interpreter Augustine brought to his interpretation of Moses' use of violence in Exodus 2 another intertext from the New Testament, namely, the Gospel story about the disciple Peter pulling out a sword and wounding one of the party who arrested Jesus before his crucifixion (John 18:10–11). Jesus strongly condemned Peter's violent act and commanded him to put the sword away. Augustine used Jesus' condemnation as justification for assuming that Moses' killing of the Egyptian was an immature and impulsive act, contrary to the will of God.[40]

A deconstructive approach to Exodus 2 and Moses' use of violence for the sake of social justice would likely seek to keep genuine gaps in the narrative open and seek to undo or "counter-read" any reading that claims an assured and inevitable conclusion from the story. Some years before the arrival of deconstructive methods in biblical studies, biblical scholar Brevard Childs made this observation about the Moses story in Exodus 2:

The Old Testament does not moralize on Moses' act of violence. Nowhere is there an explicit evaluation that either praises or condemns it. Rather, a situation is painted with great realism and sensitivity, and the reader is left

---

[40] Augustine, "Reply to Faustus the Manichean [XXII.70]," in *Writings in Connection with the Manichean Heresy*, trans. Richard Stothert Edinburgh: T. & T. Clark, 1872), 459.

to ponder on the only one meaning. It is open to misunderstanding and a variety of possible interpretations. Moses supposed that his motivation was obvious, but the Hebrew who was abusing his fellow attributed a totally different intention from that which Moses has envisioned. "Who made you a ruler over us?"[41]

The narrative of Exodus 2 itself testifies to the multiplicity of meanings that can be read onto a single act as well as a single text. The Hebrew who quarreled with Moses "read" his "text" – his act of killing the Egypt – with different eyes than Moses had intended. The author does not control the text, and subterranean meanings are always lurking just under the surface of the text, waiting to be teased out.

A Dialogical/Rhetorical Reading of Exodus 1:22–2:22. In conclusion, what might a dialogical and rhetorical approach have to contribute to our understanding of these three stories at the beginning of the book of Exodus? Staying as much as possible at the level of the "text itself" (which is never entirely possible as the other chapters in this book make clear), a dialogical and rhetorical approach might encourage an intertextual dialogue initially not with other "far away" texts like the New Testament or rabbinic midrash or the social context of an interpreter. Rather, it might promote a dialogue among the three texts "most near at hand" within Exodus 1:22–2:22 itself among the three different stories embedded there. In regard to the question of evaluating Moses' act of killing the Egyptian, one might argue that the two stories about Pharaoh's daughter and her successful rescue of the baby Moses and Moses' successful rescue of the Midianite daughters cast a positive hue to the whole chapter so that the two bracketing stories may lead a reader to also read the middle story of Moses killing the Egyptian positively as a righteous act of social justice and resistance to power, however small its effect may have been. But saving one baby (Moses) and helping one group of Midianite women were also small acts that foreshadowed and prepared for a much larger liberating action against Pharaoh's empire.

On the other hand, the relationship of the two framing positive rescue stories of baby Moses and the Midianite women to the middle story of Moses killing the Egyptian may be a relationship not of sameness but of

---

[41] Brevard S. Childs, "Moses' Slaying in the Two Testaments," *Biblical Theology in Crisis* (Philadelphia: Westminster, 1970), 182.

contrast. Moses finds a home and family, however temporary, in the two framing stories of Exodus 1:22–2:10 and Exodus 2:15b–22. Those positive endings mark the two framing tales of nonviolent action for the sake of justice as positive. In contrast, Moses only flees as a homeless fugitive at the end of the middle story of Exodus 2:11–15a, placing perhaps a more negative shroud over the use of violence for the sake of social justice.

   In the end, the dialogical approach of a Bakhtin and the long rhetorical tradition would emphasize the need to place these texts as events of real human communication within the context of real-world dialogues, faith communities, social groups, and political realities where there are actual human speakers, actors, and thinkers interacting. As that happens, the literary approach urges us as interpreters to strive to listen carefully to the details of the text, giving the text its due, even as we and the context in which we work bring a host of other influences, traditions, and commitments to the reading and hearing of these biblical texts.

EXODUS 19–20

We will now move on to illustrate briefly a variety of literary approaches to Exodus 19–20. We begin our analysis with a brief overview of the placement of Exodus 19–20 within the larger biblical context along with the contents of the two chapters. After leaving Egypt and the dramatic Red Sea event in Exodus 14–15, several scenes from Exodus 16–18 recount the stages of Israel's journey through the wilderness marked by a narrative sequence of geographical and time indicators: the "wilderness of Shur" (Exod 15:22), "the wilderness of Sin" on "the fifteenth day of the second month after they had departed from the land of Egypt" (Exod 16:1), departure from "the wilderness of Sin" (Exod 17:1), and events at "Massah and Meribah" (Exod 17:7) as well as "Rephidim" (Exod 17:8). After these wilderness events, Exodus 19:1 clearly begins a new literary unit with time and place indicators: "On the third new moon after the Israelites had gone out of the land of Egypt, on that very day, they came into the wilderness of Sinai." In the context of the larger Exodus narrative, this arrival at Sinai is not just another stage in the wilderness journey like the rest. Israel has at last come to "the mountain" where God dwells, the mountain to which God had promised to bring Moses and the Israelites after their rescue from Egypt as "a sign" of God's faithfulness (see Exod 3:12). The Israelites remain at this mountain in the wilderness of Sinai for nearly a year, which comprises the literature in the remainder of the book of Exodus, the entire book of Leviticus, and the first portion of the book of Numbers (Num 1:1–10:11), when the Israelites depart from "the wilderness of Sinai" in the second month of the second year. Thus, Exodus 19–20 marks the beginning of the large and central Sinai complex in the middle of the Pentateuch. The Sinai complex in Exodus 19–Numbers 10 is dominated by dramatic appearances of God, numerous law codes, and intervening narratives that mark a major turning point in the relationship of Israel's God and the people of Israel as God inaugurates a formal covenant relationship with God's people.

The contents and structure of Exodus 19–20 include the following elements:

Exodus 19:1–8a – Israel's arrival at "the mountain" at Sinai, God's declaration of the covenant, and the people's acceptance of the terms of the covenant

Exodus 19:8b–19 – God's dramatic appearance or theophany on Mount Sinai

Exodus 19:20–25 – Warnings about maintaining boundaries of holiness around the mountain

Exodus 20:1–17 – God's giving of the Ten Commandments on Mount Sinai

Exodus 20:18–21 – The fear of the Israelites and their request that Moses act as mediator of the words of God to them

Exodus 20:22–23:33 – The Book of the Covenant – additional laws given by God to Moses and mediated to the people

In the following paragraphs, we consider a brief sampling of constructive, deconstructive, and dialogical approaches to Exodus 19–20.

A Constructive Literary Reading of Exodus 19–20. One of the challenges in providing a constructive literary analysis of Exodus 19–20 is that most scholars agree that several different traditions and sources have been incorporated into these chapters, causing an unusual density of unevenness and tension among the various sections.[42] This is especially true

---

[42] Marc Brettler, "The Many Faces of God in Exodus 19," in *Jews, Christians, and the Theology of the Hebrew Scriptures* (SBLSymS 8; eds. Alice Ogden Bellis and Joel S. Kaminsky; Atlanta: Society of Biblical Literature, 2000), 353–56.

in Exodus 19 where the narrative action does not always follow a clear logical movement or temporal sequence. Moses climbs up Mount Sinai to speak with God a number of times in Exodus 19, but the reasons for each different ascent are not clear. Moreover, the movement of Moses up and down the mountain does not always follow a clear logical sequence. Moses will go up to the *top* of the mountain to be with God (Exod 19:3), and then suddenly Moses will appear without warning at the *bottom* of the mountain, talking to the people (Exod 19:7). No descent of Moses is narrated in between.

One constructive literary reading of Exodus 19 argues that while these disjunctions in time sequence in the narrative may indeed reflect a dense combination of sources and traditions, Exodus 19 has been constructed in its present form with an alternative mode of narrative organization based not on sequential chronology or plot (x happened and then y and then z) but on "spatial form devices." These "spatial form devices" have been identified by literary scholars in other literature; they interrupt the usual narrative flow of time with an alternative structure that focuses more on setting (space) and character. Thus, in regard to Exodus 19, Thomas Dozeman observes how redactors have given shape to the present form of Exodus 19:

The resulting structure of narrative in which spatial-form devices predominate has been likened to an orange. Like an orange, such a narrative is structured into individual pieces – similar segments of equal value – in which the movement is circular, focused on the single subject, the core. Scenes, therefore, are often juxtaposed to each other to provide a different perspective on the same core event, with the result that temporal sequence is often replaced by characterization, slow pace, lack of resolution, and repetition.[43]

Thus, the reader may discern an order and symmetry in Exodus 19 after all, based not on temporal sequence but on juxtaposed spatial segments. For example, Exodus 19:1–8a falls into two symmetrical halves, joined together by the repetition of the key verb "to call" (Hebrew *qāraʾ* in Exod 19:3 and 7) and a repetition of the actual covenant-making scene, one on top of Mount Sinai and one at the bottom of Mount Sinai. Exodus 19:1–8

---

[43] Thomas Dozeman, "Spatial Form in Exod 19:1–8a and in the Larger Sinai Narrative," *Semeia* 46 (1989): 87–101.

has the following two-part symmetry with Moses "ascending" in the first and "descending" in the second:

I. Exodus 19:3–6 – Moses on top of Mount Sinai with God – covenant making
   A. Moses "ascends" to God (Exod 19:3a)
   B. God "calls" to Moses (Exod 19:3ba)
   C. God delivers a proposal of covenant to Israel (Exod 19:3bb-6)
II. Exodus 19:7–8a – Moses at the base of Mount Sinai
   A. Moses "descends" to the people (Exod 19:7aa)
   B. Moses "calls" to the elders (Exod 19:7ab)
   C. Moses repeats the proposal of covenant (Exod 19:7b)
   D. The people accept the proposal of covenant (Exod 19:8a)

The juxtaposition of laws and narratives throughout Exodus 19–40 may be seen as structured in this manner, in which the literature is arranged around the one core event of God's revelation on Mount Sinai and the giving of the Torah:

Long sections of legislation, which correlate with the movement of Moses on Mount Sinai, suspend temporal sequence for chapters at a time. Throughout these extended divine discourses on law, the reader repeatedly loses a sense of the past, present, and future of narrated time. But this loss of narrated time serves a canonical purpose, for the result is that the reader's time becomes the significant moment for interpreting the promulgation of Torah "on this day" [Exod 19:1].[44]

In the end, Exodus 19 has its own unique coherence, logic, and overall structure that continues into Exodus 20 (with the alternation of narratives and the Ten Commandments) and on through the end of the book of Exodus.

A Deconstructive Literary Reading of Exodus 19–20. The disjunctions and tensions within Exodus 19 may be a challenge to constructive modes of literary analysis, but they are embraced and amplified by more deconstructive readings of the same text. Elements of Benjamin Sommer's analysis of Exodus 19 begin to move in a deconstructive direction. Sommer uses Exodus 19 to reflect on Jewish understandings of divine

---

[44] Ibid., 94–95.

revelation and its relationship to human interpretation. He observes that "the chapter defies a coherent sequential reading. More than any other passage in the Pentateuch, it is full of ambiguities, gaps, strange repetitions, and apparent contradictions."[45] He focuses in particular on the repeated Hebrew word, *qôl*, in Exodus 19–20, which may be translated in several different ways within the chapter:

Exodus 19:5 – God's "voice"
Exodus 19:16a – "thunder"
Exodus 19:16b – "blast" [of a trumpet]
Exodus 19:19a – "blast" [of a trumpet]
Exodus 19:19b – "thunder" [or God's "voice"?]
   "[God] would answer [Moses] in thunder" *or*
   "[God] would answer [Moses] with a voice."
Exodus 20:18a – "thunder"
Exodus 20:18b – "sound" [of the trumpet]

The ambiguity in Exodus 19:19b, in particular, raises questions about the nature of God's revelation at Sinai. Did the Israelites only hear God speak in unintelligible and terrifying "thunder" rather than an intelligible divine "voice" with words? Were all of the commandments and laws mediated through a human being, Moses? Or did the Israelites hear and receive at least some words directly from God at Mount Sinai? Exodus 19–20, Sommer argues, is ambiguous. Sommer goes on to consider a wide range of intertexts both from the Bible itself and from later postbiblical and medieval Jewish commentators to explore the theme of God's revelation at Sinai. "The oldest Jewish commentary on the Book of Exodus" in Deuteronomy 4–5 removes some of the ambiguity of Exodus 19–20, declaring plainly that Israel heard "not merely thunder but a voice articulating sounds in order to communicate meaning" (Deut 4:12–13; 5:23). Yet at the same time Deuteronomy 5:4–5 also expresses contradictory claims about the unmediated speaking of God to Israel at Sinai, on one hand (v. 4) and Moses' mediation of all of God's words to the people, on the other (v. 5).[46]

---

[45] Benjamin Sommer, "Revelation at Sinai in the Hebrew Bible and in Jewish Theology," *The Journal of Religion* 79 (1999): 426.
[46] Ibid., 433–34.

Exodus 24 functions as another biblical intertext to Exodus 19–20. The alternate portrait of God's revelation on Mount Sinai in Exodus 24 features absolutely no sound, no *qôl*, from God that the elders or priests of Israel who are permitted to climb Mount Sinai may hear. It is a purely visual revelation: "they saw the Godof Israel . . . they beheld God, and they ate and drank" (Exod 24:10–11). There is only silence in viewing the divine. This then leads Sommer to another biblical text, 1 Kings 19, in which Elijah encounters God at Mount Sinai (also known as Horeb). At this mountain of God, Elijah does not encounter the divine in the dramatic sounds, visions of howling wind, loud earthquake, or even devouring fire;but in "a sound (*qôl*) of thin utter silence" (1 Kgs 19:12). The divine word is thus silence, "an intimation of something beyond words and shapes, a trace that discloses a real and commanding presence."[47] Jewish interpreters concluded from this text that the direct word of God at Sinai was unintelligible to human beings. Divine revelation always requires human mediation and human interpretation. The "heavenly" or "primordial Torah" is like fire, according to one Jewish tradition, "real yet insubstantial, perceptible but not quite physical, ever changing yet oddly constant."[48] This view of language and revelation – the elusiveness of the divine *qôl* or "voice" – illustrates well the deconstructive suspicion of overly confident claims for stable, unified, and assured meanings in texts, including religious texts like the Bible.

   A Dialogical/Rhetorical Reading of Exodus 19–20. Mark Brettler's study of Exodus 19 also begins with the disjunctions and tensions within the chapter. He argues that Exodus 19 is a "magnet text," a text that attracts a high density of diverse traditions because of the momentous nature of the subject matter.[49] What is unique and momentous about Exodus 19–20 in its ancient Near Eastern context is that a deity, Israel's God, gives law to a particular nation, Israel (Deut 4:32–36). Typically in the ancient Near East, it is human kings or rulers who issue laws and decrees, not deities. Because God's revelation of the law at Sinai is such a central event for ancient Israel, Brettler argues, biblical editors allowed a diversity of traditions to coexist in Exodus 19–20. The editors believed that no

---

[47] Ibid., 445.
[48] Ibid., 446.
[49] Brettler, "The Many Faces of God in Exodus 19," 357.

one tradition could exhaust the meaning of this event. Thus, traditions that honored Moses alone as mediator of God's law who alone was permitted to ascend Mount Sinai (Exod 19:3) coexist with traditions that included Aaron the priest as permitted on the mountain (Exod 19:24). Remarkably, another tradition even permitted "all the people" to go up to the mountain: "When the trumpet sounds a long blast, they [all the people] may go up on the mountain" (Exod 19:13b). These conflicting traditions are not harmonized but allowed to stand together in dialogical tension.[50]

The same dialogical tension occurs with the quite varied depictions of the divine presence. God is at times depicted as hidden in "a thick cloud" (Exod 19:9) that protects humans from seeing God and dying as a result. The divine cloud in Exodus 19:16 depicts God's great power through a storm cloud with dramatic thunder and lightning accompanying it. Another image associated with the divine presence is the fire of a volcano, another image of divine power with its own distinctive character (Exod 19:18). Exodus 24 provides a counterpoint to the noisy, fiery, conflicting, and in the end mysterious images in Exodus 19. In Exodus 24, the hierarchy of who can ascend the mountain is clear and consistent (Moses at the top, elders and priests midway, people at the bottom). The atmosphere of Exodus 24 is less terrifying and more ritualistic, calm, and even quiet. No divine words are spoken. Clouds do not hide God. Instead, the text says plainly that Moses, the priests, and the elders "saw the God of Israel . . . they beheld God, and they ate and drank" (Exod 24:10–11).[51]

Unlike Sommer's more deconstructive reading, Brettler takes these dissonances within Exodus 19–20 and 24 as reflection on different modes of leadership (democracy versus hierarchy) as well as theology. Exodus 19 serves to emphasize more the mystery, power, and elusiveness of God. Exodus 24, in contrast, "is redacted in a more rationalistic vein, bringing together various sources and traditions so they would make sense, so revelation would be relatively straightforward."[52] In the end, the dialogue between Exodus 19 and 24 reminds interpreters that when "we are

[50] Ibid., 362–63.
[51] Ibid., 367.
[52] Ibid., 367.

interpreting religious texts," we will likely find "elements of both rationality and mystery within them."[53]

The literary arrangement of the Ten Commandments (Exod 20:1–17)
and the Book of the Covenant (Exod 20:22–23:19) also invited a dialogical
interpretation. The juxtaposition of the very different law codes raises
the question of the relationship between the terse and well-ordered Ten
Commandments and the more varied and seemingly unorganized laws
in Book of the Covenant. The Ten Commandments appear as more
comprehensive and ordered than the more specific and historically time-
bound laws in the Book of the Covenant. The Ten Commandments move
systematically from a narrative preamble about what God has done (Exod
20:1–2) to a list of apodictic laws concerning obligations to God (Exod
20:3–11) and finally to a list of obligations to other humans (Exod 20:12–
17). The polished and timeless qualities of the Ten Commandments have
enabled its imperatives to speak directly and immediately to communities
across time and space in different cultures and eras. In contrast, the less
organized laws in the Book of the Covenant resists attempts to discern
any underlying scheme or structure of organization. The laws are varied
in topic and in form, prompting interpreters to judge the law code to
structure or any organizing themes.

But the contrasts in form and organization between the Ten Commandments and the Book of the Covenant may serve a larger literary
function. Joe Sprinkle, for example, has argued that the varied laws of
the Book function as specific and illustrative commentary to the more
abstract and generalized Ten Commandments.[54] The laws of the Book
of the Covenant illustrate how the more abstract Ten Commandments
could enter into specific areas of Israel's common life. It is precisely
the laws' unsystematic character that invites the reader to ongoing legal
interpretation that involves negotiation of competing obligations and
values. The divine law is grounded in the stone tablets of the Ten Commandments but is then immediately applied to specific circumstances.
The dialogical relationship of the two law codes models the ongoing

---

[53] Ibid., 367.
[54] Joe Sprinkle, *The Book of the Covenant: A Literary Approach* (Sheffield: Sheffield Academic Press, 1994), 17–34. See also Dennis T. Olson, "The Jagged Cliffs of Mount Sinai:
A Theological Reading of the Book of the Covenant (Exod. 20:22–23:19)," *Interpretation*
(July 1999): 251–63.

process of ethical reflection. The interplay of the Ten Commandments and the Book of the Covenant urges the reader to join a rich dialogue of reasoned applications of specific laws in real-world circumstances and diverse rhetorical contexts.

FURTHER READING

General

Abbott, H. Porter. *The Cambridge Introduction to Narrative*. Cambridge: Cambridge University Press, 2005.

Amit, Yairah. *Reading Biblical Narratives, Literary Criticism and the Hebrew Bible*. Minneapolis: Fortress, 2001.

Barry, Peter. *Beginning Theory: An Introduction to Literary and Cultural Theory*. Manchester: Manchester University Press, 2002.

Berlin, Adele. *Poetics and Interpretation of Biblical Narrative*. Sheffield: Almond Press, 1983.

Culler, Jonathan. *Literary Theory. A Very Short Introduction*. New York: Oxford, 2000.

_____. *On Deconstruction: Theory and Criticism after Structuralism*. Ithaca, NY: Cornell University Press, 2007.

Fokkelman, J. P. *Reading Biblical Narrative, An Introductory Guide*. Trans. Ineke Smit. Louisville, KY: Westminster John Knox, 1999.

Green, Barbara. *Mikhail Bakhtin and Biblical Scholarship, An Introduction*. Atlanta, GA: Society of Biblical Literature, 2000.

Greenstein, Edward. "Deconstruction and Biblical Narrative." *Prooftexts* 9 (1989): 43–71.

Gunn, David, and Danna Nolan Fewell. *Narrative in the Hebrew Bible*. New York: Oxford University Press, 1993.

Meynet, Roland. "Rhetorical Analysis, An Introduction to Biblical Rhetoric." JSOT-Sup 256. Sheffield: Sheffield Academic, 1998.

Morson, Gary Saul, and Caryl Emerson. *Mikhail Bakhtin, Creation of a Prosaics*. Stanford: Stanford University Press, 1990.

Patrick, Dale. *The Rhetoric of Revelation in the Hebrew Bible*. Minneapolis: Fortress, 1999.

_____, and Allen Scult. *Rhetoric and Biblical Interpretation*. JSOTSup 82. Sheffield: Almond, 1990.

Watson, Wilfred. *Classical Hebrew Poetry: A Guide to Its Techniques*. New York: T & T Clark, 2005.

Literary and Rhetorical Criticism of Exodus

Carroll, Robert. "Strange Fire: Abstract of Presence Absent in the Text: Meditations on Exodus 3." JSOT 61 (1994): 39–58.

Davies, John A. *A Royal Priesthood, Literary and Intertextual Perspectives on an Image of Israel in Exodus 19.6*. New York: T & T Clark, 2004.

Leder, Arie C. "The Coherence of Exodus, Narrative Unity and Meaning." *CTJ* 36 (2001): 251–69.

Liss, Hanna. "The Imaginary Sanctuary: The Priestly Code as an Example of Fictional Literature in the Hebrew Bible," pages 663–89 in *Judah and Judeans in the Persian Period*. Edited by Oded Lipschits. Winona Lake, IN: Eisenbrauns, 2006.

Polak, Frank. "Water, Rock, and Wood: Structure and Thought Pattern in the Exodus Narrative." *Journal of the Ancient Near Eastern Society* 25 (1997): 19–42.

Schreckhise, Robert L. "The Rhetoric of the Expressions in the Song by the Sea (Exodus 15, 1–18)." SJOT 21 (2007): 201–17.

Siebert-Hommes, Jopie. *Let the Daughters Live! The Literary Architecture of Exodus 1–2 As a Key for Interpretation*. Biblical Interpretation Series 37. Leiden: Brill, 1999.

Smith, Mark. *The Pilgrimage Pattern in Exodus*. Sheffield: Sheffield Academic Press, 1997.

2

Genre Criticism

KENTON L. SPARKS

THE METHODOLOGY OF GENRE CRITICISM

Genre is a loan word from the French that means "kind" or "type." The term is widely used with reference to human discourse; to inquire about the genre of verbal discourse, whether of a spoken utterance or written text, is to ask about the sort of discourse that it is. Utterances might be "commands," "questions," "poems," or "stories," just as texts might be "biographies," "histories," "letters," or "newspaper articles." When we identify verbal discourse using one of these labels, we imply that we know something about how that type of discourse works and that we have the competence to understand it to some degree. If we have this skill as interpreters of literature, scholars would say that we have *generic* or *literary competence.* Our objective in the present article is modestly to pursue generic competence as readers of the Bible and, more specifically, as readers of the Book of Exodus. The quest begins with a bit of historical reflection on form criticism, which is the theoretical forerunner of genre criticism.

The Origins and Nature of Form Criticism

It would be accurate to say that prior to the Enlightenment (c. eighteenth cent.), the Bible's genre was foremost understood as "divine word." By this I do not mean to say that pre-Enlightenment scholars failed to notice that different types of literature were in the Bible; I mean instead that, whatever these other genres were, they were considered secondary to the Bible's status as divine discourse. And because the Bible was a divine book,

both Jews and Christians interpreted it differently from other books. They
anticipated that their respective Bibles would provide a single, coherent
understanding of God and theology. As a result, when two biblical laws
seemed to contradict each other, the Jewish rabbis would resolve the
contradiction by employing one of their interpretive rules, such as *kelal
upherat* ("the general and the particular"),[1] or by interpreting one or
both conflicting texts as allegories. Early Christians also used allegories
for this purpose.[2] The details of these interpretive strategies are not
important; the important point is that the traditional understanding of
the Bible's genre as "divine word" significantly affected the secondary
generic judgments made by Jews and Christians about its human genre.
Equally important for our understanding of early interpretation is the fact
that for much of Western history, biblical interpreters underestimated the
historical distance that separated them from the world of the biblical text.
Traditional interpreters, whether they lived in the fifth, tenth, or fifteenth
centuries, never doubted that their world was also the world that God
created, the world where Adam and Eve once lived, the world of the great
flood, and the world populated by the descendants of Noah's sons, Ham,
Shem, and Japheth.[3] Christians and Jews alike usually assumed that a
seamless fabric connected their world with the biblical world. So the
Bible was a divine book, and its cultural world was our world.

During the late medieval period, and especially during the subsequent
Renaissance period, this understanding of the biblical world was gradually shattered by the rise of historical consciousness. Scholars studying
Latin and Greek texts, and the classical historical contexts described in
them and assumed by them, began to realize that human languages and
traditions change radically over the course of time. At first this observation was not rigorously applied to the Church and the Bible, but eventually scholars turned their critical eye on these religious institutions. Just as

---

[1] That is, the general rule expressed in one text can be modified or circumscribed by
    texts that are more particular in their import. See J. Bowker, *The Targums and Rabbinic
    Literature: An Introduction to Jewish Interpretation of Scripture* (Cambridge: University
    Press, 1969), 315; see also Richard N. Longenecker, *Biblical Exegesis in the Apostolic
    Period* (2nd ed.; Grand Rapids, MI: Eerdmans, 1999), 18–24.
[2] See Frances Young, "Alexandrian and Antiochene Exegesis," in *A History of Biblical
    Interpretation: The Ancient Period* (Vol. 1; Grand Rapids, MI: Eerdmans, 2003), 334–54.
[3] For this characterization of Calvin and of the precritical tradition in general, see Hans
    W. Frei, *The Eclipse of Biblical Narrative* (New Haven: Yale, 1974), 1–50.

the Reformation uncovered the historically contingent nature of Church tradition and doctrine, so the Enlightenment revealed that the Bible was a product of many different historical and cultural perspectives. These developments laid the groundwork for the first critical engagements with the Bible's genres.

Scholars of the Enlightenment and early post-Enlightenment eras attended closely to the historically and socially conditioned nature of the Bible's human genres. One thinks immediately of the Jewish scholar, Baruch Spinoza, or of the Christian scholar David Strauss. But the father of the generic study of the Bible was undoubtedly Hermann Gunkel (1862–1932).[4] Gunkel was a theologian and Bible scholar, but he was also an avid reader of the German folklore collections then newly published by the Brothers Grimm. He noticed how often the primitive oral myths, legends, folktales, and fairy tales of Germany reminded him of the stories in the Hebrew Bible. On this comparative basis, he proposed that much of the pentateuchal narrative was not historical in the conventional sense but was instead traditional narrative, which included not only historical recollections but also a blend of myths, legends, folktales, and fairy tales. Consequently, he viewed the Pentateuch as the work of a collector (*Sammler*) of old oral traditions rather than as the product of a full-fledged author. So, whereas some of his contemporaries inquired about the "book" of Exodus, Gunkel was more interested in the origins and development of the various oral legends that stood behind the book, such as those concerning Israel's descent into Egypt, Moses, Sinai, the Wilderness, the Passover, and the Exodus event. Gunkel's method for studying the text came to be known as *Form Criticism*, so-called because it gave careful attention to the "form" or structure of biblical traditions.

Form criticism's narrow focus on the Bible's small, oral units of tradition was never a necessary limitation. This limitation was an accident, which resulted from an artificial boundary that developed between *literary* or *source criticism*, which focused on the longer written sources used to compose the Bible, and form criticism, which sought to discern the nature and character of the smaller tradition units. But in fact, all units of verbal discourse – whether large or small, oral or written – have a generic

---

[4] For selections from the works of Spinoza, Strauss, and Gunkel, see William Yarchin, *History of Biblical Interpretation* (Peabody, MA: Hendrickson, 2004), 195–207, 218–248.

character that can be considered. Consequently, not too long after form criticism developed, scholars began to speak freely about the forms (or genres) of whole books, or large parts of books, rather than of very small text units.

How have form critics determined the genres of biblical texts? Gunkel and his followers have generally identified the *Gattung* (genre) of a text on the basis of *mood, form,* and *Sitz im Leben.*[5] Mood referred to the internal dispositions of the author; form, to the structure or elements in the discourse; and *Sitz im Leben,* to the "life setting" or context that produced the genre. Every text that shared these three features was judged to be of the same genre. Gunkel's work on the Psalms provides an example. He identified the genre of "individual lament Psalms" on the following bases:

> **mood:** the text expresses grief and sadness.
> **form:** these feelings are expressed from a first person ("I") perspective, and are followed by a request for help from God.
> **setting:** the text was composed and used in a private devotional setting.

When drawing this generic conclusion about a Psalm, Gunkel did not mean that it was "probably" or "sometimes" used as he describes. In his opinion, it was the very nature of the case that any Psalm exhibiting these features originated and was used in private devotional settings.

It is fairly easy to recognize, however, that there are serious flaws in this approach. For common sense tells us that the "I" laments – like modern hymns that use the word "I" – could have been written for use by the congregation as a whole. And even if they were not, this would not have prevented religious congregations from singing them. This example illustrates the obvious tension between the rigidity of the form critical method and the actual fluidity of generic traits. What accounts for the theoretical rigidity form criticism? First, Gunkel and his followers were very interested in reconstructing the social history of Israel, especially of "primitive" Israelite society. By rigidly forcing each text into a particular category that reflected a particular social context, they believed that they could make it speak a clear word about that social history. Second, in what turns out to be a related matter, Gunkel was deeply influenced by

---

[5] See Hermann Gunkel, *The Psalms: A Form-Critical Introduction* (trans. Th. M. Horner; Philadelphia: Fortress, 1967), 10.

the Neoclassical notion of generic purity. For the Neoclassicists, a text was ideally composed in one, and only one, genre. This is why in his work on the Psalms and legends, Gunkel's list of genres had to conclude by tossing in a category called "mixed genres."[6] His need for a "mixed genre" category modestly reveals that there is a theoretical flaw in form criticism as it is usually construed.

James Muilenburg was among the first biblical scholars to put his finger on the problem. He noted that when the form critics classify texts into generic categories on the threefold basis of mood, form, and setting, their tendency is to focus only or mainly on the similarities of the texts and to overlook or underappreciate the differences. In order to compensate for this oversight, Muilenburg proposed that biblical scholars add *rhetorical criticism* to their theoretical chest of research tools.[7] Rhetorical criticism begins where form criticism ends by closely examining texts of the same genre to determine what distinguishes them from each other. So whereas a form critic might point out that Psalms 8 and 22 are "individual lament psalms," the rhetorical critic will go on carefully attending to the differences between these laments.

The Rise of Genre Criticism

I say all of this not merely for history's sake but mainly so that we can clearly understand why this chapter is entitled *genre criticism* rather than *form criticism*. As we have just noted, rhetorical criticism developed to correct a theoretical flaw in form criticism, but this flaw itself was not actually recognized by Muilenburg and the early rhetorical critics. The chief difficulty with form criticism is that it drinks deeply from the well of *generic realism* rather than from the theoretically superior spring of *generic conceptualism*.[8] This heady comment requires a word of explanation.

---

[6] Gunkel, *The Psalms*, 36–39; Hermann Gunkel, *The Legends of Genesis* (trans. W. F. Albright; New York: Schocken, 1964), 34–35.

[7] James Muilenburg, "Form Criticism and Beyond," *JBL* 88 (1969): 1–18.

[8] For the purposes of this discussion, the practical significance of "conceptualism" for generic study is the same as for two other views of genre, "nominalism" and "moderate realism." For the subtle theoretical distinctions, see K. W. Hempfer, *Gattungstheorie: Information und Synthese* (Uni-Taschenbücher 133; Munich: Wilhelm Fink, 1963); for a basic introduction, see Frederick Garber et al., "Genre," *The New Princeton Encyclopedia of Poetry and Poetics* (ed. A. Preminger and T. V. F. Brogan; Princeton, NJ: Princeton University Press, 1993), 456–59.

When it comes to interpretation, strict generic realists tend to believe that generic categories (such as "myth," "legend," "historiography" and "wisdom literature") have an existence apart from the writing and interpretation of texts. Within this theoretical perspective, our goal as interpreters is to discover the essence of these preexisting categories ("What is historiography?") and to place the correct texts into those categories ("Is the book of Exodus historiography?"). This generic approach stands behind the modern scholarly debates about the definition of genres like "wisdom literature" and "historiography"; these debates assume that there is a "correct" definition of "historiography" and that scholars are competing to find it. One can easily sense the circularity involved in this dispute. One scholar labels various texts as "historiography" and then uses those texts both to define the genre and to exclude other texts from it; the next scholar disagrees, perhaps by beginning with a different set of texts or perhaps by asserting a different definition of historiography, which then dictates the texts that fit. These debates are interminable and fail to appreciate the insights of generic conceptualism.

Generic conceptualists recognize that human beings create generic categories as we interpret literature. There is no such thing as *the* correct definition of "myth," and every application of the term to literature implies the definition of the person using the term. Confusion naturally arises with the use of shorthand labels like "myth," "legend," "wisdom," and "historiography" because scholars are apt to define these terms differently. Implied in this observation is that there is no one-to-one correlation between text and genre. Because we create and give labels to generic categories, a text can fit many different generic categories at the same time. Consider the biblical books of Ruth and Lamentations as an example. While a traditional form critic (a generic realist) will tend to believe that these books either are or are not of the same genre, the conceptualist will think otherwise. If our generic category is "Hebrew texts" or "short books" or "festival scrolls," then Ruth and Lamentations will be of the same genre. If, however, our generic category is "narrative literature" or "literature about women," then Ruth is in, Lamentations is out. The main point, from a conceptualist point of view, is that readers create generic categories as we classify together texts that share a common trait or traits. Interpretation succeeds when these common traits are correctly identified because this elucidates our understanding of the text we are reading. So, while the form critics were on the right track when they used the threefold criteria of mood, form, and setting to classify biblical texts, they erred at three critical points: first, they errantly assumed that these criteria dictated the one and only genre of the text; second, they overlooked the fact that these three elements represent only a few of the many traits one can employ to create and form generic categories; and third, they failed to understand that generic categories are the taxonomic creations of interpreters. Genre criticism capitalizes on the comparative insights of form criticism but corrects these theoretical flaws.

Before proceeding further, one word of clarification is in order. I have so far discussed form criticism in the past tense, as if it has been wholly supplanted by genre criticism and is no longer practiced. But in fact, there are still many scholars who practice form criticism in precisely the way that I have described it, and many other scholars who are attempting to "reform" form criticism by making adjustments to it, often in the direction of generic conceptualism.[9] The result is that the term *form criticism* means many things in contemporary scholarship; it is often synonymous with *genre criticism*.

Genre Criticism in Theory and Practice

At this point we can consider genre criticism in more detail. Generic theory is a complicated matter about which scholars have many debates and arguments, but this needn't prevent us from appreciating the basic theoretical issues and from adopting a working theory of genre for our study of Exodus. An adequate grasp of generic theory will involve both sides of human discourse. Here I refer, on the one hand, to the writer (or speaker), and, on the other hand, to the reader (or listener). Let us begin with the writer's perspective. All scholars agree that genre reflects the ground rules shared by authors and readers. Just as an author must follow the rules of grammar to be understood, so the author must adhere to the generic "rules" that govern the larger shape and order of the discourse. In the case of a letter, for instance, the writer knows to begin with a salutation, "Dear Elizabeth," followed by the body of the letter, a

---

[9] See Marvin A. Sweeney and Ehud Ben Zvi, eds., *The Changing Face of Form Criticism for the Twenty-First Century* (Grand Rapids, MI: Eerdmans, 2003).

complimentary conclusion, and a signature. If the author fails to follow
these conventions, readers may misunderstand or be confused by the
discourse. Put theoretically, genre functions "to mediate between speaker
and hearer by establishing a common *dynamics* capable of ruling both
the production of the discourse as a work of a certain kind and its
interpretation according to rules provided by the genre."[10]

Is genre therefore a straitjacket that more or less forces authors to
follow a narrow set of established conventions? The answer is "yes" and
"no." Indeed, authors must follow certain conventions to be understood
by readers. On the other hand, because every text is in some respects
unique, it follows that authors also enjoy a certain amount of literary
freedom. This is in part because authors can combine previously existing generic conventions in unique ways (thus making new buildings
out of old bricks), and in part because of the metaphorical capacity of
human thought and discourse. The metaphor "God is a mighty rock,"
for instance, communicates something about God's dependability by
symbolically linking it with "rock." The creative capacity to use a symbol
in this way is native to human intelligence but differs in kind and scope
from person to person. So authors are free to combine generic categories
and even to make creative symbolic leaps so long as readers can recognize and understand the creative moves. Fortunately, informed readers
in the author's community can usually follow the author's creative path
without too much trouble. But if the author exercises poor judgment in
these creative decisions, confused readers will be the result.

Which brings us to the other side of the communication event. How
do readers, as interpreters, make sense of a text that is new to them? It is
widely recognized that human beings make sense of our experiences in
an interpretive process that depends on comparison and classification.
For instance, when I am about to eat some new and exotic fruit that I've
never tasted before, I will initially form an expectation about what it will
taste like by comparing it with the shapes, colors, smells, and textures
of other fruits that I've tasted before. Once I have actually tasted it, of
course, I will quickly discover how close my initial "guess" was, and I will
usually go on to explain the actual taste in terms of fruits that I and others

---

[10]   Paul Ricouer, "The Hermeneutical Function of Distanciation," *Philosophy Today* 17
        (1973): 129–41.

already know: "It tastes like a peach, but is tart like a lemon and fibrous like a Mango." All interpretation is like this, insofar as we make sense of what is new by classifying and comparing it with what we have seen or experienced before. The main point is that as we discuss the literary genres of Exodus, we should remember that this generic activity is only a small part of the practically infinite train of generic judgments and categories that permeate our life experience.

The process of comparison and classification tacitly permeates our communication, both oral and written; we do this unconsciously because we have *generic competence* – the ability to recognize "types" and "kinds" of discourse and then to make adjustments for new and unique combinations. So long as we are communicating within our own cultural setting, this generic activity generally works quite well. But when we are interpreting literature from a time and culture different from our own, as we must in our reading of Exodus, we do not naturally possess generic competence. We must pursue it by employing genre criticism, which is an explicit attempt to gain generic competence by comparing the text we are reading with similar texts. The result, it is hoped, is that this comparison will reveal generic patterns that prevailed in that distant context; we will be able to understand how the ancient text "worked" or "fit" within its social world. These comments imply that *genre criticism is not a method* in the sense that one can simply follow a few steps and arrive at the proper conclusions. Rather, *genre criticism is a complex interpretive exercise that seeks to understand the nature, meaning, and significance of a text by creatively comparing it with similar texts and/or traditions.*

Although genre criticism is not a method per se, it is certainly possible to outline some of the essential theoretical elements and practical activities involved in generic criticism. Generic comparison begins with a particular text – let us call it the "target text" – that we wish to understand. Our initial reading of that text depends upon residual generic competence, as we recognize in the text various traits and features that appear in other texts we've read or studied before. This opening engagement with the text normally results in perceptions of modest understanding and partial confusion; genre criticism seeks to clear up the confusion and to critically challenge and/or confirm the perception that we have understood the text correctly. This critical end is pursued by comparing our target text with texts and traditions that are similar to it, with a

view to identifying both similarities and differences. The genre (or genres) implied in this comparison is referred to as an *analytical genre,* so
named because the generic category is created for purposes of technical
analysis.

In the case of the Hebrew Bible, the primary source of comparative
exemplars is the Bible itself. That is, just as we learn the meaning of
an English word by seeing how it's actually used in different situations,
so we learn how particular Hebrew genres worked by seeing them used
many times. We are wise to pursue an understanding of Psalm 100,
for example, by comparing it with the other 149 psalms preserved in
the Hebrew canon. A second source of comparative exemplars for our
study of the Hebrew Bible is the ancient Near East, whose societies
produced many texts that are similar to parts of the Hebrew Bible.[11] These
ancient Near Eastern texts are especially important when the number
of biblical exemplars of a genre is small, which makes it difficult to
understand how the genre's conventions work. Moreover, even when the
exemplars of a genre seem plentiful in the Bible, we sometimes have
great difficulty determining how these texts actually "worked" because
we can't determine their original social setting. The ancient Near Eastern
texts often help us resolve this contextual question. As a result, our
understanding of the biblical genres will never be very good without the
help of similar ancient Near Eastern texts. A third source of comparative
exemplars is the anthropological evidence from humanity at large. These
comparative exemplars are important when our biblical and ancient Near
Eastern exemplars do not answer important interpretive questions. As
an example, scholars have often wondered whether the long genealogies
in Genesis and Chronicles preserve accurate historical memories. When
we turn to the ancient Near Eastern parallels, however, these are too few
to be helpful and, to make matters worse, we can't easily tell whether
they preserve accurate information. Consequently, much of what we
know about the biblical genealogies has been gleaned by examining how
oral genealogies are used in living societies. That these genealogies are
oral, and not textual, highlights the fact that the comparative evidence
used in genre criticism needn't be textual; as the word *genre* implies,
any similarity in "type" or "kind" between the biblical text and human

---

[11] The standard comparative resource is Kenton L. Sparks, *Ancient Texts for the Study of
the Hebrew Bible* (Peabody, MA: Hendrickson, 2005).

tradition is fair game. As a case in point from the book of Exodus, one might legitimately compare the birth narrative of Moses – in which the infant foundling was raised by Pharaoh's daughter – with modern studies of foundlings and their childhood experiences; the comparative genre in this case would be "foundling traditions," or something of the sort. At any rate, it is clear that there is no end to the comparative possibilities that suit genre criticism.

Because the traits and features of any text appear in wide variety of other texts, generic comparison is never as simple as finding *the* genre of a biblical text from among a sample of comparative texts. In the case of the book of Exodus, for example, scholars have frequently compared parts of it to "historiography" (Exod 1–18), "law codes," "treaty texts" (Exod 19–24), "prescriptive rituals" (Exod 25–40), "legends" (stories that explain the origins of religious institutions), "religious propaganda" (Exod 32–34), and "biography" (parts of the book are about the life of Moses). Because each biblical text shares features from many generic categories, the best generic judgments about the biblical text will be made by those with the most exposure to, and best grasp of, the many genres found in the Bible, the ancient Near East, and human cultures farther afield.

Whenever we group texts together as members of the same generic category, it is preferable (if possible) to clarify the causes of their similarity. Two commonly cited causes are *cultural diffusion* and *phenomenology*.[12] In the first instance, the two texts are similar because the same stream of tradition has influenced them. Scholars have often suggested, for instance, that the laws of Exodus are similar to ancient Near Eastern laws because the biblical author either read ancient Near Eastern legal texts or was exposed to their features through long-standing legal traditions. In the second instance, phenomenology, the similarities are not the result of cultural borrowing but rather of parallel developments taking place in otherwise diverse cultural or social settings. A good example of a phenomenological parallel would be the similarity between the holy mountain of God in Exodus and the sacred mountains found in other cultures and religions.[13]

---

[12] See Ninian Smart, "Comparative-Historical Methods," *ER* 3:571–74; Meir Malul, *Comparative Method in Ancient Near Eastern and Biblical Legal Studies* (AOAT 227; Neukirchen-Vluyn: Neukirchener Verlag, 1990).

[13] Mircea Eliade, *The Sacred & The Profane: The Nature of Religion* (New York: Harcourt Brace Jovanovich, 1959), 37–41.

In keeping with the concerns of the early rhetorical critics, the comparative activity of genre criticism always involves attention to both similarities and differences. This is particularly important in the comparative study of biblical literature, which often employs generic traits and features from the ancient Near East but also subverts or reverses them in certain ways. The cela or holy place in the Exodus tabernacle provides a good example. While its conception of sacred space for God's dwelling stands very close to ancient Near Eastern practice, the absence of a divine statue in the central cela of the temple was unique in the ancient world.

Given the pervasive interest of genre criticism in all aspects and levels of textual interpretation, a natural question arises at this point. What is the relationship between genre criticism and some of the other critical tools discussed in this book, such as source criticism, redaction criticism, literary criticism, rhetorical criticism, liberation criticism, postcolonial criticism, and feminist criticism? Technically speaking, because all of these critical approaches involve comparison, classification, and judgments about the *kind* of text one is reading, they are best understood as legitimate aspects of genre criticism rather than as wholly discrete approaches to textual interpretation. But practically speaking, the need for these different "criticisms" arises for the same reason that we have different kinds of medical specialties. Textual interpretation is complex, so we benefit most when we focus on certain aspects of the text before trying to make sense of the whole. Attending to the sources used in a text (source criticism), to its editorial history (redaction criticism), to its rhetorical details (literary and rhetorical criticism), and to the perspective of its author or contemporary readers on human freedom, power, social location, and gender (liberation, postcolonial, and feminist criticisms) ultimately helps us pursue a fuller understanding of the text's genre. And to correctly understand a text's genre is nothing other than to understand its meaning and significance, for the ancients, and for us.

GENRE CRITICISM AND THE BOOK OF EXODUS

Before we embark on a detailed look at Exodus 1–2 and 19–20, it is helpful to survey the range of generic judgments that scholars have made respecting the book as a whole. Such a survey elucidates the generic complexity of Exodus as well as of the Pentateuch itself. We shall consider the book in three parts, focusing respectively on Exodus 1–18, 19–24, and 25–40.

Exodus 1–18

Exodus 1–18 is a narrative complex that includes at least two major literary components, "P" and "non-P," which begin in Genesis and end in the book of Numbers. The P material is attributed to an author called the "Priestly Writer," while non-P is often credited to an author referred to as the Yahwist (J) and, secondarily, to another author called the Elohist (E). Professor Boorer discusses these sources at some length in the chapter on source and redaction criticism, so we needn't belabor the point here. The present discussion will simply refer to these two narrative components as P and non-P. Our task is to characterize the genres of each, and then to consider the genre of the final whole. We will begin with non-P.

In some form or fashion, most modern scholarship on the non-P layer of the Pentateuch follows the lead of Hermann Gunkel's student, Hugo Gressmann, who believed that this narrative brings together a range of traditions that are older than the narrative itself.[14] This means that non-P is not a work of creative fiction, even if some of its sources originated as oral or literary fictions. There are two basic approaches at this point regarding non-P. One approach, which closely follows the lead of Gunkel and Gressmann, is reflected in the work of Rolf Rendtorff, Erhard Blum, and David Carr. These scholars assume that significant blocks of tradition, some smaller and others larger, already existed when non-P was assembled.[15] On this account of non-P, the editor who knitted these traditions together did not radically reshape the sources but mainly

---

[14] Hugo Gressmann, *Mose und seine Zeit* (Göttingen: Vandenhoeck & Ruprecht, 1913).

[15] Rolf Rendtorff, *The Problem of the Process of Transmission in the Pentateuch* (trans. J. J. Scullion; JSOTSup 89; Sheffield: Sheffield Academic Press, 1990); Erhard Blum, *Die Komposition der Vätergeschichte* (WMANT 57; Neukirchen: Neukirchener Verlag, 1984); idem, *Studien zur Komposition des Pentateuch* (BZAW 189; Berlin: de Gruyter, 1990); David M. Carr, *Reading the Fractures of Genesis: Historical and Literary Approaches* (Louisville, KY: Westminster John Knox, 1996). An increasingly popular variation of this theory holds that the non-P Pentateuch was not assembled before the composition of P. Scholars holding this view agree that the pre-Pentateuchal traditions developed into large blocks or complexes of tradition, but they date the combing of these traditions later than Rendtorff, Blum, and Carr (although Blum seems to be shifting in this direction of late). For further discussion, see Konrad Schmid, *Erzväter und Exodus: Untersuchungen zur doppelten Begründung der Ursprünge Israels innerhalb der Geschichtsbücher des Alten Testaments* (WMANT 81; Neukirchen-Vluyn: Neukirchener Verlag, 1999).

preserved them as he found them.[16] If the editor contributed anything
to the narrative, it was a theological veneer that subtly tied the whole
together with a common theme. This theme is generally identified as the
"promise" to the forefathers, Abraham, Isaac, and Jacob. Fundamental
to this model of non-P is that the traditions used in it underwent a
long process of growth and development prior to the assembly of non-P.
Consequently, non-P potentially draws upon traditions that date as early
as nascent Israel and as late as the editor, who is usually dated to the
Exilic or post-Exilic period (sixth century B.C.E.).

The other approach to non-P follows the lead of Gerhard von Rad,
who attributed non-P to an historian who took up disparate sources and
used them to create a national history of early Israel.[17] This historian
is known as the Yahwist (J), mainly because he uses the divine name
"Yahweh" in the early parts of his narrative. Von Rad dated the Yahwist's
historical effort to the tenth century B.C.E., connecting it with the rise of
the Israelite state under Solomon and with the appearance of scribal and
scholarly activities in Solomon's royal courts. Why did von Rad associate
the rise of Hebrew historiography with this "Solomonic Enlightenment?"
His comparative exemplars were the rise of Greek historiography, usually associated with the so-called Ionian Enlightenment (sixth century
B.C.E.), and rise of modern historiography, associated with the modern
Enlightenment proper. Hence, for von Rad, a key generic feature of historiography is the critical, Enlightenment-style thinking that supposedly
stands behind it; true historians know how to consult and sift through
historical sources and arrange them into a sensible narrative of the past.
Without that process of critical reflection, there is no history writing.

While von Rad believed that J's history contained considerable older
material, the newer rendition of his theory, offered by John Van Seters,
heads in a different direction. Van Seters admits that J reflects old sources,
but his J historian dates much later than von Rad's (to the sixth century)
and hence is more remote from the early Israelite experience. Moreover,

---

[16] Blum refers to this composition as the "deuteronomistische Komposition" (KD), the
name reflecting the influence of Deuteronomy's ideas on its editor.
[17] Gerhard von Rad, *The Problem of the Hexateuch and Other Essays* (Edinburgh: Oliver
& Boyd, 1965); John Van Seters, *Prologue to History: The Yahwist as Historian in Genesis*
(Louisville, KY: Westminster John Knox, 1992); idem, *The Life of Moses: The Yahwist as
Historian in Exodus-Numbers* (Louisville, KY: Westminster John Knox, 1994).

Van Seters postulates a different relationship between J and the Greeks. Whereas von Rad compared J to the "critical" historiography of writers like Thucydides and Herodotus, Van Seters finds better analogues in the very early Greek historians, such as the logographers. Unlike the critical historians, these authors did not sift through their sources to discover "what actually happened"; their primary aim was to preserve traditions and entertain readers. As a result, the earliest Greek historians simply repeated whatever their sources said (whether this seemed historically accurate or not) and, when it suited their purpose, they creatively shaped the sources to make a good story. Van Seters believes that their genre, which he calls "antiquarian historiography," is very similar to the genre of J's work. If there is a difference between the Yahwist and the early Greek historians, it would be that J's history is more thematically unified than the Greek histories. According to Van Seters, the historian's primary thematic agenda was to link his narrative closely with that of the promises made to the Israelite forefathers. Respecting the book of Exodus, the call of Moses and the subsequent deliverance of Israel from slavery reflect God's plan to keep his covenant with Abraham and his children.

I should point out that, in my opinion, both approaches to non-P actually present us with a historian of sorts. If we define historiography as "a narrative of past events based on earlier sources," then in either case we have a purveyor of the past, who took up older sources and joined them to create a coherent history of early Israel. The two views are separated mainly by their respective judgments about what kind of sources the author/editor had available, and about how much the author/editor shaped and influenced the final form of non-P. This is a debate that we cannot sort out in this introductory venue, but two implications of the discussion are important. First, it is clear that the Israelite history in non-P is entirely different from a modern history book, for its author/editor was not trying to recover and narrate the events of history as they actually occurred. And second, it is equally clear that non-P drew upon a variety of earlier and smaller traditions, each with its own generic character and history. We will consider some of these smaller generic units and features in our more detailed discussion of Exodus 1–2.

What shall we say about P's contribution to Exodus 1–18? As we see in Professor Boorer's discussion of P, most scholars (with notable exceptions) believe that P was written *after* non-P (or JE) and was in some

respects a revision of, or response to, the earlier non-P narrative. This
conclusion is based on the many cases in which P provides an alternative view of events or traditions already in non-P. This suggests that P
is, generically speaking, both a mimetic text (it intentionally imitates
non-P) and a polemical text (it sometimes works against the viewpoints
of non-P). There is an ongoing scholarly debate about P's basic literary
strategy, namely, about whether P originated as a self-standing document (the compositional theory, thus making P an alternative to non-P)
or only as an addition to the non-P narrative (the supplemental theory,
thus making P a revision of non-P).[18] A majority of scholars prefer the
compositional theory, in part because of comparative considerations.
The Hebrew Bible provides an actual example of a self-standing priestly
text with revisionary aims. I have in mind the books of Chronicles, which
provided a priestly alternative to the history narrated in the earlier books
of Samuel and Kings.[19] Again, these issues are discussed in more detail
by Professor Boorer and so needn't detain us here. The main point is
that, if one wishes to consider the genre of P, the comparative texts that
most naturally enlighten us are the non-P Pentateuch (which P sought to
revise) and Chronicles (the text that is most like P). And because non-P
tends to be dated to the late monarchy or early exile in contemporary
research, P's dependence on non-P suggests that, like Chronicles, it dates
to the post-Exilic period. Establishing this Exilic/post-Exilic *Sitz im Leben*
for P has important generic implications.

Because P imitates non-P, it initially has the look and feel of a work
that was composed by an historian, but in fact its basic structure was
provided by non-P, as was most of its source material. Insofar as P differs
from non-P, this is not so much the result of differing historical sources
as it is of differing perspectives. For according to most scholars, P is
largely a work of theological and literary invention. P's treatment of the
priesthood provides an example.[20] The Priestly writer informs us that

---

[18] For orientation and bibliography, see Kenton L. Sparks, *The Pentateuch: An Annotated
Bibliography* (IBR Bibliographies 1; Grand Rapids, MI: Baker, 2002), 22–36.

[19] See W. Johnstone, "Reactivating the Chronicles Analogy in Pentateuchal Studies with
Special Reference to the Sinai Pericope in Exodus," *ZAW* 99 (1987): 16–37.

[20] See Aelred Cody, *The History of the Old Testament Priesthood* (AnBib 35; Rome: Pon-
tifical Biblical Institute, 1969); Lester L. Grabbe, *Priests, Prophets, Diviners, Sages: A
Socio-Historical Study of Religious Specialists in Ancient Israel* (Valley Forge, PA: Trinity
Press, 1995). For bibliography, see Sparks, *The Pentateuch*, 95–96.

only the sons of Aaron can serve as priests, a limitation that he traces all the way back to Moses. This contrasts sharply with our other biblical sources, in which men from the tribe of Levi, or even from the other Israelite tribes, can serve priestly functions (see Deut 17:9; 18:1, 6–7, 21:5; 1 Sam 7); the first biblical text that limits the priesthood in the style of P is Ezekiel, which dates to the Exilic period (see Ezekiel 44). It follows, then, that every P story which assumes priestly hegemony over the Levites during the Mosaic period was *invented* during the post-Exilic period, in whole or part, to defend priestly prerogatives and power (see Numbers 1–4, 8, 16). From this we learn something important about P's generic activity: P supports its cultic, religious, and theological viewpoints by making them appear to be very old and Mosaic and, hence, of divine origin. This generic judgment is reinforced by comparative evidence from the ancient Near East, where Mesopotamian and Egyptian priests often invented stories whose purpose was to secure their power and influence or to advance their theological agendas.[21] It is not a surprise, then, that Israelite priests did the same.

If P's narrative has been invented in this way, shall we also refer to its genre as "fiction"? This question is more difficult to answer than one might think. For though we know that P has created a portrait of the history that is not historically accurate, and also that he used literary invention to do it, we cannot easily tell whether P thought of his work as creative fiction or as a work that tells us how history "must have been." In other words, it may be that in P's opinion, the many theological and historical points that he is making really must have been true, even in the days of Moses. I say this because in the similar case of historical revision in the post-Exilic priestly book of Chronicles, there is some evidence that the chronicler actually thought that history worked out as he was suggesting.[22]

What shall we say about the genre of Exodus 1–18 as a whole, which is a combination of the very different views of P and non-P? What was

---

[21] Some examples include the Cruciform Monument of Maništušu, the Autobiography of Kurigalzu, the Agum-kakrime Inscription, and the Sin of Sargon (all from Mesopotamia), as well as the Bentresh Stela and Famine Stela from Egypt. For bibliography and summaries of these texts, see Sparks, *Ancient Texts for the Study of the Hebrew Bible*, 282, 289–91, 296–97.

[22] William Schniedewind, "The Source Citations of Manasseh: King Manasseh in History and Homily," *VT* 41 (1991): 450–61.

the objective or purpose of those who created this document? It would seem that there are three possibilities.[23] First, it is possible that P is only a supplement of non-P, in which case the authors of P wanted to provide readers with a new "edition" of Israel's history. This would mean that in its final form, Exodus 1–18 was designed to advance the theological perspectives of P. A second possibility is that we are dealing with a "compromise document," created when the community that embraced the P story forged a theological agreement with those who embraced non-P. This would explain why two competing viewpoints appear in the text; in terms of interpretation, it would mean that the text was produced by those who cared more about the unity of Judaism than about the particular perspectives advanced by either P or non-P. Finally, it is possible to characterize the narrative as an "anthology," created when an editor who combined P and non-P in his quest to preserve Israelite traditions; in this case, we are not dealing with two communities who arrived at a compromise but rather with an individual editor who was untroubled by the conflicting viewpoints in his sources.

Exodus 19–24

Having considered Exodus 1–18, let us now turn to the "Sinai Pericope" in Exodus 19–24. Here we find the story of God's powerful revelation to Israel on the mountain. For generations this story has stirred the imaginations of lay readers and theologians; for biblical scholars, this tale has become one of the most perplexing in the Pentateuch. Why does Moses, in his intercessory role between God and the people, move up and down the mountain in such a confusing and haphazard way? And why does the text contain so many theological tensions? Is God so holy that he must be hidden in a cloud (Exod 19:9), or did Moses, Aaron, Nadab, Abihu, and the elders of Israel actually "see God" (Exod 24:9–11)? Is it Moses alone who is the real intercessor for Israel, or is Aaron also included (cf. Exod 19, esp. v. 24; and Exod 24, esp. vv. 1 and 9)? The complexity of this text is compounded by its generic variety, which includes the divine mountain,

[23] See Gary N. Knoppers and Bernard M. Levinson, *The Pentateuch as Torah: New Models for Understanding Its Promulgation and Acceptance* (Winona Lake, WI: Eisenbrauns, 2007).

the theophany, a covenant, and a law code. All of these genres are native to the ancient Near East, so their mere presence is not perplexing for us; perplexing in that only in the Bible do we find all of these genres combined into a single text. Because we'll attend to the divine mountain and theophany motifs in our detailed look at Exodus 19–20, our attention in this overview is devoted to the covenantal and legal genres.

God's covenant with Israel is the primary subject of the Sinai Pericope, but this theme doesn't appear out of thin air. The entire book of Exodus can be generically understood as a "charter myth," such as one finds in living cultures and in certain texts from the ancient Near East.[24] Charter myths tell the story of a society's origins and, in doing so, provide the ideological foundations for the culture and its institutions.[25] In the case of Exodus, the book teaches that Israel is fundamentally a society delivered from slavery by Yahweh and therefore a nation that covenantally belongs to him. So the text is generically polemical in that it defends a monotheistic devotion to Yahweh. I should point out that the use of "myth" to describe Exodus is potentially confusing. Scholars often use the term as shorthand for "stories about the gods," but it is sometimes used – as it is here – to refer to *any* story that serves a foundational role in society. Also, though it is true that "myth" nearly always implies "invented" in the fictional sense, this does not mean that the Exodus story reflects no history. Most scholars would concede that the Exodus tradition reflects genuine history in some form or fashion, so one might speak here of "mythologized history."[26] But whatever label we use, the narrative in Exodus – the "charter myth" – accentuates the exclusive relationship between Yahweh and Israel.

---

[24] Karel van der Toorn, "The Exodus as Charter Myth," in *Religious Identity and the Invention of Tradition* (ed. J. W. van Henten and A. Houtepen; Studies in Theology and Religion 3; Leiden: Brill, 2001), 128–43; Rainer Albertz, "Exodus: Liberation History against Chart Myth," in *Religious Identity and the Invention of Tradition* (ed. J. W. van Henten and A. Houtepen; Studies in Theology and Religion 3; Leiden: Brill, 2001), 128–43.

[25] B. Malinowski, *Magic, Science and Religion and Other Essays* (Boston: Beacon, 1948), 120.

[26] See Albertz, "Exodus: Liberation History against Chart Myth," 135; Hans-Peter Müller, "History-oriented Foundation Myths in Israel and its Environment," in *Religious Identity and the Invention of Tradition* (ed. J. W. van Henten and A. Houtepen; Studies in Theology and Religion 3; Leiden: Brill, 2001), 169–90.

In the ancient Near East exclusive relationships, such as the one involving Yahweh and Israel, were formally expressed through covenants and
treaties. It has long been recognized that the covenant referred to in
Exodus, and elsewhere in the Pentateuch, is related to the genre of international treaties that foreign nations enacted with each other.[27] Some
of these treaties are best described as "vassal treaties," inasmuch as they
involved a more powerful king or overlord who dictated the treaty's
terms to a weaker vassal. It is this type of treaty, the vassal treaty, that
has been most closely compared to the biblical covenants. But in the
case of Exodus, the formal generic relationship is not as close as one
finds, for example, in Deuteronomy, where the author directly imitated
Neo-Assyrian vassal treaties.[28] In Exodus generally, and in Sinai pericope
specifically, it is rather as if the author alludes to a written treaty whose
existence is assumed.[29] Some of the treaty features that are explicitly
included in Exodus 19–24 can be discerned by comparing the text with
a list of features found in other ancient Near Eastern treaties. There is
of course no "master list" of these treaty elements, but among the most
common treaty features are the following, here given in the order that
they often appear: (1) the identification of the document as a treaty;
(2) identification of the treaty's parties; (3) a historical prologue that
reviews past relations between the parties; (4) stipulations that the vassal
must obey; (5) provisions for the deposit of the document; (6) directions
for future readings of the document; (7) a list of divine witnesses to the
treaty; (7) blessings for obedience to the treaty stipulations; (8) curses for
disobedience. Sometimes the treaty texts also mention the oaths that were
taken by the vassals and a sacrifice and meal at the ratification ceremony,
but even when these elements are not mentioned, we can reasonably
presume that they were features of the treaty ceremony.

[27] The classic but now dated studies were G. E. Mendenhall, "Ancient Oriental and Biblical
Law," *BA* 17 (1954): 26–46; Dennis J. McCarthy, *Treaty and Covenant* (2nd ed.; AnBib
21a. Rome: Pontifical Biblical Institute, 1978).
[28] R. Frankena, "The Vassal-Treaties of Esarhaddon and the Dating of Deuteronomy," in
1940–1965 Oudtestamentlich Werkgezelschap in Nederland (OtSt 14; Leiden: Brill, 1965),
122–54; Moshe Weinfeld, *Deuteronomy and the Deuteronomic School* (Oxford: Oxford
University Press, 1972), 116–29.
[29] As noted by William H. C. Propp, *Exodus* (AB; 2 vols.; Garden City, NY: Doubleday,
1999–2006), 2.34–35.

Among these listed features, the stipulations (#4) are the most readily discernible in Exodus, because they make up the bulk of the text in Exodus 20:1–17 (the Decalogue) and Exodus 20:22–23:19 (the "Covenant Code"). We will return to these stipulations in a moment. Other discernible features include identification of the document as a treaty (see Exod 19:5, 24:7), identification of the parties (Exod 19), a very brief historical prologue (Exod 19:3–4), and blessings for obedience (Exod 19:5–6). Curses are not mentioned but may be implied by the sacrifices and meal, given that the sacrificed animal often symbolized the disobedient vassal in ancient treaty rituals.[30] The oath is specifically mentioned as well, when the people declare that "all that Yahweh has spoken we will do, and we will be obedient" (Exod 24:7). It must be remembered that the Sinai pericope is a composite text, so that some of these features may be attributed to one or another of the text's editors. But overall, the impression is clear enough: this central portion of Exodus reflects the generic features of an international treaty.

The presence of stipulations in the form of a "Covenant Code" (Exod 20:22–23:19) is not a surprise in a text that we judge to be a treaty, but the stipulations themselves are nothing like treaty stipulations. Treaty stipulations have mainly to do with matters governing the relationship between the treaty's parties, whereas in these laws we have stipulations concerning jurisprudence, criminal law, and civil law. By this I mean that one does not find in Near Eastern treaties stipulations that concern murder, perjury, slavery, marriage, personal injury, property, and criminal law. In this respect, this collection of Hebrew law – variously known as the Covenant Code or the Book of the Covenant – stands very close to ancient Near Eastern lawcodes, such as Hammurabi's famous code.[31] The similarities are more than general, in fact. In some cases the laws of Covenant Code and the Code of Hammurabi are uncannily similar. Consider, for example, the slave and ox laws from the two codes.

---

[30] See Sefire text 1, pt. 4 in Joseph A. Fitzmeyer, *The Aramaic Inscriptions of Sefire* (rev. ed., BibOr 19/A; Editrice Pontificio Istituto Biblico, 1995).

[31] See Martha T. Roth, *Law Collections from Mesopotamia and Asia Minor* (2nd ed.; Writing from the Ancient World 6; Atlanta: Scholars Press, 1997), 70–142.

Covenant Code	Code of Hammurabi
When you buy a male Hebrew slave, he shall serve six years, but in the seventh he shall go out a free person, without debt (Exod 21:2).	If an obligation is outstanding against a man and he sells or gives into debt service his wife, his son, or his daughter, they shall perform service in the house of their buyer or of the one who holds them in debt service for three years; their release shall be secured in the fourth year (CH §117).
When an ox gores a man or a woman to death, the ox shall be stoned, and its flesh shall not be eaten; but the owner of the ox shall be clear. But if the ox has been accustomed to gore in the past, and its owner has been warned but has not kept it in, and it kills a man or a woman, the ox shall be stoned, and its owner also shall be put to death (Exod 21:28–9).	If an ox gores to death a man while it is passing through the streets, that case has no basis for a claim. If an ox is a known gorer, and the authorities of his city quarter notify him that it is a known gorer, but he does not blunt (?) its horns or control his ox, and that ox gores to death a member of the *awilu*–class, he (the owner) shall give 30 shekels of silver (CH §250–51).

Scholars generally give two different explanations for these generic similarities. One explanation is that both texts drew upon a common legal tradition, which was widely disseminated in the ancient world.[32] The other explanation is more direct. While not denying a common legal tradition, it postulates that the author of the Covenant Code knew and intentionally imitated Hammurabi's laws. This "direct influence" view was popular when the Code of Hammurabi was first discovered in the nineteenth century, but it gradually fell into disfavor. David P. Wright has recently reinvigorated the theory by arguing that the Covenant Code follows the Code of Hammurabi closely in both content and order.[33] Wright dates the composition of the Covenant Code to the Neo-Assyrian period,

[32] Shalom M. Paul, *Studies in the Book of the Covenant in the Light of Cuneiform and Biblical Law* (VTSup 18; Leiden: E. J. Brill, 1970); Hans J. Boecker, *Law and the Administration of Justice in the Old Testament and Ancient East* (Minneapolis: Augsburg, 1980).

[33] David P. Wright, "The Laws of Hammurabi as a Source for the Covenant Collection (Exodus 20:23–23:19)," *Maarav* 10 (2003): 11–88.

where it was a response to Mesopotamian imperialism. Another recent advocate of this view, John Van Seters, dates the composition of the Covenant Code to the Exilic period, a context which provides obvious points of contact between the Hebrew and Babylonian legal traditions (Van Seters attributes the code to his Yahwist historian).[34] But readers should note that at present this reading of the Covenant Code remains a minority viewpoint, and it has been vigorously challenged.[35] It will be interesting to see if it finally wins the day. But regardless, the scholarly consensus is that the laws of the Covenant Code cannot be understood well apart from a comparative understanding of ancient Near Eastern law and jurisprudence. We cannot trace out all of these implications here, but one is worth mentioning. In spite of the thousands and thousands of texts that archaeologists have unearthed in Near Eastern excavations, there does not appear to be a single case in which one of the law codes – such as Hammurabi's Code – was substantively used to adjudicate law.[36] It would seem, then, that the laws were not "codes" in the modern legal sense but rather works of political propaganda, in which kings illustrated their regime's justice by publishing examples of their judicial rulings. This observation suits the size of law codes themselves, which invariably fall short of providing the full-orbed legal coverage needed in substantive law. The fact that the Covenant Code was even shorter than the ancient Near Eastern codes suggests that it was probably not proffered as substantive law but was composed for some other reason. In my opinion, the most likely possibility is that mentioned above: that the Covenant Code is an example of elite emulation written to imitate Hammurabi's laws.

We should note that any serious study of the Covenant Code will involve comparisons with its closest generic cousins, which are not the ancient Near Eastern laws but rather the law codes of the Hebrew Bible itself. These include the Deuteronomic Code (Deut 12–26), the Holiness Code (Lev 17–26), and the Priestly Code (belonging to the P author and

---

[34] John Van Seters, *A Law Book for the Diaspora: Revision in the Study of the Covenant Code* (Oxford: University Press, 2003).

[35] Bernard M. Levinson, *Deuteronomy and the Hermeneutics of Legal Innovation* (New York and Oxford: Oxford University Press, 1997); Bruce Wells, "The Covenant Code and Near Eastern Legal Traditions: A Response to David P. Wright," *Maarav* 13 (2006): 85–118.

[36] For comments, see Martha T. Roth, *Law Collections from Mesopotamia and Asia Minor* (2nd ed.; SBLWAW 6; Atlanta: Scholars, 1997), 4–7.

found in various parts of Exodus, Leviticus, and Numbers). It is precisely by comparing the differing judgments of these codes that one notices the unique perspectives and concerns of each author. I will highlight just one example, which provides the background needed for our discussion of Exod 25–40.

One of the most obvious differences between the major Hebrew law-codes is their view of Israel's sacrificial cult, specifically regarding *where* animal sacrifices can be offered. It seems that the Covenant Code permitted sacrifices at multiple locations (Exod 20:24–26), but Deuteronomy's laws allowed this only before the construction of Solomon's temple (Deut 12:1–10). Once constructed, that temple became the one place where sacrifices could be legitimately offered (Deut 12:11–14). The Priestly Code seems to radicalize this Deuteronomic perspective. Whereas Deuteronomy freely admits that no single place for sacrifice existed prior to Israel's settlement in the land, the P code claims that God provided a central place for sacrifices from the very beginning of Israel's history (see Exod 25:1–9). This mobile "temple" was really a portable tent, which allowed Yahweh to dwell with his people before their settlement in Palestine, as they wandered in the wilderness for a generation. The second half of Exodus is the story of this tent, which is often called the "tabernacle" (from a Latin word that means "tent").

Exodus 25–40

The Priestly Writer's tabernacle in Exodus 25–40 has been compared with three different but closely related Mesopotamian genres. Foremost, it has been compared to Mesopotamian temple construction narratives.[37] These texts normally follow a five-part literary *topos*, which includes (1) the circumstances that prompted the divine decision to build; (2) preparations for construction; (3) description and construction of the building; (4) dedication rituals for the temple; and (5) promise or request for blessings upon the temple's builder. As it turns out, all of these features appear in Exodus 25–40; there is little doubt that its author was influenced

---

[37] Victor A. Hurowitz, "The Priestly Account of the Building of the Tabernacle," *BASOR* 105 (1985): 21–30; idem., *I Have Built You an Exalted House: Temple Building in the Bible in Light of Mesopotamian and Northwest Semitic Writings* (JSOTSup 115; Sheffield: Sheffield Academic Press, 1992),

by the Mesopotamian temple construction genre. Secondly, the tabernacle construction narrative has been compared to Mesopotamian rituals for manufacturing idols of the gods.[38] According to these ritual texts, an idol could only be prepared if one followed blueprints and rituals provided by the gods. If these plans were followed properly, and with reverence, the deity would finally inhabit the once lifeless idol. Now this is precisely how things work in the tabernacle construction narrative of Exodus. Moses is told, "In accordance with all that I show you concerning the pattern of the tabernacle and of all its furniture, so you shall make it." He is then given very detailed plans for the structure, which he carries out "just as Yahweh instructed him." The story then ends with the expected result: "the glory of Yahweh filled the tabernacle" (Exod 40:35). The third Mesopotamian genre that has been compared to the temple construction narratives are the temple topographies.[39] The bulk of the texts are not geographical exercises, as the name might imply, but rather theological and cosmological explorations of various cult shrines. Temples are listed along with their furnishings and features, and these are in turn provided with theological interpretations. Some of the topographies are metrological, providing detailed measurements of temples and their floor plans. Now anyone familiar with the tabernacle narrative in Exodus will immediately see the similarities. Scholars and lay readers alike have often commented about the inexplicably painstaking detail of its tabernacle description. Perhaps we finally have an explanation for this feature. Like the Mesopotamians before them, the Israelites accentuated the holiness of their sacred space by describing it in minute detail.

The foregoing discussion raises an interesting question: Why is the Priestly Writer's work so often similar to Mesopotamian traditions? In order to explore this question, we shall have to consider not only P's work in Exodus but in the Pentateuch as a whole. For many years, scholars have recognized that the Priestly creation story in Genesis 1 appears to be a

---

[38] See Propp, *Exodus*, 2.495–96; Kenton L. Sparks, "*Enūma Elish* and Priestly Mimesis: Elite Emulation in Nascent Judaism," *JBL* 126 (2007): 625–48; cf. C. Walker and Michael B. Dick, "The Induction of the Cult Image in Ancient Mesopotamia: The Mesopotamian mīs pî Ritual," in *Born in Heaven, Made on Earth* (ed. M. B. Dick; Winona Lake, WI: Eisenbrauns, 1999), 55–121.

[39] For the topographies themselves, see A. R. George, *Babylonian Topographical Texts* (OLA 40; Leuven: Peeters, 1992). For discussion, see Sparks, "*Enūma Elish* and Priestly Mimesis."

polemical response to the Babylonian creation myth, *Enuma Elish*.[40] P seems to have taken up that Babylonian story and recast it in Hebrew garb, so that the Sabbath rest and Hebrew monotheism were accentuated. The monotheistic message was pressed forward by depersonifying features of the older story. Whereas in the Babylonian account the creator deity, Marduk, created the cosmos by splitting open the body of the sea-demon, Tiamat, in Genesis this is accomplished when God divides the impersonal waters of the *tehom* (cf. Tiamat). The supposed connection between Genesis 1 and *Enuma Elish* has recently been reinforced by other evidence, which shows that P has not only mimicked the myth but also the ritual used in connection with it, the *kuppuru*. P's Yom Kippur ritual in Leviticus 16 essentially has the same name as the *kuppuru*, and both rites used blood to cleanse the temple's cela at the turn of the year. In fact, once one is looking for it, there is extensive evidence that P is adapting Mesopotamian traditions throughout his work. Take, for example, P's list of primeval heroes in Genesis 5 and their long life spans; this is very similar to the list of long-lived, pre-Flood heroes in the Mesopotamian tradition.[41] The similarities between P and Mesopotamian tradition are so great that it is very likely that P is intentionally copying them. But why would P mimic these Mesopotamian traditions?

We can never read the mind of an ancient author, but in my opinion it is very likely that in P we are dealing with a genre that scholars call *elite emulation*.[42] The genre appears when a peripheral society, oppressed and threatened by another group, borrows literary and cultural images of power from the oppressor. An example is provided by the Native American Cuna people in Panama, where the women continue to wear traditional Cuna garb while the men – borrowing images of prestige and power from the Europeans – wear suit coats and ties.[43] Similarly, it may well be that P's community lived in a context where Mesopotamian culture was deemed a threat to Jewish society. If P was written during

[40] For bibliography relevant to this paragraph, see Sparks, "*Enūma Elish* and Priestly Mimesis."

[41] Sparks, *Ancient Texts for the Study of the Hebrew Bible*, 345–48.

[42] Carolyn R. Higginbotham, *Egyptianization and Elite Emulation in Ramesside Palestine: Governance and Accommodation on the Imperial Periphery* (Culture and History of the Ancient Near East; Leiden: Brill, 2000).

[43] Michael T. Taussig, *Mimesis and Alterity: A Particular History of the Senses* (New York: Routledge, 1993).

or more likely after the Babylonian exile, as the evidence suggests, then many Jews were either living in Mesopotamia or were under its cultural influence. The Priestly Writer's use of elite emulation would make sense in that context, and his tabernacle construction narrative in Exodus suggests that this is precisely how he worked. P sought to bestow upon Israel, and upon Israel's religion, that air of antiquity and authority that was attached to all things Mesopotamian.

The foregoing discussion suggests that P's portrait of the tabernacle is generically fictional in two respects. First, it is historically fictional because there was never such an institution in early Israel's history. This is why none of the earlier Hebrew traditions – neither non-P (J) nor Deuteronomy – know of the tabernacle's existence prior to the exile. Second, the tabernacle account is fictional because it is in fact a literary text, which was never intended as a guide for building the tabernacle. It was instead a polemical text, which depicted Israel's religious cult using the symbols of Mesopotamian power in order to subvert (or perhaps even to accommodate) that foreign and oppressive power. So, while it is quite true that tent-like sanctuaries were known in the ancient world and may have been used by the Israelites in certain times and places,[44] this contextual detail casts only a thin veneer of verisimilitude on what is otherwise a creative piece of theological literature.

Having discussed the overall generic context of the book of Exodus, we are now in a position to look at two text units in more detail. We shall begin with Exodus 1–2 before moving on to discuss Exodus 19–20.

EXODUS 1–2

This short narrative sequence explains the circumstances that caused Egypt to enslave Israel and relates to readers the story of Moses's birth and his self-imposed exile in Midian, where he met and received a call from God. The pericope begins with a list of Hebrews who originally migrated to Egypt (Exod 1:1–5). Jacob is listed, along with his twelve sons – each the eponymous ancestor of an Israelite tribe. The list is suitably described as a *segmented genealogy*, insofar as it lists twelve genealogical "branches"

---

[44] Daniel E. Fleming, "Mari's Large Public Tent and the Priestly Sanctuary," *VT* 50 (2000): 484–98.

of Jacob (his twelve sons), but it is also a *tribal list* because each son is supposedly the forefather of an Israelite tribe.

Comparative studies reveal that the genealogies of living cultures and the ancient Near East rarely served the historical function that one finds in modern genealogies.[45] More often the genealogies were ideological texts, which enumerated social relationships and defined the contours of social practice. One result of this function is that genealogies are often fluid, since they must adjust to the changing ebb and flow of as-lived social history. Scholars believe that Israel's genealogical tribal lists behaved in a similar fashion.[46] The lists were ideological, in that they expressed the identity of "ideal" Israel. The earliest lists were ten-tribe lists, such as we find in the Song of Deborah (Judg 5). These lists did not include the southern tribes of Judah and Simeon, nor did they include the priestly Levite tribe. As the tribal lists expanded with the addition of new tribal identities, the ideal number of tribes was increased to twelve. Though the number of significant tribes eventually reached thirteen, the number twelve was always preserved in the lists by making certain adjustments. Whenever Joseph was represented by his sons, Ephraim and Manasseh (which would create thirteen tribes), the Levi tribe was eliminated from the list because of its special priestly status; whenever Levi was included, Joseph alone represented Ephraim and Manasseh. The list in Exodus 1 is of the latter type. The fact that the text enumerates twelve tribes, including the southern tribes of Judah and Simeon, shows that it is a late version of the tribal list tradition. Consequently, as it stands this part of Exodus was not written early in Israel's history. It dates sometime after the fall of the northern kingdom in 722 B.C.E., for it was then that Judah inherited the name "Israel" from its fallen sister to the north. So the nation involved in the Exodus story is "greater Israel," in the sense that tribes from the north (Israel) and south (Judah) shared in the experience.

Exodus 1:6–8, which begins "Then Joseph died, and all his brothers, and that whole generation. . . . Now a new king arose over Egypt, who did not know Joseph," is a transition formula, which partly repeats what

---

[45] Robert R. Wilson, *Genealogy and History in the Biblical World* (YNER 7; New Haven, CT; London: Yale University Press, 1977).

[46] For bibliography and discussion, see Kenton L. Sparks, "Genesis 49 and the Tribal List Tradition in Ancient Israel," *ZAW* 115 (2003): 327–47.

is said at the end of Genesis (Gen 50:26) and is akin to the formula used at the beginning of Judges (Judg 2:8–10). It therefore serves the purpose of marking the beginning of a new book (Exodus), and it does so by introducing the cause of Israel's enslavement. The cause, we are told, is that the new king was unaware of the special relationship once forged between Egypt and Israel through Joseph. This motif, in which a change of regimes results in a change of political alliances and fortunes, is prominent in the well-known Egyptian story of Sinuhe;[47] like many literary motifs, this one was inspired by real patterns in ancient political behavior.

One indicator that a story is fictional is the presence of internal features and motifs that cannot be squared with historical realities or with normal human behavior. In the case of Exodus 1:9–22 there are many such indicators. We are told that the Egyptian king, upon noticing that there were more Israelites than Egyptians, proceeded to strategically eliminate his Hebrew slave labor by working them to death and, this failing, by having them summarily killed upon their birth stools. This latter plan failed because the two midwives responsible for birthing the Hebrew children refused to cooperate. The main point from a generic standpoint is that none of this is historically plausible because there cannot have been as many Israelites as Egyptians,[48] no king would have tried to kill all of his male slaves if he also wished to use them as slave labor, and two midwives cannot have been responsible for the thousands of births the text suggests would have taken place. The fact that the Egyptian king is anonymous in the story, and remains so throughout the book of Exodus, is further evidence that we are dealing with fictional (or at least, fictionalized) literature. So, while there were undoubtedly historical realities in the early Israelite experience that modestly inspired the ancient story of the Exodus, the story in its present form shows many signs of fictional shaping late in Israel's history.

Pharaoh's desire to eradicate the Hebrew slaves sets the stage for the birth of the Israelite savior, Moses. Having failed on two attempts to control the Israelite population, Pharaoh finally elected to have every

---

[47] See *ANET* 18–23.
[48] For estimates of the early Israelite settlement in Canaan based on the archaeological data, see Israel Finkelstein, *The Archaeology of the Israelite Settlement* (Jerusalem: Israel Exploration Society, 1988).

male Hebrew child thrown into the Nile River – death would be certain,
by water and crocodile. Many readers will already know how baby Moses
was saved from this fate by placing him in a basket among the river-
side reeds. The baby was fortuitously found and raised by an Egyptian
princess, thus equipping him – or so it would seem – with a strategic
position for helping his enslaved brethren. This is Moses' birth story, in
a nutshell. Now scholars have recognized for some time that this story of
a foundling, who is providentially saved and rises to power and prominence, is probably more legend than history. It is similar to several other
ancient Near Eastern hero stories and is especially close to the "Sargon
Birth Legend."[49] In that story a priestess, vowed to chastity, became pregnant and was forced to bear her child in secrecy. After the child's birth, the
priestess placed him in a basket and set it among the reeds at the river's
edge. A water drawer found and raised the child, but it was the goddess
Ishtar who gave him his big career break: she took a liking to Sargon and
made him king of Akkad. This story is ostensibly about Sargon the Great,
who ruled Akkad from circa 2334 to 2279 B.C.E., although most scholars
believe that the story was actually written centuries later by the Sargon
II (r. 721–705 B.C.E.), a Neo-Assyrian king who wrote this text in honor
of his namesake. If this last supposition is right, then it is likely that the
birth story of Moses was modeled after Sargon's birth legend at some
point during or after Sargon II's reign.

Is there any harder evidence that this story was borrowed by the
Israelite author of Exodus? Indeed, there is. The artificial attachment of
the concealment theme to the Moses story is suggested by the sudden and
unexplained disappearance of the infant-killing motif after Moses was
found at the river's edge. Rabbinic tradition attempted to account for
this strange feature: "Moses was cast into the Nile to make the [Egyptian]
astrologers think that Israel's savior had already been thrown into the
Nile, so that from that day on they would call off the search for him.
Indeed from that day on, the decree was annulled, for they divined that
Israel's savior had already been attacked by water."[50] Although the rabbinic solution might strike us as artificial, the rabbis correctly recognized

---

[49] Brian Lewis, *The Sargon Legend: A Study of the Akkadian Text and the Tale of the Hero
Who Was Exposed at Birth* (ASOR Dissertation Series 4; Cambridge, Mass.: ASOR,
1980); see also Propp, *Exodus*, 1.159–60.

[50] Moshe Greenberg, *Understanding Exodus* (New York: Behrman House for the Melton
Research Center of the Jewish Theological Seminary of America, 1969), 39.

the problem. The infant-killing motif and the resulting concealment do not cohere with the Moses story as nicely as in the Sargon Birth Legend. This suggests that the Hebrew writer took up the motif from the Sargon legend, where it fit very satisfactorily, and applied it to Moses in order to portray Israel's lawgiver as a similar hero. Why was this done? It has been suggested that the biblical presentations of Moses were reshaped from time to time in order to counter political and theological challenges from Assyria, Babylon, and Persia.[51] In the case of the exposure motif, this may reflect an attempt to contrast the heroic exploits of Moses with the enslaving presence of the Neo-Assyrian king Sargon II. But even if the text has no direct association with Sargon II, it was certainly designed to portray Moses using heroic tropes from the ancient Near Eastern literary tradition.

Though the birth story may be anti-Assyrian, if Brevard Childs is right it is not wholly opposed to foreign peoples and cultures. Childs has categorized it as a "historicized wisdom tale" written by a sage scribe.[52] Childs' judgment is not based on the form of the literature itself but rather on other generic criteria that he associates with scholarly wisdom circles. For example, Childs points out that Pharaoh's daughter, upon discovering the infant Moses in his basket, feels "compassion" on the child and wishes to adopt it as her own. In his opinion, this degree of ethnic inclusivism, which is willing to depict foreign royalty in such positive terms, is indicative of the international and cosmopolitan values of the wisdom tradition. We needn't go into the other details adduced by Childs in his article to recognize the benefit of his work. Even if his wisdom thesis is ultimately wrong, it was the comparative process itself – in which Childs brought the text into conversation with other biblical texts and traditions – that highlighted the ethnically inclusive proclivities of the biblical author. That is, in the final analysis, Childs has helped us recognize that this text certainly falls within that category of texts – that genre of texts – which reflect inclusive rather than exclusive ethnic perspectives (cf. Gen 16:1; Exod 2:21–22; Ezra 9–10; Neh 13:1–3).

Exodus 2:1–15 explains how Moses came to reside in the land of Midian. It contains two episodes that foreshadow his future role in Israel's

---

[51] Eckhart Otto, "Mose und das Gesetz: Die Mose-Figur als Gegenentwurf politischer Theologie zur neuassyrischen Königsideologie im 7. Jh v. Chr," in *Mose: Agypten und das Alte Testament* (ed. E. Otto; SBS 189; Stuttgart: BKW, 2000), 43–83.

[52] Brevard S. Childs, "The Birth of Moses," *JBL* 84 (1965): 109–22.

history. First, Moses kills an Egyptian who is beating a Hebrew slave (thus anticipating his role as Israel's savior), and second, Moses intercedes in an altercation between two Hebrews (thus anticipating his role as a law-giver and judge). The two episodes are linked in that, during the second episode, Moses learns that the Egyptian blood on his hands is known to Pharaoh. So Moses flees to the eastern desert, to Midian. As William Propp has pointed out, this story reflects a common folktale pattern, in which the "naïve prince ventures outside the palace to witness com-mon life and is permanently transformed."[53] The "disillusioned prince" genre has been documented in numerous cultural settings and also in the ancient Near East, where one finds it in the Sumerian story of "Gilgamesh and the Land of the Living."[54] The result in these stories is that the prince forsakes the life of luxury and comfort in order to accomplish something more important. But Moses, as yet, does not know what that great task will be. So the reader has been generically primed for the revelation of that quest.

Exodus 2:16–22 picks up the story in Midian, where Moses meets and marries his wife (Zipporah) and becomes acquainted with her father, who is a "priest of Midian." Michael Martin has pointed out that the genre of this story is a classic "betrothal journey narrative," such as one finds in the Hebrew stories of Isaac, Jacob, Saul, David, and Tobit/Tobias.[55] The schema for this genre generally includes the following elements: (1) the groom-to-be travels to a foreign country; (2) he meets a young woman or women at a well; (3) someone draws water; (4) a gift is given or a service is performed that ingratiates the suitor with the woman and/or her family; (5) the suitor reveals his identity; (6) the woman/women rush home with a report of his arrival; and (7) a betrothal is arranged, usually in connection with a meal.[56] In this rendition of the schema, the key innovations appear in #4–5. The service that Moses renders reveals yet again that he is a savior figure, who first delivered a Hebrew slave

---

[53] Propp, *Exodus*, 1.165–66.

[54] See motif P14.19 in Stith Thompson's standard folkore manual, *Motif-Index of Folk-Literature* (Bloomington: Indiana University, 1955); for more on the Gilgamesh tale, see the discussion and bibliography in Sparks, *Ancient Texts for the Study of the Hebrew Bible*, 275–78.

[55] See Robert Alter, *The Art of Biblical Narrative* (New York: Basic, 1982), 47–62; Michael W. Martin, "Betrothal Journey Narratives," *CBQ* 70 (2008): 505–23.

[56] Adapted Martin, "Betrothal Journey Narratives," 507–8.

from an Egyptian and now delivers women from oppressive shepherds (Exod 2:17). The author is helping readers to see that, though Moses will eventually deny his qualifications as a deliverer (Exod 3:11), his life itself tells another story. Moses is not only competent; he is also humble. The other innovation, according to Martin, is that Moses does not reveal his identity, as is done in all other betrothal journey stories. This highlights the ambiguity surrounding Moses identity in his own eyes and in the eyes of others. He is a Hebrew, but the Midianites identify him as an "Egyptian" (Exod 2:19); he is a fugitive and so cannot reveal his identity, but in the great task to follow the Israelites will have to accept him, not only as a fellow Hebrew but as their deliverer. What we are witnessing is the (literary) creation of an Israelite hero.

Exodus 2 ends with an intervention by the narrator, who tells us what is occurring in Egypt and in the heavens during Moses's long exile in Midian (Exod 2:23–25). The Pharaoh who sought Moses's life has died, the Israelites have been crying out for help, and God – hearing that cry – has remembered his covenant with Abraham, Isaac, and Jacob. This sets the stage for the call of Moses in chapter 3. Generically speaking, the content of the narrator's intervention is evidence of the larger historiographic work into which the Moses story, and Exodus story, have been set. The book of Exodus picks up where Genesis left off, thus anticipating that God will fulfill the patriarchal promises, not only by delivering Israel from slavery, but by giving Israel its land in Canaan.

EXODUS 19–20

The main themes of Exodus 19 are the covenant and the theophany atop Mt. Sinai. Let us begin with the covenant theme. According to Exodus 19, Moses ascends the mountain, receives the terms of the covenant, and then returns to the people with God's offer. When the people accept, they are invited to approach YHWH and to partially ascend the mountain at its foot, to what was essentially the border between profane space and the holy presence of God. Frank Polak points out that this is precisely how ancient treaties were enacted.[57] Messengers from one party took the

---

[57] Frank H. Polak, "The Covenant at Mount Sinai in Light of Texts from Mari," in *Sefer Moshe: The Moshe Weinfeld Jubilee Volume* (ed. Ch. Cohen, A. Hurvitz, and Sh. M. Paul; Winona Lake, IN: Eisenbrauns, 2004), 119–34.

treaty proposal to the other and, if these were accepted, the two parties would meet at their common border to ratify the treaty. This suggests that the procedures in Exodus 19 should be understood generically as treaty negotiations, in the tradition of ancient Near Eastern political agreements. If this is right, then it implies that Moses' speech to the people in Exodus 19:7 included a summary of the covenant's obligations, even though these are not enumerated. This would explain the response of the people in Exodus 19:8, "We will do everything Yahweh has said."

After the Israelites accepted the treaty's basic terms, the stage was set for God's appearance on the mountain. The closest ancient Near Eastern parallel to the divine mountain is undoubtedly Baal's Mt. Zaphon, which in Ugaritic lore was the dwelling place of that powerful storm god.[58] The parallels between Sinai and Zaphon are straightforward and informative, but here the genre is not literary but rather a matter of religious typology. The biblical author is employing the imagery of the cosmic mountain – inherited from Israel's polytheistic Canaanite heritage – to show that YHWH is the one and only God of Israel. It is difficult to judge from the text whether the original viewpoint was monotheistic or only henotheistic (admitting the existence of other gods), but the cosmic-mountain motif was certainly a generic attempt to say that Yahweh was the only legitimate God for Israel. And in the final form of Exodus, the message of this text is unabashedly monotheistic.

The theophany itself has been compared to other biblical theophanies, in which God powerfully appears with an entourage of smoke and fire.[59] According to Jorg Jeremias, this genre refers not merely to God's presence but rather to his dramatic arrival when coming from somewhere else.[60] Hence, the book of Exodus presents the reader with an apparent theological inconsistency.[61] If we place the image of the cosmic mountain in the context of this theophanic genre, the result is a

---

[58] The standard discussion is R. J. Clifford, *The Cosmic Mountain in Canaan and the Old Testament* (HSM 4; Cambridge: Harvard, 1972).

[59] See Judg 5:4–5, Nahum 1:2, Hab 3:3–15, Micah 1:3–4 and numerous Psalms.

[60] Jorg Jeremias, *Theophanie: Die Geschichte einer alttestamentlichen Gattung* (WMANT 10; Neukirchen-Vluyn: Neukirchen Verlag, 1965).

[61] E.g., 1 Kgs 8:13. For discussion, see T. N. D. Mettinger, *The Dethronement of Sabaoth: Studies in Shem and Kabod Theologies* (ConBOT 18; Lund: Gleerup, 1982), 19–37; M. Görg, "Die Gattung des sogenannten Tempelweihspruches (1 Kg 8, 12f.)," *UF* 6 (1974): 55–63.

subtle tension between the image of YHWH's permanent dwelling on Mt. Zion (as implied by the cosmic mountain motif) and the image of YHWH's mobility (as implied by the theophany). According to Thomas Dozeman, this odd juxtaposition of generic images arises from tensions between the earliest tradition, which understood YHWH's dwelling as a permanent location, and later editorial changes that accentuated God's freedom to come and go as he wills.[62] These editorial changes (by the Deuteronomistic and Priestly editors) reveal an important generic aspect of the Sinai pericope. Tradents would have edited it in this way only because successive generations of Israelites viewed *this* text as central to Israelite theology. One reason for the text's importance resides in what comes after Exodus 19.

The theophany in Exodus 19 provides a suitable prelude to the actual law of God, which begins in Exodus 20 with one of the best known of biblical texts: the Ten Commandments or, as it is called in the Bible, the Decalogue (literally "Ten Words"). These titles do not come from the text of Exodus 20 but, rather, from two other ten-law lists, which appear in Deuteronomy 5 and in Exodus 34.[63] Of these lists, the first, in Deuteronomy, is most similar to the list in Exodus 20. In both of these texts, the Ten Commandments appear at the very beginning of the respective lawcodes of the Covenant Code and the Deuteronomic Code and serve as a kind of summary or basis for the laws that follow. The other list of ten laws, which is also called the "Ten Words," appears in Exodus 34:10–26. The curious thing about this list is that, though it purports to be a "second printing" of the original Ten Commandments listed in Exodus 20, its actual commands – which focus on ritual matters – are very different from those found in Exodus 20 and Deuteronomy 5. Scholars often refer to this as the "Ritual Decalogue." We will discuss this below, but the important point is that we have three biblical "Decalogues" to consider in our generic deliberations.

The other source of comparative texts for the study of the Decalogue is the ancient Near Eastern law codes. If we begin with these texts, the most salient comparative point is this: though there are many general and specific similarities between the biblical and ancient Near Eastern laws

---

[62] Thomas B. Dozeman, *God on the Mountain: A Study of Redaction, Theology and Canon in Exodus 19–24* (Atlanta: Scholars, 1989).

[63] Deuteronomy actually refers to this list as the "Ten Words" in Deut 10:4.

and treaties, there appears to be no instance in which the ancient Near
Eastern cultures produced a brief "summary code" of ten (or seven, or
twelve, etc.) laws, commands or stipulations which introduced and served
as the ideological foundation for their written lawcodes and treaties. The
closest one parallel is the Egyptian instructions, which are much longer
than the Decalogue but sometimes include lists of moral and ethical
directives. So, though it is hard to imagine that ancient Near Eastern
societies failed to produce any sort of "Decalogue," it remains the case the
Hebrew Decalogue is unique in antiquity. The Decalogue is also unique in
that it does not enumerate for the Israelite judiciary the penalties due for
wrongdoers; any penalties or rewards are assumed to come from God's
hand. We see this in the second, third, and fifth commands, where God
promises blessings or punishment depending on Israel's obedience to the
commands, and also in the final commandment against coveting, where
only God can judge the covetousness of the heart. Among the ancient
Near Eastern texts, this inward look at the heart appears only in the
treaties, where overlords often demanded that vassals be faithful "with a
whole heart."[64] Taken together, this suggests that the author of Exodus
was influenced by a number of ancient Near Eastern generic traditions,
including treaties and laws, and probably by wisdom literature as well.

Scholars have tended to offer one of two very different explanations for
the Decalogue's uniqueness. One approach postulates that the Decalogue
is one of the oldest (if not *the* oldest) collections of Hebrew law and,
consequently, that it served as the foundation or core around which the
other Israelite laws grew. Because of the Decalogue's relative simplicity,
these scholars often associate the Decalogue with Israel's earliest and
simplest social contexts, when the Hebrews were nomadic and/or living
in relatively small villages.[65] If these scholars are right, then the present
shape of Exodus and Deuteronomy – which makes the Decalogue the
introduction and basis of the law code – reflects the actual history of
the Pentateuch's legal development. Other scholars reverse the history,
arguing that the Decalogue is not an early law collection but rather the

[64] This feature is most prominent in the Neo-Assyrian loyalty oaths. See Simo Parpola
and K. Watanabe, *Neo-Assyrian Treaties and Loyalty Oaths* (SAA 2; Helsinki: Helsinki
University Press, 1988).
[65] Moshe Weinfeld, "The Decalogue: Its Significance, Uniqueness, and Place in Israel's
Tradition," in *Religion and Law: Biblical-Judaic and Islam Perspectives* (ed. E. B. Firmage;
Winona Lake, IN: Eisenbrauns, 1990), 3–47; Ron E. Tappy, "The Code of Kinship in
the Ten Commandments," *RB* 107 (2000): 321–27.

late summary and final fruit of Hebrew law.[66] In past years this view was often espoused because the ethical character of the Decalogue, which lacks judicial penalties and focuses on inward aspects of the person, seemed to reflect the perspectives of Israel's ethically sensitive prophetic tradition, but this is no longer the case.[67] In contemporary scholarship a late date for the Decalogue is based on the observation that its mono-Yahwism probably developed fairly late in Israel's history,[68] and on the fact that our earliest Hebrew texts (especially the early prophets) do not mention the Decalogue. I will return to this matter later.

While the debate about the date of the Decalogue is not unimportant, it would seem that the final verdict remains the same: the editors of both Exodus and Deuteronomy wanted readers to understand the Ten Commandments as the fundamental expression of Israel's ethical and legal principles. The two primary renditions of the Decalogue bear this out generically, for a comparison of them with the other Hebrew laws shows that they are unique in three obvious respects: they stand at the beginning of the law, they are the only laws uttered by God himself, and they are the only laws etched into the two tablets of stone.[69] Although some scholars have downplayed the distinctiveness of the Decalogue among the Hebrew laws,[70] the actual *effects* of the biblical text reveals its uniqueness. The Rabbis tell us about one of these effects, when they explain that liturgical uses of the Decalogue were eventually discontinued because some Jews began to consider the Decalogue the only law given at Sinai.[71] The Jews advocating a "Decalogue-only" perspective acquired the idea from the biblical authors, who really did draw a fairly sharp distinction between the Decalogue and Israel's other laws.

The distinctiveness of the Decalogue in Jewish thought is borne out further by the fact that we have three versions of the "Ten Words," one of them so different that it bears the title "Ritual Decalogue" (Exod 34).

---

[66] R. G. Kratz, "Der Dekalog im Exodusbuch," *VT* 44 (1994): 205–38.

[67] See the discussion of Johann J. Stamm and Maurice E. Andrew, *The Ten Commandments in Recent Research* (SBT² 2; London: SCM Press, 1967), 22–35.

[68] Mark S. Smith, *The Origins of Biblical Monotheism: Israel's Polytheistic Background and the Ugaritic Texts* (Oxford: University Press, 2001).

[69] Norbert, Lohfink, "Kennt das Alte Testament einen Unterschied von 'Gebot' und 'Gesetz' Zur bibeltheolgischen Einstufung des Dekalogs," *JBTh* 4 (1989): 63–89.

[70] Frank Crüsemann, *The Torah: Theology and Social History of Old Testament Law* (Philadelphia: Fortress, 1996), 351–61.

[71] See the Talmud (b. Ber. 11b) and discussion in Nahum Sarna, *Exodus* (JPS Torah Commentary; Philadelphia: Jewish Publication Society, 1991), 109.

That these three Decalogues differ and at the same time make similar claims to serve as the foundation of Jewish thought is surely significant. It would seem that the Decalogue – with its twin stone tablets – became the genre in which competing claims for the basis of Jewish religion were played out. The Decalogues of Exodus 20 and Deuteronomy 5 are very similar and, hence, so were the respective viewpoints of the authors; the major difference between them is revealed in the Sabbath law, where Deuteronomy 5 makes it a commemoration of the escape from Egypt whereas Exodus 20 makes it a commemoration of God's rest on the seventh day of creation. This difference reveals that the editors of the two Decalogues embraced divergent starting points for history, inasmuch as Deuteronomy began with Israel's exodus from Egypt and Exodus 20 – which modern scholars attribute to Priestly editors – began with the creation of humanity as a whole. Given that the Priestly Writer was responding to and sometimes mimicking Mesopotamian tradition (see above discussion), a likely explanation is that his Decalogue was here competing with Mesopotamian theologies that credited the creation to foreign deities (especially to Babylon's high god, Marduk).

Although it is difficult to be sure in these matters, the very unusual Decalogue of Exodus 34, with its list of ritual commands, probably dates after the standard Decalogue tradition reflected in Exodus 20 and Deuteronomy 5.[72] I suggest this because the author enumerates it as a second edition of the two tablets, given by God after the first set was broken. The implication would be that Israel's most pressing need after the first covenant tablets were broken was not another copy of the same laws but rather a new set of laws – another "covenant" (see Exod 34:10) – which would insure that the most important rites and festivals were properly observed and that the most dangerous rites – especially the creation of idols – were avoided.

But why, we may ask, was the first Decalogue composed? And was it written early in Israel's history, as some scholars believe, or later in history, as the majority of scholars suggest? On this matter, my own view is that there is some truth in both perspectives. On the one hand, we have a short list of Israel's "sins" in Hosea, a prophet of the eighth

---

[72] For an opposing view, which doubts that Exodus 34 offers an alternative Decalogue, see Propp, *Exodus*, 2.150.

century B.C.E., which closely parallels the sixth, seventh, eighth, and ninth commandments of the Decalogue.[73] Given that Hosea complains about Israel's broken covenant and neglect of the law, and given, too, that he mentions a "prophet" who led Israel out of Egypt (undoubtedly Moses), one cannot help but see a connection between Hosea and the Decalogue. By no means does this mean that Hosea knew the Decalogue or something like it; it does mean, however, that the existence of an early "Decalogue-like" list cannot be gainsaid. On the other hand, in my view, the real issue at hand is why the Israelites would have found it necessary to espouse certain laws as literally "written in stone" and "from the mouth of God" when they had so many other laws that were authoritative. The answer, I think, is generic, and indicates that the Decalogue originated as the solution to a problem in later Judaism. As time wore on, it became clear to Jewish scribes that some of the laws in the emerging Israelite canon apparently contradicted each other; at the very least, it was clear that some of the laws had changed. I suspect that the scribes who composed the Decalogue, in a search for conceptual religious stability, were willing to make a generic distinction between the "permanent" universal commands of the Decalogue and the more fluid legal traditions of the Pentateuch as a whole. As we saw earlier, we know for a fact that some Jews were deeply influenced by this legal distinction, but in the end Rabbinic Judaism went in a different direction.

CONCLUSIONS

We may conclude our deliberations with these brief observations. Although most scholars believe that the Exodus and Moses stories preserve a limited core of ancient Israelite tradition, a generically sensitive reading of Exodus as a whole, and of Exodus 1–2, 19–20 specifically, shows that even the earliest traditions preserved in the book – whatever they may be – are not historical records in any straightforward sense but were long ago shaped to address the religious concerns of communities who lived long after the birth of Israel. In the end, this produced a book that includes a staggering variety of generic diversity that, in turn, reflects the multiplicity of authors and editors who contributed to the book. In

[73] See HosEa 4:2 and comments by William Rainey Harper, *A Critical and Exegetical Commentary on Amos and Hosea* (New York: Scribners, 1905), 250.

most instances this generic evidence provides a better sense of the general audience addressed by the text, but in some cases it permits us to go beyond even this, to identify more specific social and historical situations that must have concerned the authors and editors. These observations obviously leave us with many dangling questions and perplexing interpretive problems, but they also advance us considerably as competent readers of the book of Exodus.

FOR FURTHER READING

Beebee, T. O. *The Ideology of Genre: A Comparative Study of Generic Instability.* University Park: Pennsylvania State University Press, 1994.
Ben-Amos, Dan, ed. *Folklore Genres.* Austin: University of Texas Press, 1976.
Duff, David, ed. *Modern Genre Theory.* Harlow: Longman, 2000.
Ehrlich, Carl, ed. *From an Antique Land: An Introduction to Ancient Near Eastern Literature.* New York: Rowman & Littlefield, 2008.
Hallo, W. W. "Compare and Contrast: The Contextual Approach to Biblical Literature." In W. W. Hallo, B. W. Jones, and G. L. Mattingly, eds. *The Bible in the Light of Cuneiform Literature.* Scripture in Context 3. Lewiston, NY: Mellen, 1990: 1–30.
Hayes, J. H., ed. *Old Testament Form Criticism.* San Antonio, TX: Trinity University Press, 1974.
McKenzie, Steven L. *How to Read the Bible: History, Prophecy, Literature – Why Modern Readers Need to Know the Difference, and What It Means for Faith Today.* Oxford; New York: Oxford University Press, 2005.
Niditch, Susan. *Oral World and Written Word: Ancient Israelite Literature.* Library of Ancient Israel. Louisville, KY: Westminster John Knox, 1996.
Rosmarin, Adena. *The Power of Genre.* Minneapolis: University of Minnesota Press, 1985.
Sparks, Kenton L. *Ancient Texts for the Study of the Hebrew Bible.* Peabody, MA: Hendrickson, 2005.
Sweeney, M. A., and E. Ben Zvi, eds. *The Changing Face of Form Criticism for the Twenty-First Century.* Grand Rapids, MI: Eerdmans, 2003.
Talmon, Sh. "The Comparative Method in Biblical Interpretation-Principles and Problems." In *Congress Volume: Göttingen.* VTSup 29. Leiden: E. J. Brill, 1978: 320–56.
Todorov, Tzvetan. *Genres in Discourse.* Cambridge: Cambridge University Press, 1990.
Vanstiphout, H. L. J., ed. *Genre in Mesopotamian Literature.* Leiden: Brill, 2005.

3

Source and Redaction Criticism

SUZANNE BOORER

Source and redaction criticism are two related methodologies that come under the broader umbrella of the historical critical approach, which seeks to interpret texts within their original historical contexts. The aim of source and redaction criticism is to discern the history of the literary composition of the text. They seek to explore the diachronic dimensions of the text by identifying the literary sources or layers of which the text is composed, their relative chronology, and how they have been brought together and edited over time to eventually form the text as we now have it. Source criticism as such focuses on identifying the earlier written sources of which the present text is comprised, and, if possible, discerning the date and original historical context of each, and to interpret them in relation to these. Redaction criticism focuses on the stages and processes, and something of the intent, whereby these written sources were combined with each other and/or redacted (or edited) to give the final form of the text. As such these methods are interrelated: source criticism takes the text apart into its earlier written components; redaction criticism puts the text back together again and shows the rationale behind each of the stages identified.

THE METHODOLOGY OF SOURCE CRITICISM

Source criticism grew out of the study of Pentateuch, which, especially from the nineteenth century onward, was recognized not as the work of one author but as a composite text, made up of several written sources. Even now, the term source criticism tends to be used specifically and

almost exclusively in relation to Pentateuchal studies. Indeed, the terminology of *source criticism* reflects the view that predominated in much of
the twentieth century arising from the application of this method to the
Pentateuchal text, and therefore the book of Exodus; that this complex
text is composed from parallel continuous sources J, E, P.[1] Before dis-
cussing the results of source criticism in the interpretation of the book
of Exodus, it is important to understand how source criticism works as
a method.

Source criticism, in seeking to identify the written sources of which
the text is composed, relies on a number of literary criteria that work
together to help in the discerning process. These criteria are: repetitions
and doublets; discrepancies or inconsistencies; differences in style, terminology, and/or theological perspective; coherence/incoherence within
the passage; and coherence or not with the wider context. None of these
are reliable on their own; however, working in harmony they can provide
cumulative support for the identification of written sources. This is provided that allowance is made for the possibility that some features of the
text may be better explained as resulting from the preliterary accumula-
tion or transmission of disparate oral traditions; that is, form critical and
traditiohistorical considerations can influence the application of these
criteria. It will be helpful to discuss the strengths and limitations of each
of these criteria, and the way in which they must work together, in order
to gain a better understanding of the subtlety of the art of source critical
analysis.[2]

First, the repetition of elements within a story or repetition of episodes
in different versions can be an indication of the presence of more than one
written source. However, such repetition, particularly within an episode,
may simply be stylistic, part of the writer's art.[3] The case for more than one

---

[1] Source criticism is also referred to in contemporary writings as *classical literary criticism*,
    or in older publications as simply *literary criticism*. For a critique of the terminology of
    source criticism, see Rolf Knierim, "Criticism of Literary Features, Form, Tradition and
    Redaction," in *The Hebrew Bible and Its Modern Interpreters* (ed. Douglas A. Knight
    and Gene M. Tucker; Chico, CA: Scholars Press, 1985), 130–31; John Barton, "Source
    Criticism," in *ABD* 6: 162–65, 164.

[2] For excellent discussions of source critical criteria and their appropriate use, see Claus
    Westermann, *Genesis 1–11* (London: SPCK, 1984), 575–84; Odil Steck, *Old Testament
    Exegesis: A Guide to the Methodology* (2nd ed.; trans. J. D. Nogalski; Atlanta: Scholars
    Press, 1998), 54–58.

[3] See Robert Alter, *The Art of Biblical Narrative* (New York: Basic Books, 1981), 88–113.

written source is strengthened considerably if the repetitions or doublets coincide with other observations such as inconsistencies or discrepancies, differences in style, terminology, and perspective. Even then, some caution is required, for such repetitions need to be weighed in light of the possibility of oral variants having been taken up, or worked together, within the one document. This possibility needs also to be taken into consideration in the use of the second criterion of observed discrepancies between episodes or between details within a narrative. However, a good case can be made for the possibility of the existence of more than one literary source if such discrepancies in detail between repeated elements appear to be part of different literary contexts, with consistent differences in style, terminology, and/or perspective in relation to each other. Such literary contexts, representing different literary sources, may be discerned where the repetitions and discrepancies are: between separate episodes; or within the one narrative where the intertwining of written sources creates inconsistencies and problems of coherence.

The third criterion of differences in style, terminology, and perspective has always been important in the practice of source criticism. This criterion is particularly helpful in relation to texts that seem to show a consistent and unified style, which in the Pentateuch and therefore Exodus, applies in particular to the Priestly material (P).[4] Priestly texts are discerned from their style, terminology, interests, and perspective, but even here source critics do not use these observations alone: these coincide with perceived repetitions and discrepancies with surrounding (non-Priestly) material. The criterion of style and terminology is less helpful in relation to the non-Priestly material in the Pentateuch, since this material seems to reflect a history of collection and transmission of oral traditions that were eventually written down. Hence the variation in terminology, style, and perspective may in large part reflect preliterary stages rather than different written sources.[5] One detail in terminology, the alternation of the divine name (whether Elohim or YHWH), has traditionally been used by source critics to distinguish different literary sources. However, at its best this has only been relied on in harmony

---

[4] Deuteronomic or Deuteronomistic material in the Pentateuch is largely identified also on the grounds of style and terminology.

[5] Recently, however, the existence of oral tradition behind these texts has been disputed: see, for example, the work of John Van Seters, discussed later in this chapter.

with observations regarding repetition, discrepancy, style, perspective, and coherence. In addition, within Exodus the divine name terminology is not all that helpful, since after the revelation of the divine name, YHWH, in Exodus 3 and 6 the distinction between the use of YHWH and Elohim is no longer definitive.

Finally, the criterion of coherence is concerned with the issue of narrative thread or progression of thought, but also with consistency in style, terminology, perspective. This comes into play on two fronts. First, the issue of coherence can be a consideration within a particular passage: if the coherence of the text is interrupted by a passage that displays repetition, discrepancy, different style, or terminology, but then is resumed, it is quite possible that two different literary sources have been interspersed with each other within the one passage, or another literary hand has inserted a passage into the original. Second, the source critic will look at the wider context, within Exodus or even the whole Pentateuch, in order to see if there are signs of coherence with other passages, in narrative progression, style, terminology, and perspective in order to determine the extent and nature of the written sources identified.

From all this it can be seen that source criticism is no mechanical enterprise, but an art that entails the cautious weighing of cumulative and interdependent observations regarding repetitions and doublets; discrepancies or inconsistencies; differences in style, terminology, and/or theological perspective; coherence/incoherence within the passage; and coherence or not with the wider context.

The Methodology of Redaction Criticism

The term *redaction criticism* was first coined by W. Marxsen in 1956 in relation to the interpretation of the Gospels, but was practiced much earlier in Pentateuchal studies. Historically, redaction criticism emerged in relation to, and was a consequence of, the source criticism of the Pentateuch. Based on the insight that the Pentateuch is a composite literary text in which different literary sources are still discernible, and yet, displays a certain coherence, redaction criticism sought to trace the process and rationale by which the distinct literary sources were brought together. Redaction criticism focuses on each stage of the editing or redactional process in which written sources were combined, reshaped, and/or supplemented to form a new text, or level of text, up until the eventual formation of its final form. It seeks to explore the intent of each level of redaction in its relative chronological order, and if possible in relation to its specific historical context.

In order to understand how redaction criticism operates, it is helpful to outline the types of evidence perceived in the text that suggests the work or hand of a redactor or editor.[6] First, there is the ordering and arranging of existing literary texts. This can be quite difficult to discern, but when there seems to be certain coherence or pattern to the arrangement of different literary sources in relation to each other beyond the mere collection or cataloguing of existing texts, the hand and rationale of a redactor may be discerned. Second, there may be evidence of the redactor's hand in the reshaping of literary sources themselves as they are preserved in the formation of the text. Third, the redactor's hand can be seen in the addition of short linking passages that may consist only of a few words, often as a means of integrating originally separate literary sources into a more coherent narrative. And, finally, there may be the addition of explicit interpretative passages, often in a common style, that show in a clear fashion the intention of the redactor in presenting the existing text, or the theological message that such a redactor wishes to communicate. In sum, it is in the linking, arrangement, reshaping, and/or commenting on, the existing literary sources that the hand and intention of the redactor is discerned. And it is the task of redaction criticism to discern when and how this process occurs at each stage from the earliest literary level up to the final form of the text.

Clearly the extent and role of the redactor at various levels in this process can vary considerably, ranging from a minimalist position of presenting little more than an anthology of texts to extensive reshaping and supplementing almost akin to the work of an author (albeit still based on existing literary text). Indeed, it will be seen when we trace the history of interpretation of the book of Exodus that although the methods of source and redaction criticism are, in their essentials, consistent over time, the particular role of the redactor, and even the particular nuance of the meaning of redaction criticism, varies to a certain extent

---

[6] For helpful discussions of redaction criticism, see John Barton, "Redaction Criticism," *ABD* 5: 644–47; Steck, *Old Testament Exegesis*, 75–93.

depending on the conclusions drawn, or the particular model advocated, with regard to the composition and formation of the text. For example, in the earlier days of the application of source criticism the focus of interpretation was primarily on the delineation, chronological ordering, and characteristics of the literary sources, with less attention given to the process of redaction, seen primarily (though by no means exclusively) in terms of the combining of the sources. In contrast, in more recent times, redaction criticism of the Pentateuchal text has become increasingly a major focus; and, especially with the questioning in some contemporary circles of the existence of the traditionally formulated continuous literary sources, in particular J and E, there is a tendency to perceive the redactional process primarily in terms of levels of supplementation. In addition, intrinsic to the various views put forward over time are changing perceptions, not only of the redactional process and its interrelation with source criticism, but also with regard to the relationship between redaction criticism and form and traditiohistorical criticism. And not only the nature of redaction, but inevitably also conceptions regarding the nature of the sources, have varied over time, ranging, for example, from continuous and originally parallel strands – themselves the work of schools of collectors, or redactors, or the intentional creation of an author with a specific theological intention – to successive levels of redaction or supplementation, to even the denial of their existence, at least with regard to J and E. To this history of interpretation of the Pentateuch, and Exodus in particular, in terms of source and redaction criticism over the last two hundred years or so we will now turn.[7]

The Development of Source and Redaction Criticism of the Pentateuch

The view that the Pentateuch was a literary composite began to emerge increasingly in the seventeenth century. Rationalists such as Hobbes, Spinoza, and Simon used criteria such as anachronisms, repetitions,

---

[7] I have drawn on the following works, particularly where specific works of scholars are not cited: John H. Hayes, *An Introduction to Old Testament Study* (Nashville: Abingdon, 1979), 106–20, 155–97; Ronald E. Clements, *One Hundred Years of Old Testament Interpretation* (Philadelphia: Westminster, 1976); Suzanne Boorer, *The Promise of the Land as Oath: A Key to the Formation of the Pentateuch* (BZAW 205; Berlin: de Gruyter, 1992), 5–33; and in particular the in-depth analysis of E. W. Nicholson, *The Pentateuch in the Twentieth Century: The Legacy of Julius Wellhausen* (Oxford: Oxford University Press, 1998).

inconsistencies, contradictions, variety in style, and evidence of editorial activity to argue against Mosaic authorship. Their work therefore
represents the roots of the source-critical method.

In the eighteen century, source-critical criteria such as repetition, style,
and in particular the alternation of the divine names were applied to the
book of Genesis, and two main continuous parallel sources, E (= present
day P) and J were identified,[8] although these were thought to have been
put together by Moses. This so-called *older documentary hypothesis* is
associated with the work of Witter (1711), Astruc (1753), and EichHorn
(1780). Ilgen (1798) was the first to identify a third continuous source
in Genesis, which he called E2 (= present-day E). Although by the end
of the eighteenth century, two other models of literary composition,
the fragmentary hypothesis and the supplementary hypothesis, were
competing with this model of continuous sources, it was the latter that
won out in the nineteenth century.

The nineteenth century extended the source-critical work done on the
book of Genesis to Exodus, indeed the whole Pentateuch, and formulated
what came to be known as the *newer documentary hypothesis*. Using the
same source-critical criteria of repetition, discrepancies, alternation of
the divine name, differences in style and perspective, and coherence,
attention was given to refining and extending the assignment of material
to the continuous parallel sources already identified, of E1 (= P), J, and
E2 (= E), and, importantly, on the relative ordering of these sources
and their dating. De Wette (1805) identified Deuteronomy (D) as the law
book of Josiah's reform in 621 B.C.E., something that later became crucial
in the relative dating of the other sources. Hupfeld (1853) worked out
the details of Ilgen's E2, ordering the sources in the sequence E1 (= P),
J, E2 (=E), D. In the 1860s Graf and Kuenen, foreshadowed by, and
building on, the work of Reuss (1834), worked out the relative ordering
and dating of the sources as, from earlier to later, J, E, D, P; that is, they
established P (Priestly source) as the latest of the sources rather than the
earliest. Most famously, Julius Wellhausen, summarized and popularized
this view of four parallel and continuous sources in the chronological
order of J, E, D, P.[9] He presented the source-critical arguments for this in

---

[8] E (= P) uses the name Elohim and J uses the name YHWH in Genesis.
[9] Julius Wellhausen, *Geschichte Israels I* (Berlin, 1978). Published subsequently as *Prolegomena zur Geschichte Israels* (2nd ed.; Berlin: G. Reimer, 1883). English Translation,
Prolegomena to the History of Ancient Israel (New York: Meridian Books, 1957).

such a logical and cogent fashion that it became, in its essentials, almost universally accepted for most of the twentieth century, and still today it is adhered to by many, or at least forms the starting point in relation to the proposal of alternative views.

Before this, in a work first published in 1876–1877, Wellhausen had unfolded in detail his source-critical analysis of the text of Genesis–Joshua.[10] Although conceiving the literary composition of the text primarily in terms of the interweaving of the four continuous sources, he also identified additions and supplements, as well as the hand of redactors in the formation of the text. J and E were each supplemented before being combined by a redactor, the Jehovist (RJE). RJE combined J and E, reshaping them and working in his own material (in a style close to that of Deuteronomy) in such a way that this redactor is conceived of, particularly in the Sinai material, not as a compiler, but closer to an author. Wellhausen identified other Deuteronomistic styled texts as expansions added to the Jehovist's work, before another redactor (Rd) combined JE with D (= Deuteronomy, which itself had undergone a complex process of growth). This was further supplemented, before being combined with the later Priestly Code – itself the product of an originally independent narrative (= Q) expanded by Priestly legislation – to form the Hexateuch. *Geschichte Israel I*, then, focused primarily on arguments for the relative chronology of the sources, which Wellhausen perceived as reflecting the views of the time of their respective composition, with J dated to the ninth century, E to the eighth century, D to the seventh century, and P to the fifth century B.C.E.

Wellhausen's position dominated Pentateuchal studies at the turn of the twentieth century. In the early twentieth century, while working within Wellhausen's framework, there was a tendency to refine the definition of the sources further. For example, J was divided into originally independent documents by R. Smend (1912, J1 and J2), O. Eissfeldt (1922, a "lay source," L, and J), G. Fohrer (1923, a "Nomadic" document, N, and J), and J. Morgenstern (1927, a "Kenite source," K, and J). Although most adhered to an E source, its fragmentary nature was acknowledged, and its existence was questioned by P. Volz and W. Rudolph (1933), who argued that the material classified as E represented glosses and additions

---

[10] Julius Wellhausen, *Die Composition des Hexateuchs und der historischen Bucher des Alten Testaments* (Berlin: G. Reimer, 1889).

to J rather than elements of a continuous source. G. von Rad (1934) divided P into two narrative strands (PA and PB). The complexities of Wellhausen's portrayal of the processes of redaction were maintained, along with the acknowledgment of texts in Deuteronomistic style in Exodus in particular.

With the rise of form criticism in the early twentieth century, however, it was increasingly acknowledged that some of the repetitions, discrepancies, and differences in terminology and style, could be due to the diversity of traditions at a preliterary level, rather than being evidence of different literary levels. Eventually this tended to halt somewhat the tendency towards more and more minute division of sources into different strands and levels. The focus of form criticism on the smaller units behind the literary sources led H. Gunkel and his student H. Gressmann, writing on Exodus, to view the sources J and E as collections and cycles of tradition, rather than, as Wellhausen maintained, deliberate literary creations of authors; although they still maintained that P was effectively the work of an author. Inevitably, with the influence of form criticism and tradition history, and the recognition of an extended history of tradition behind the sources, it was increasingly acknowledged that the sources, including P, contained a great deal of material that was much earlier than the date of their composition. At this stage form and traditiohistorical criticism and the existence of sources worked out in terms of the classical source-critical criteria were basically seen as complementary approaches operating alongside each other in the interpretation of the Pentateuchal text. This was to remain the case at least until the 1970s.

A significant turning point in the history of source and redaction criticism is represented by G. von Rad's 1938 essay.[11] In this essay, von Rad brought together form, source and redaction criticism into a creative partnership that produced a new perspective on the interpretation of the sources, in particular J. It reversed the increasing tendency to fragment the text in the practice of source criticism and form criticism in the first decades of the twentieth century. Von Rad focused rather on the process of the coming together of traditions to form the shape of the text as a whole, that is, the integrating process that belongs to the realm

[11] Gerhard von Rad, *Das Formgeschichtliche Problem des Pentateuch* (BWANT 26; Stuttgart, 1938). English Translation, "The Form-Critical Problem of the Hexateuch," in *The Problem of the Hexateuch and Other Essays* (trans. E. Dicken; Edinburgh: Oliver & Boyd, 1966), 1–78.

of redaction criticism, but specifically in relation to the combining of traditions, including oral traditions, to form the literary source J to which he attributed the basic structure of the Hexateuch. He accepted and assumed the results of source criticism and applied form criticism to the source J, inquiring about the origins of its structure, its setting, and its intention. He argued that the origins of the shape of J are to be found in the cultic confessional credo of the settlement tradition (Deut 26:5b–9). The "author" of J used this as a framework and incorporated other inherited traditions, some also with roots in the cult, such as the Sinai tradition, to form his work. The Yahwist incorporated the Sinai complex, expanded the patriarchal traditions, and structured and added Genesis 2–11 (J). The result was a document with an overall theological purpose that functioned to address the setting in which it was composed, that is, for von Rad, the Davidic/Solomonic kingdom of tenth-century Israel. Thus the literary source J has now become a theological document, composed by an "author," in stark contrast to Gunkel's conception of J as a collection of material. For von Rad, J was the most important source, since E and P followed the shape and pattern of J, albeit with their own original theological nuances.

M. Noth built on von Rad's hypothesis but shifted focus more to the earlier traditions behind the written sources, and the tradition history through which they might have passed before becoming fixed in the literary sources, J and E.[12] His research into the preliterary stages led him to postulate a basic form of the tradition (G) upon which J and E drew. G, which could have been either oral or written, emerged in the premonarchical period and already comprised the combined and expanded themes of "Guidance out of Egypt," "Guidance into the Arable land," "Promise to the Patriarchs," "Guidance in the Wilderness," and "Revelation at Sinai," that form the shape and structure of the Pentateuch. J and E, therefore, represent later literary recensions of this common tradition. Like von Rad, Noth saw J as the product of an author, but with the smaller role of adding Genesis 2–11 (J) only, as he inherited the expanded patriarchal tradition and the Sinai tradition from G. E and P were also the products of authors. With regard to P, Noth saw the basic narrative, Pg, as the product of an author who was familiar with JE but composed his

---

[12] Martin Noth, *A History of Pentateuchal Traditions* (trans. Bernhard W. Anderson; Englewood Cliffs, NJ: Prentice Hall, 1972).

own independent narrative, integrating earlier traditions and subordinating them to his overall purpose. This was later supplemented by laws (Ps). Like von Rad, the theology of each of the sources was important for Noth for he assigned to each a specific overall theological intention. Deuteronomy he saw as quite separate from J, E, and P, forming part of the Deuteronomistic History (DtrH), which extended to the end of 2 Kings. The process of redaction comprised: the combining of J and E by a redactor (RJE) who used J as a literary base and expanded it with fragments from E; the subsequent combining of JE with P by a redactor (R JEP), this time using P as the literary base and fitting JE into this, to form JEP. Only later was JEP combined with DtrH, and therefore with Deuteronomy. Noth did recognize texts in Deuteronomistic style within Genesis–Numbers (e.g., Exod 13:3–16; 19:3b–9a; 32:9–14) but made little of them, referring to them rather vaguely as Deuteronomistic additions, but definitely not as part of a Deuteronomistic redaction.

These works of von Rad and Noth dominated Pentateuchal study for a generation, especially with regard to source and redaction criticism. In particular, the shift to seeing the sources as theological with an overall purpose or intention was taken up and explored, particularly in the 1960s and 1970s.[13]

Indeed, at least up until the 1970s the paradigm of continuous sources, J and E (however fragmentary), and an originally independent P narrative (Pg), with their redaction in stages into JE and then JEP, was held by the large majority of scholars. Even today, there are still many who hold to this position in its essentials.[14] Of some dispute, among the advocates of this paradigm, is the existence and nature of E. Although many, after Noth, see E as an originally independent continuous source, albeit preserved in fragmentary form, there are a number of dissenting voices that follow in the steps of Volz and Rudolph (1933), maintaining that so-called E texts represent supplements to J or a later redaction of J. With regard to P, although the majority of scholars who hold to the essentials of the continuous source paradigm maintain Pg as an originally

---

[13] See, for example, Walter Brueggemann and Hans W. Wolff, eds., *The Vitality of Old Testament Traditions* (2nd ed.; Atlanta: John Knox, 1982); A. W. Jenks, *The Elohist and North Israelite Tradition* (Cambridge, MA: Harvard, 1965).

[14] See, for example, the recent detailed defense of this position by Nicholson, *The Pentateuch*; and the recent commentary by William H. Propp, *Exodus 1–18; Exodus 19–40* (AB; New York: Doubleday, 1999, 2006).

independent continuous source, F. M. Cross argued for P as a redaction, maintaining that P supplements JE, especially in Exodus and Numbers, with framing elements, and much of its own material (especially in the Sinai section),[15] and this has had some influence on current scholarship.

However, it is the nature of J, and related texts in Deuteronomistic (Dtr) style in Genesis–Numbers, that have received most attention, particularly from the 1970s onward. This has led to views that, not only strain at the edges of this paradigm of the redaction of continuous sources so dominant from Wellhausen onward and for the generation after von Rad and Noth, but indeed break away from it to give different models of the literary formation of the Pentateuch, and Exodus in particular.

In the 1960s some attention began to be given specifically to the texts in Deuteronomistic (Dtr) style, found especially in Exodus (e.g., Exod 13:3–16; 19:3–6), with regard to their possible date of composition and relationship to J. C. Brekelmans (1966), N. Lohfink (1963, 1984), and W. Fuss (1972) identified these texts as earlier than equivalent texts in Deuteronomy (and therefore as pre-Deuteronomic or "proto-Deutero-nomic").[16] They tended to identify their composition closely to the redactor who put J and E together, a position akin to that of Wellhausen. More recently, E. W. Nicholson (1998) has argued that many of these texts are pre-Deuteronomic, but at different levels of composition from each other, and represent the work of the Jehovist, defined as a school of theologians.[17] Also in the 1960s L. Perlitt (1969), in arguing for the formulation of covenant theology as arising from Deuteronomic circles, highlighted the issue of the possible contribution of Dtr editors to the redaction of Exodus.[18] Consequently, there arose a greater focus on the process of redaction whereby the Deuteronomistic History (DtrH) was brought together with JE in Genesis–Numbers to give a pre-P text extending from Genesis–Kings. For example, P. Weimar (1977) postulated more than one level of Dtr texts in Genesis–Numbers, with a Jehovist who combined J and E, that was then supplemented by Dtr1 (the first Deuteronomistic redactor), which in turn was joined with DtrH

---

[15] Frank M. Cross, *Canaanite Myth and Hebrew Epic* (Cambridge: Harvard University Press, 1973).

[16] See Boorer, *The Promise of the Land*, 20.

[17] Nicholson, *The Pentateuch*, 241, 244–45.

[18] See Nicholson, *The Pentateuch*, 90–91.

by Dtr2 (the second Deuteronomistic redactor).[19] More important, however, the interest in the relationship between J, the Dtr style texts in Genesis–Numbers, Deuteronomy, and the DtrH eventually led to different conceptions of J than had hitherto been proposed, and even to the denial of J's existence altogether.

An important figure in these developments is H. H. Schmid, who, although focusing on the dating of J, blurred the distinction between J and DtrH, such that his work can be seen as something of a stepping stone to other more radical views with regard to the nature of the non-Priestly material in Genesis–Numbers.[20] Against the prevalent view, after von Rad, that J is to be dated to the tenth century B.C.E., Schmid argued for the dating of J after the pre-Exilic prophets and approximately contemporaneous with Deuteronomy/DtrH, that is somewhere around Exilic times. He conceived of J as a multilayered work both in its literary formation and theological outlook, which comprised a coherent inner-Yahwistic redaction that allowed him still to speak of a "Yahwist" (somewhere in between Gunkel's collector and von Rad's author). This process of redaction in J is so close to the Dtr process of redaction in DtrH that they in effect blur into each other, and their relative chronology cannot be determined. Thus, Schmid's view, though still more or less within Noth's paradigm, strains it to the limit, such that although J and DtrH represent two works, they are so out of focus that they phase into each other.

J. Van Seters also takes seriously the Dtr styled texts within the non-Priestly material in Genesis–Numbers and advocates a late date for J, but in so doing puts forward a different paradigm for the literary composition of the Pentateuch, indeed for Genesis–Kings, from that of Noth.[21] Dismissing the view that cumulative oral tradition lies behind J, Van Seters has argued that J was more or less composed by an author on one level as a literary extension of DtrH, and is to be dated to the late

---

[19] See Boorer, *The Promise of the Land*, 23.
[20] H. H. Schmid, *Der Sogenannte Yahwist: Beobachtungen und Fragen zu Pentateuch-forschung* (Zurich: Theologischen, 1976).
[21] See especially, John Van Seters, *In Search of History: Historiography in the Ancient World and the Origins of Biblical History* (New Haven, CT: Yale University Press, 1983); Idem, *Prologue to History: The Yahwist as Historian in Genesis* (Louisville, KY: Westminster/John Knox, 1992); Idem, *The Life of Moses: The Yahwist as Historian in Exodus–Numbers* (Louisville, KY: Westminster/John Knox, 1994).

Exilic/post-Exilic period. Thus, J is perceived, in this model, as later and literarily dependent on DtrH. J never stood alone, but as an extension or prologue to DtrH supplemented DtrH's account of conquest in Joshua and composed the non-P text of Genesis–Numbers to form a work extending from Genesis–2 Kings. The Dtr style texts in Genesis–Numbers, then, are explained as part of J's style, as J's writing has been influenced by DtrH. P is a later redaction that supplemented J (or strictly speaking the non-P text of Genesis–2 Kings, i.e., J + DtrH) all at one level, extending from Genesis–Judges 2. In this paradigm, then, E is virtually nonexistent, while J, though the product of a creative author, can also be described as a redaction since it supplements DtrH, and P is a redaction. In the work of van Seters the conception of parallel and continuous sources that were combined in stages by redaction is abandoned; rather, the "sources" have become successive stages in the redaction of DtrH. This supplementary model is quite different from the traditional model resulting from source and redaction criticism almost universally adhered to up until the 1970s.

The work of R. Rendtorff has also pointed scholarship in yet another direction, and has proposed quite a different model again.[22] Rendtorff is critical of what he sees as the all too easy acceptance in previous scholarship, particularly by von Rad and Noth, of the compatibility of the results of classical source criticism, of parallel and continuous sources J, E, P, and form and traditiohistorical criticism. Instead, he argues, that if form criticism and traditiohistorical criticism are more rigorously applied, tracing through the stages of growth from the earliest to the latest, then one does not end up with the traditional continuous sources J, E, and P at all, but with a different model of the growth and composition of the Pentateuch altogether. In this process, he maintains that literary (or source) criticism as a method is important, although it must not be confused with the theory of sources: literary criticism should be carried out in the service of tradition history, that is, literary critical questions should be put at all stages of the traditiohistorical enquiry. The way in which Rendtorff actually goes about this, however, shows that his conception of tradition

[22] Rolf Rendtorff, *The Problem of the Process of Transmission in the Pentateuch* (trans. J. J. Scullion; Sheffield: JSOT, 1990); trans. of *Das übclicfcungs gcs chicht liche Problem des Pentateuch* (BZAW 147; Berlin: de Gruyter, 1977).

history seems to be confined to the literary level. Hence the way in which literary criticism is applied in the service of this tradition history is in terms of the successive literary or redactional stages, involving the editorial combining of already existing texts, to form the text as we now have it. Limiting his literary critical observations more or less to explicit formulations and cross references, he argues that what emerges in working from the earlier to the later stages of redaction is not a continuous source J, but distinct blocks of material, each of which were edited or redacted in a number of stages separately and in different ways from each other until the time of Deuteronomic–Deuteronomistic circles. These complexes of tradition comprise: the patriarchal traditions (edited in stages in terms of the promises); the exodus tradition (not edited in terms of the promises); the Sinai complex; the wilderness wandering complex; and the occupation of the land complex. These complexes of tradition were first linked together by Deuteronomistic texts that have similar formulations and occur at key points in Genesis–Numbers. These represent the editing of a Deuteronomic–Deuteronomistic school to whom he attributes the shaping of Genesis–Numbers, the composition of Deuteronomy, and the formation of the text up to Kings, without defining specifically any relative levels within them. He has argued also that it is possible to discern P texts that supplement Genesis–Exodus 6 only. These P texts include chronological and theological additions, with Exod 2:23–25; 6:2–9 functioning to link together the patriarchal and exodus traditions. Although clearly a different model of the formation of the text from that of Van Seters, Rendtorff's position has in common with Van Seters a focus: on the written level of texts, with little or no consideration of possible oral levels; and, most importantly, on redactional or editorial activity as the key process in the literary composition of the Pentateuchal text.

Finally, it is important to mention the work of E. Blum, as it represents a recent and increasingly influential comprehensive study of the formation of the Pentateuch in the school of Rendtorff. However, his position diverges significantly from that of Rendtorff particularly in relation to Exodus onward.[23] Like Rendtorff, his focus is on the editing of the written text, he abandons the notion of continuous sources and

---

[23] Erhard Blum, *Studien zur Komposition des Pentateuch* (BZAW 189; Berlin: de Gruyter, 1990).

originally independent sources, J, E, and P, and he perceives the patriarchal narratives as separate from the Exodus narratives, until their linking
together at a late stage in the formation of the Pentateuch.[24] However,
unlike Rendtorff, he speaks in terms of two main stages in the formation of the Pentateuch, KD (a Deuteronomistic "composition") and KP
(a Priestly "composition"), the former comprising the non-P material
extending throughout Exodus–Numbers at least, and the latter comprising substantially Genesis–Numbers as we now have it. KD is the work
of Deuteronomistic editors who took up earlier pre-Exilic (but post-722
B.C.E.) written narratives, in particular a narrative of the life of Moses,
and redacted them, that is, reworked and supplemented them, adding
texts that they composed, in such a way as to form a theologically coherent
composition layer. KD was composed in the early post-Exilic period, after
the DtrH and under its influence. Given its distinctive literary nature,
however, KD was not composed as a prologue to the DtrH, but as an
independent work. KD, in turn, was redacted by later Priestly writers
who produced a well-crafted composition, KP, through reworking KD
and incorporating other already existing written narratives as well as
composing their own texts. This KP, then, is perceived by Blum, neither
as a "source" nor as a "redaction," as it is not an independent source, but
neither does redaction adequately describe it: rather, it is best described
as *compositional*, that is, as a composition layer or simply a composition.
In this way the text of Genesis–Numbers was formed.

The different models of the literary composition and formation of the
Pentateuchal text, including Exodus, formulated by Van Seters, Rendtorff
and Blum, stand alongside the more traditional paradigm, still held by
many, of continuous parallel sources (in particular J and P) combined in
stages by redactors to form the present text. It remains to be seen which
will become the dominant paradigm in the twenty-first century.

It is clear from this history of interpretation that source and redaction
criticism of the Pentateuch, including Exodus, have interacted closely,

---

[24] In *Studien*, he attributes this to the hand of Deuteronomistic editors (his KD), but,
more recently, he has argued that the connection between Genesis and Exodus was
first made still later by P (i.e., his KP); see E. Blum, "The Literary Connection between
the Books of Genesis and Exodus and the end of the book of Joshua," in *A Farewell
to the Yahwist: The Composition of the Pentateuch in Recent European Interpretation*
(ed. Thomas B. Dozeman and Konrad Schmid; Atlanta: Society of Biblical Literature,
2006), 89–106.

albeit in various ways, not only with each other, but also with form criticism and traditiohistorical criticism. In addition, it can be said that source and redaction criticism have the potential to interact creatively and fruitfully with rhetorical criticism: in particular, stylistic features of a composite literary text, such as repetition and the juxtaposition of different styles and perspectives not only contribute to the possible redactional intent of the text, but form the basis for exploring its rhetorical impact. Thus, source and redaction criticism interact in dynamic ways with form or genre criticism and rhetorical criticism.

It remains to illustrate concretely the application of source and redaction criticism to Exodus 1–2 and Exodus 19–20.

EXODUS 1–2

Using the criteria of repetition, style, terminology, coherence within this text, and with the wider context in Genesis and Exodus, it is relatively easy to identify Priestly material (P) in these chapters from non-Priestly material. The Priestly material comprises: Exodus 1:1–5, 7, 13–14; 2:23bc–25. Therefore, Exodus 1:6, 8–12, 15–22; 2:1–23a are delineated as non-P. The reasons are as follows.

Repetitions can be seen in the following motifs: the transition from the Jacob generation to Israel as a nation in Exodus 1:1–5, 7 and Exodus 1:6, 8; the Israelites as numerous and strong in Exodus 1:7 and Exodus 1:9, 12, 20; and the imposition of slavery by the Egyptians in Exodus 1:13–14 and Exodus 1:11. Corresponding to these repetitions there are differences in the way these motifs are expressed, particularly in style and terminology.

In Exodus 1:1–5, 7 the transition from the patriarchs to Israel as a nation is effected by the play on the word *Israel* between verse 1, where it signifies the patriarch Jacob, and verse 7 where it signifies the nation of Israel; whereas in Exodus 1:6, 8 the change in generations is expressed formulaically (see the parallel in Judg 2:8, 10) in terms of the death of Joseph and his generation and the emergence of a new king who did not know Joseph.[25] Moreover, the interest in genealogies and lists of names,

---

[25] Some commentators, for example, Martin Noth (*Exodus: A Commentary* [Philadelphia: Westminster, 1962] 19–20), J. P. Hyatt (*Exodus* [Grand Rapids, MI: Eerdmans, 1980] 56–7), and George W. Coats (*Exodus 1–18* [Grand Rapids, MI: Eerdmans, 1999] 22), see verse 6 as belonging to P. However, I agree with those who see verse 6 as going with v. 8

as found in verses 1–5, is typical of texts commonly identified as P in Genesis (e.g., Gen 46:8–27). The terminology in Exodus 1:7 consists of a combination of terms that occur in P texts, Genesis 1, 9, and 17: *šāraṣ* (swarm, Gen 1:20, 21; 9:7), *pārâ* (be fruitful), and *mil'û 'et-hā'āreṣ* (fill the earth, Gen 1:28; 9:1), and *bim'ōd mě'ōd* (very very much, Gen 17:2, 6). The motif of a numerous and strong nation found in Exodus 1:7 in the form of a statement is repeated in Exodus 1:9 but this time as direct speech, and in comparative terms as more numerous (*rābâ*) and stronger (*'āṣam*) than the Egyptians (see also Exod 1:12, 20). Although verses 7, 9, 20 have in common the word (*'āṣam*, strong), verses 9, 20 lack any of the distinctively P terminology found in Exodus 1:7. Finally, the motif of oppression or slavery is expressed in Exodus 1:13–14 in a repetitive style, using the terminology of the root, *'ābad*, both as a verb and a noun, repeated five times, along with the chiastic use of *běpārek* (with duress), found only in Priestly texts (e.g., Lev 25:43, 46), surrounding motifs of bitterness and harshness. In contrast, in Exodus 1:11 the imposition of forced labor (*siblôt*) is a way of dealing shrewdly, a strategy designed to stop them multiplying and escaping from the land (v. 10). For all these reasons, then, Exodus 1:1–5, 7, 1–14 and Exodus 1:6, 8, 10–12 are seen as belonging to at least two different written sources: the former to P in contrast to the latter which are not P.

With regard to the rest of the material in Exodus 1–2, the criterion of coherence, along with style and terminology, becomes particularly important in separating out P from the non-P material. Exodus 1:13–14 (P), with its focus on the harshness of the slavery, interrupts the plot, or sequence of the narrative, in the non-P material, for Exodus 1:8–12, which moves from dealing shrewdly by oppressing the Israelites lest they multiply (vv. 10–11), to the ironic consequence of this that they do multiply (v. 12), finds its next logical step in the attempts to reduce their numbers through genocide in Exodus 1:15–22. Exodus 2:23bc–25 resumes and moves on coherently from Exodus 1:13–14. It refers to the *slavery* (*'ăbōdâ*, repeated twice) used in Exodus 1:13–14, and goes on to state that God heard their groaning (*nǎ'āqâ*), remembered (*zākar*) his covenant with the patriarchs and took notice of them, with the emphasis on *God*

because of the close parallel with Judges 2:8, 10 that expresses the change of generations (see, for example, Brevard S. Childs, *Exodus: A Commentary* [London: SCM, 1974] 2–3, Propp, *Exodus 1–18*, 126).

which is repeated five times. This coherence between Exodus 1:13–14 and Exodus 2:23bc, the fact that God's *remembering* is a distinctive P motif (Gen 8:1; 9:15–16), and its repetitive style identifies Exodus 2:23bc–25 as P. This is reinforced by the continuation of these motifs in Exodus 6:2–8, generally recognized as P's version of the call of Moses. Exodus 2:23bc–25, in turn, interrupts its immediate context that has Moses in Midian (Exod 2:11–22) where he subsequently receives his call (Exod 3:1ff), directing attention back to the slavery in Egypt.

Along with the criteria of repetition, style, terminology, and coherence within Exodus 1–2, all working together to separate P, from non-P, material, the criterion of the coherence of Exodus 1:1–5, 7, 13–14; 2:23bc-25 (P) with the wider context in Genesis and Exodus has also been part of our discussion. It will be helpful at this point to summarize and unfold this in more detail. Exodus 1:1–5 recapitulates Gen 46:8–27 (P) with minor variations,[26] and uses this along with Exodus 1:7 to form a transition, after the death of Jacob's generation in Genesis 50:12–13, 22–23 (P),[27] from the patriarchs to the nation Israel. Exodus 1:7 in its terminology parallels both Genesis 1:28; 9:1, 7, and Genesis 17:2, 6, thereby seeing the rise of the nation Israel as the fulfillment of the Abrahamic covenantal promise, and aligning its fruitfulness with that of all humanity in the cosmic setting. The situation of this nation in the grip of harsh slavery in Exodus 1:13–14 forms the necessary backdrop, and leads coherently to God's response to this situation of remembering his covenant with the patriarchs in Exodus 2:23bc–25. This, in turn, leads to the promise of the exodus to (and through) Moses in Exodus 6:2–8 (P). Exodus 6:2–8, in typical P style, resumes what has been said before and coherently moves on from there: thus, Exodus 6:4–5 refers back to the remembrance of the covenant with Abraham, Isaac, and Jacob and the groaning of the Israelites linked with their slavery as stated in Exodus 2:23bc–24, and then moves on to

---

[26] Because of this repetition, some commentators, such as Propp (*Exodus 1–18*, 125) see Exodus 1:1–5 as the work of a redactor (RP) that is later than P as such. This is possible. However, I would maintain along with, for example, Noth (*Exodus*, 20), Childs (*Exodus*, 2), and Blum (*Studien*, 202) that these verses are on the same level as Exodus 1:7, 13–14; 2:23bc–25, as Exodus 1:1–5 is typical of P's technique of structuring the narrative by means of genealogies and lists throughout Genesis.

[27] The death of Joseph is not stated explicitly in P, but it is quite possible that P's notice of his death was dropped in favor of non-P material in Genesis 50:26; Exodus 1:6 by a redactor.

the next stage involving the promise of exodus and possession of the promised land.

This consistency in style, terminology, and coherence with P passages prior to and following Exodus 1:1–5, 7, 13–14; 2:23bc–25 reinforces the identity of these verses as belonging to P. It also raises the issue of the nature of this P material in Exodus 1–2, as to whether it forms part of a continuous and originally independent source (i.e., Pg) or whether it should be seen as a redaction that supplements the non-P material.

The main argument cited by those who see P as a redaction in this context is that there is a gap in its coherence, as it does not introduce Moses as such: Moses appears abruptly in Exodus 6:2 and therefore P must be a redactor who incorporated the non-P material that describes the birth of Moses and something of his background in Exodus 2:1–22.[28] This carries some weight. However, I would argue that this is overridden by considerations of the coherence that we have seen between the P passages, with their style of resumption and progression in terms of the key points highlighted in summary fashion. The style and economy of P's prose does not necessarily need explicitly to introduce a figure so well known as Moses. On the grounds of coherence, then, as well as the many parallels with the non-P material, I would agree with the majority of scholars, that the P narrative here in Exodus 1–2 is part of an originally independent narrative source extending back into Genesis and forward at least through Exodus. Moreover, I agree with the generally held view that P here is later than the non-P material in its context, given P's style of summarizing statements that would seem to extract what P sees to be the essence of the storytelling style non-P material.

Having separated out the P source, what can now be said about the literary composition of the non-P material, Exodus 1:6, 8–12, 15–22; 2:1–23a?

The only possible repetition or doublet within this material is found in Exodus 1:15–21 and Exodus 1:22, both of which describe the killing of the Israelite boys, but by different people (the midwives, the Egyptians) and by different means (killing them on the birth stool, throwing them into the Nile). Consequently, verses 15–21 and verse 22 are often attributed

---

[28] See, for example, Cross, *Canaanite Myth*, 317–18; Van Seters, *The Life of Moses*, 20, 23; and Blum, *Studien*, 240.

to different written sources; and those scholars who adhere to the view that the non-P material in the Pentateuch comprises the sources J and E usually attribute Exodus 1:15–21 to E, and Exodus 1:22, as its doublet to J.[29] Exodus 1:15–21 is seen as E primarily because of the divine name *Elohim* (God) in verses 17, 20, 21, and because of the motif of the fear of God in verses 17, 21, which occurs in other texts thought to be E (e.g., Gen 20:8, 11; 22:17; Exod 3:6; 18:21; 20:18, 20).[30] This is possible, but the evidence is quite slim, given the fragmentary nature of any of the texts thought to be E in the wider context of Genesis and Exodus. Also, given the fact that there is no mention of YHWH in verse 22 or any of the other non-P material in Exodus 1–2, the criterion of the alternation of the divine name does not carry much weight in this context. It is also quite possible to see verses 15–21 as an isolated story taken up from the tradition. Alternatively, verse 22 could be seen as the next step in the sequence of the story, the second strategy to try and reduce the Israelite population by killing the boys, especially given the use of *rābâ* (multiply) and *ʿāṣam* (strong) in verse 20 as in Exodus 1:9, which is usually seen as of a piece with verse 22.[31]

With regard to the non-P material before and after Exodus 1:15–22, it can be argued that, allowing for the possible taking up of motifs or stories from the tradition, there is (along with vv. [15–21] 22) enough coherence to advocate a continuous literary source, at least within Exodus 1–2. There is a coherent progression of thought in terms of cause and effect between Exodus 1:6, 8–12, (15–21), 22. After the death of Joseph, the new king of a new era sees that the Israelites are more numerous and powerful than the Egyptians (vv. 6, 8–9) and so he thinks up the plan to enslave them, in order to stop their numbers increasing and their escaping from the land (vv. 10–11). But when ironically the plan backfires and their number still increases (v. 12), the next strategy is genocide in verses 15–21, 22. Verse 22, the intention to drown the boys in the Nile (*yĕʾōr*), then, forms the necessary backdrop for the story of Moses' birth and rescue in Exodus 2:1–10, explaining the reason for hiding Moses, ironically, in the Nile

[29] See, for example, Noth, *Exodus*, 23–24; Propp, *Exodus 1–18*, 138.
[30] See Hans W. Wolff, "The Elohistic Fragments in the Pentateuch," in Brueggemann and Wolff, *The Vitality*, 67–82.
[31] See Hyatt (*Exodus*, 61) who attributes all of verses 15–22 to E; Van Seters (*The Life of Moses*, 23) who attributes all the non-P material in Exodus 1 to his late J.

($yĕ'ōr$, v. 3), from where he is adopted into Pharaoh's household. Exodus 2:11–15a, though fairly loosely connected to this through the repetition of the verb $gādal$ (grow up, vv. 10 and 11), follows coherently in terms of narrative plot, with the adult Moses killing an Egyptian in defense of a Hebrew, thus picking up on the motifs in Exodus 2:1–10 of his Hebrew birth and nurturing, and adoption as an Egyptian. Exodus 2:15b–22, the scene at the well that leads to Moses' marriage, then, follows coherently. It takes place in Midian to which he has fled as a result of killing the Egyptian, and displays links with Exodus 2:11–15a in terms of the common motif of Moses' active concern for justice for the weaker party that crosses the bounds of different nationalities.[32]

In terms of source criticism, this coherence in narrative progression supports the view that Exodus 1:6, 8–12, 22; 2:1–22[33] at least belongs to the one written source. Any slight unevennesses, such as the loose connection between Exodus 2:10 and 11, can be explained, using form and traditiohistorical criticism, as the incorporation of a story from the tradition (Exod 2:1–10). It is possible, also, that the scene at the well as a whole draws on a traditional story, since in form-critical terms the scenario of betrothal following a meeting at a well follows a typical structure that allows it to be seen as a distinctive genre (see the similar type of stories in Gen 24:10ff; 29:1ff). Alternatively, the story narrated here could be a literary construction, using the literary convention of the woman at the well type scene to portray Moses as the liberator of the oppressed.[34]

Exodus 1:8–12, 22 as it stands would definitely appear to be a literary construction, composed intentionally both as a backdrop to the introduction of Moses in Exodus 2:1–10, and as an introduction to the wider context that follows in the non-P material throughout Exodus 1–14. The motifs of the large numbers of the Israelites, their oppression through slavery, and genocide have been woven together in a seemingly deliberate cause and effect sequence that leads to Exodus 2:1–10. Exodus 1:8–12, 22 is a rather artificial construction, however, as it is not particularly logical or historically credible to want to kill off your slave force.[35] But this

---

[32] See Childs, *Exodus*, 32, and 29–30 for further observations of stylistic features especially in Exodus 2:11–15.

[33] Exodus 2:23a can be seen to follow on from Exodus 2:22, but begins another episode that would seem to be continued in Exodus 4:19.

[34] Alter, *The Art of Biblical Narrative*, 47–62.

[35] See Childs, *Exodus*, 11.

apparent illogical construction can be explained, not only by its function as leading to the introduction of Moses in Exodus 2:1–10, but by the distilling together of motifs important in the wider context outside of Exodus 1–2. Thus, the motif of great numbers looks back to, and signifies the fulfillment of, the promise of descendants to the patriarchs in the non-P material in Genesis (e.g., Gen 12:1–3; 28:14). Indeed the theme of Israel as stronger (ʿāṣam) than a foreign nation in whose territory they are residing as in Exodus 1:9–10 is found also in the wider context, in Genesis 26:16 and Numbers 22:5–6 (non-P). The motif of slavery forms the backdrop for the exodus, since this is the reason for God's rescue of them out of Egypt (Exod 3–14 [non-P]): Exodus 1:10 foreshadows this by stating explicitly that one of the goals of the plan to oppress them is, ironically, to stop them from escaping from the land. And, finally, the motif of genocide is necessary for the introduction of Moses in Exodus 2:10 as the leader of the exodus, the one who fights for justice for the oppressed (Exod 2:11–22).

What can be concluded from all of this concerning the nature of this literary source in Exodus 1–2, that I prefer to call non-P?[36] Within Exodus 1–2 it would seem to form a coherent literary composition that both draws on existing tradition but also comprises its own literary composition, designed to bring together traditional motifs into a coherent whole. This coherent whole forms a bridging function in that: it encompasses the transition from the time of Joseph to the era of the nation of Israel, whose numbers fulfill the patriarchal promise; sets the scene of the situation of oppression as the basis for the exodus; and introduces Moses, as a Hebrew with Egyptian associations who acts for the justice of those who are oppressed, thus foreshadowing his role as leader of the exodus. Because this material looks back to non-P texts in Genesis, and acts as an introduction to the whole of the non-P material in Exodus 1–14, I would argue that the non-P material in Exodus 1–2 is part of a much larger continuous account in Genesis and Exodus at least.[37]

---

[36] We could call it J – although in Exodus 1–2 there is no mention of YHWH, or any other terminology that would label it as such so such an identification would be on the grounds of related texts outside of Exodus 1–2.

[37] I agree with D. Carr ("What is Required to Identify Pre-Priestly Narrative Connections between Genesis and Exodus? Some General Reflections on Specific Cases," in Dozemann and Schmid, *A Farewell to the Yahwist?*, 159–80), against the views of those in the Rendtorff school (such as J. Gertz, K. Schmid,) who argue that there is no continuous

Finally, since the P and non-P material in Exodus 1–2 represent two continuous originally independent sources, the work of redaction here consists primarily of the intertwining of these sources. This has been done such that the different ways in which the P and non-P material affect the transition from the patriarchal era to the nation Israel are complimentary. The new situation of Israel as a numerous nation clearly arises after the death of Joseph (Exod 1:6, 7), and the speech of the new king in the new era about a plan to deal with the large number of Israelites comes clearly after, and on the basis of, the statement of their multiplication and strength, that fulfills the patriarchal promises and imitates the whole creation (Exod 1:7, 8ff). P's statement in Exodus 1:13–14, coming as it does after the ironic backfiring of the slavery plan that leads to them multiplying more in verse 12, has the effect of portraying the Egyptians as pursuing their futile strategy of slavery even more harshly before resorting in verses 15–22 to the even more extreme measure of genocide, thus showing an escalation in the Egyptians' ruthless behavior. And, finally, the insertion of Exodus 2:23bc–25 (P) into the scene of Moses in Midian brings attention back to the slavery and suffering of the Israelites, which in the meantime and even after Pharaoh's death (v. 23a) continues unrelentingly, as that which catches God's attention and stirs his memory, and thus begins the train of events leading to the exodus, beginning with the call of Moses (Exod 3:1ff).

EXODUS 19–20

The history of the literary composition of Exodus 19–20 remains, like the cloud on Mount Sinai, shrouded in mystery. That these chapters are a literary composite is not disputed. However, opinion with regard to the details of this is so varied that it is well nigh impossible to reach any definitive conclusions in relation to the possible written sources and/or redaction of this notoriously difficult text. There is general agreement that Exodus 19:1–2a at least is Priestly material and that in these chapters

source linking Genesis and Exodus before P using the sole criterion of explicit literary cross references, that there are other indications of unity and continuity across these texts such as plays on motifs and narrative progression; and that allowance must be made for the omission of explicit transitions in the non-P material, explained by the work of a later redactor giving preference to P when combining them.

(unlike Exodus 1–2) there is evidence of Deuteronomistic style redaction, especially in Exodus 19:3b–8. However, the views that have been put forward with regard to the rest of the text of Exodus 19–20 are almost as many and varied as those outlined in our history of interpretation of the Pentateuch, and indeed they tend to reflect it.

For example, older source critics divide the bulk of Exodus 19–20 into continuous sources J and E (including the Decalogue), that were then intertwined with each other by a redactor RJE. However, with regard to the details, especially in Exodus 19, there are a range of views: for example, Baentsch (1903) attributes Exodus 19:9, 11–13a, 15, 18, 20, 21, 25 to J, and Exodus 19:2b, 3a, 10, 13b–14, 16–17, 19 to E;[38] whereas Noth attributes Exodus 19:2b, 10–13a, 14–15, 16aα, 18, (20–25) to J, and Exodus 19:3a, 13b, 16aβ–17, 19 to E.[39] Childs in his classic commentary on Exodus reflects the paradigm that dominated the mid-twentieth century.[40] He divides the text into continuous sources J and E that were later combined by a pre-Deuteronomic RJE redactor who is responsible for the shape of Exodus 19–24 (32–33) 34.[41] However, using form and traditiohistorical criticism, he explains most of the unevennesses and tensions in the text in terms of the fusion of two different oral traditions regarding the Mosaic office before J and E: the basic content of the dominant form of the tradition is reflected in Exodus 19:10–11, 16–17; 20:18–20 (and Exod 24:3–8); and the content of the other form of the tradition is reflected in Exodus 19:9, 19, 20 (and Exod 34). Although the former corresponds roughly to the E source and the latter corresponds roughly to J, according to Childs, both literary sources drew on the preliterary combination of these traditions: hence the tensions within each of the literary sources are a reflection of the tension already there in the oral tradition. Finally, at the other end of the spectrum from Childs, T. Dozeman, working within Rendtorff's basic framework, treats the Sinai complex, and Exodus 19–20, 24 in particular, as an independent block of tradition and seeks to trace its tradition history, perceived not in terms of continuous sources at all, but

---

[38] Cited in Childs, *Exodus*, 345–46.
[39] Noth, *A History of Pentateuchal Traditions*, 31, 36. Noth also saw (with most) Exodus 20:18–21 as E, and Exodus 20:1–17 as a secondary insertion into E.
[40] Childs, *Exodus*, 349–60.
[41] Including moving Exodus 20:18–20 after the Decalogue (which before RJE was part of E) in order to insert the Book of the Covenant.

in terms of successive literary layers of redaction by creative theologians whose work represents planned theological editing.[42] There is a basic stratum which is a single tradition (the mountain of God tradition) comprising Exodus 19:2b–3a, 10ab–11a, 12aa, 13b–15a, 16ab–17; 24:4ab–5; a late pre-Exilic/Exilic Deuteronomistic redaction that reinterpreted it by supplementing it with the texts, Exodus 19:3b–5bc, 6b–8a, 8b–9a, 19; 20:1–17, 18–20; 20:21–23:33; 24:3–4aa, 7; and finally, a Priestly redaction, the final redaction of the Sinai complex, that added Exodus 19:1–2a, 5bb–6a, 11b, 12ab–13, 15b, 16aa, 18, 20–25; 24:1–2, 5, 6, 8, 9–11, 15b–18a.[43]

Given this, all that I can hope to achieve here, within the limits of a brief discussion, is to point to features of this text that are of greatest significance in exploring it in terms of source and redaction criticism, and along the way to raise questions, clarify some of the issues, and offer some tentative suggestions. Hopefully this discussion will at least show how the methods of source and redaction criticism operate in relation to another, and much more complex, text; and be helpful for the reader who may wish to critically explore further the multiple positions reached by scholars who have sought to analyze the history of the literary composition of this text in great detail.

I will start from what appear to be the later layers and work backwards to what seems to be earlier: this coincides with proceeding from the relatively certain into, increasingly, the realm of speculation.

Exodus 19:1–2a is generally recognized as P material. This is clear from its repetitive style, its precise attention to dating (see Exod 12:2), the terminology of "on that day" (*bayyôm hazzeh*), see Genesis 7:11; Leviticus 8:34; 16:30 [P]), and in particular its continuity and coherence with other P itinerary notices that structure the P material in Exodus (and Numbers) (e.g., Exod 16:1; 17:1abα).[44] The priority given to the date of their coming

---

[42] T. Dozeman, *God on the Mountain: A Study of Redaction Theology and Canon in Exodus 19–24* (Atlanta, GA: Scholars Press, 1989).

[43] Other recent views that have moved away from the traditional view of continuous sources J and E are those of: Blum (*Studien*, 45–51, 92–93) who attributes the bulk of Exodus 19–20 to his post-DtrH KD composition, whose hand can be seen especially in Exodus 19:3b–8; 20:22; 24:1–2, 9–11; and Van Seters (*The Life of Moses*, 247–89) who attributes Exodus 19:2–11, 13b–19; 20:18–26 to his post-DtrH Yahwist (J) and Exodus 19:1, 12–13a, 20–25; 20:1–17 to a later Priestly redaction layer.

[44] Therefore I would see this as part of the P narrative source (Pg) that continues in Exodus 24:15b–18 with a description of theophany and Moses' ascent into the cloud that parallels the theophany material in Exodus 19:9–19; 20:18–21.

to the wilderness of Sinai explains the unevenness in the order of verse 1 and verse 2a. The repetition regarding their camping there between verse 2a and verse 2b is generally taken as an indication that verse 2b is non-P.

Exodus 19:3b–8 is Dtr redaction, inserted into the underlying narrative of verse 3a and verses 9ff. There is a discrepancy between verse 3a and verse 3b in terms of where Moses is located, corresponding with a change in the divine name; that is whether he has gone up to God, or is at a distance from YHWH who calls from the mountain. Verse 3b is therefore differentiated from verse 3a, which introduces verses 3b–8a, coherent unit. YHWH tells Moses what to say to the Israelites (vv. 3b–6), which he duly does (v. 7), followed by the response of the people affirming their obedience to what YHWH has spoken (v. 8a). The terminology in verses 4–5 is clearly Deuteronomic/Deuteronomistic: "you have seen" what YHWH has done for Israel (v. 4a) is characteristic of Dtr (see Deut 4:3; 10:21; 11:7; 29:2; Josh 23:3); the imagery of being borne on eagle's wings has a parallel in Deut 32:11; listening/obeying expressed in conditional form (v. 5a) is found in Deut 11:13; 15:5; 28:1; and Israel as YHWH's "treasured possession" (*sĕgullâ*. V. 5bα) occurs in Deuteronomy 7:6; 14:2; 26:18.[45] While the terminology in verses 5bβ–6 is not strictly Dtr, it seems to be quite late (Exilic/post-Exilic) because the concept of the whole earth as belonging to YHWH (v. 5bβ) echoes the theology of Isaiah 40ff, Israel as a kingdom of priests (v. 6a) finds its closest parallel in Isaiah 61:6,[46] and Israel as a holy nation (v. 6a) finds a close parallel in Deuteronomy 7:6 (where it is also linked with Israel as YHWH's *sĕgullâ*)[47] and in the Holiness Code (see Lev 19:2; 20:26; 21:8; 22:9, 15).[48] Exodus 19:9a goes in a different direction from verses 3b–8, introducing the motif of theophany in order for Moses' authority to be recognized by the people, and is part of the context into which verses 3b–8 has been inserted. The criterion of coherence clinches the fact that verses 3b–8 is a later insertion, as verses 3b–8 introduces the motif of covenant prematurely in terms of the

[45]   See Nicholson, *The Pentateuch*, 189–90.
[46]   See E. W. Nicholson, "The Covenant Ritual in Exodus 24:3–8," *VT* 32 (1982): 74–86, 77.
[47]   Although Deuteronomy refers only to a holy *people* (Deut 7:6; 14:2, 21; 26:19) and never a holy *nation*.
[48]   Dozeman (*God on the Mountain*, pp. 94–98) argues that verses 5bb–6a represent part of his Priestly redaction.

surrounding context, that is before the theophany (Exod 19;10ff) and the giving of the law (Exod 20:1ff), thus anticipating the conclusion of the covenant in Exodus 24:3–8.[49]

Exodus 20:22–23 also represents a Dtr redaction that has been inserted into the text. It starts in very similar fashion to Exodus 19:3b–4a, as a YHWH speech to Moses, telling him what he is to say to the Israelites, beginning with, "You have seen" (v. 22b, see Exod 19:4a). This, along with the motif of YHWH speaking to the people out of heaven, which is paralleled in Deuteronomy 4:36a, marks verse 22 as Dtr. The command against making gods of silver and gold in verse 23 also has a parallel in Deuteronomy 4:15ff. Verses 22–23 are differentiated from their context in that: the descriptions of theophany in Exodus 19:10–19 and Exodus 20:18–21 do not have YHWH speaking from heaven but, rather, in storm and volcanic phenomena associated with the top of the mountain; and the altar laws in Exodus 20:24–26, which verses 22–23 introduce, use the second person singular, rather than the second person plural address of verses 22–23, and are thought to reflect quite ancient law as part of the Book of the Covenant (Exod 21:1ff).[50] It is quite likely, therefore, that Exodus 20:22–23 was inserted into the context by a Dtr hand in order to introduce, and even also include in its present context, the Book of the Covenant law code in Exodus 20:24–26; 21:1ff.[51]

Given the increasingly held view that the law codes in Exodus 20 had their own history of transmission largely independent of their present context,[52] and the laws in Exodus 20:24–26 appear to have been

---

[49] Nicholson ("The Covenant Ritual in Exodus 24:3–8") sees Exodus 19:6a as part of verses 3b–8 as a later comment on the ritual of Exodus 24:3–8 which he interprets as sanctification ritual. Cf. Van Seters (*The Life of Moses*, 273) who argues that verses 3b–8 are part of his post-DtrH J, who in writing his text copied the ordering in Deuteronomy 4–5. However, I perceive the surrounding context in Exodus 19:3a, 9ff as earlier than verses 3b–8 into which it was later inserted and therefore would argue either that the hand that inserted verses 3b–8 only may have been copying Deuteronomy 4, or, more likely, Deuteronomy 4 copied the redacted text of Exodus 19 at this point.

[50] See Childs, *Exodus*, 466. However, the expression, "where I cause my name to be remembered" is quite close to Dtr expressions such as found in Deuteronomy 5:11 and 1 Kings 8:29.

[51] There seems to be some disruption here with regard to the ordering of the laws of the Book of the Covenant, as the title for the rest of the laws in Exodus 21:1 comes after the altar law in Exodus 20:23–24.

[52] See Brevard S. Childs, *Introduction to the Old Testament as Scripture* (Philadelphia: Fortress, 1979) 65.

introduced and included by a Dtr redactor who composed Exodus 20:22–23, what can be said of the Decalogue in Exodus 20:1–17?

Exodus 20:1–17 clearly stands out from its immediate context in Exodus 19:9–25; 20:18–21, as in Exodus 20:1 God speaks directly whereas in the context, with its central theme of theophany, Moses is mediator of God's words. In addition, Exodus 19:25 breaks off abruptly, not stating what Moses said, and Exodus 20:1 does not follow from Exodus 19:25 coherently. Furthermore, Exodus 20:18–21 follows coherently from Exodus 19:19. All this suggests that Exodus 20:1–17 has been secondarily inserted into its present context. But at what point was it inserted and by whom? Views have ranged, for example, from it being an insertion between Exodus 19:19 and Exodus 20:18–21 at an early stage, that is in the E source,[53] to its insertion at a later stage than this as the work of a pre-Deuteronomic redactor who combined J and E (RJE) and shaped Exodus 19–24 as a whole,[54] to its insertion very late by a (post-DtrH) Dtr redactor who was responsible for giving Exodus 20, if not the whole of Exodus 19–20, its present shape.[55]

Evidence for Exodus 20:1–17 having been incorporated by a Dtr redactor of some description is reasonably strong. Exodus 20:1–17 parallels very closely Deuteronomy 5:6–21, and contains some typical Deuteronomic expressions, such as "the house of slavery" (v. 2, see Deut 5:6; 6:12; 7:8; 8:14; 13:5, 10), "jealous God" (v. 5, see Deut 4:24; 6:15; Josh 24:19), and long life in the land gifted by YHWH (v. 12b, see Deut 4:40; 5:33; 11:9; 30:18; 32:47). However, Exodus 20:11 is clearly Priestly, paralleling Genesis 1:1–2:3 (P). The ordering of the Decalogue in Exodus 20:1–17, where it is followed by reference to theophany and the people's request for Moses to mediate because of fear of death, is found in the same sequence in Deuteronomy 5 (vv. 6–21 the Decalogue; vv. 22–31 theophany and request). However, whether Deuteronomy 5:6–21 is earlier or later than Exodus 20 needs to be taken into consideration.

Nicholson argues that the same Dtr redactor who inserted Exodus 20:1–17 also composed Exodus 20:22–23, thus linking the Decalogue with

---

[53] See Noth, *A History of Pentateuchal Traditions*, 36.
[54] See Childs, *Exodus*, 350.
[55] See E. W. Nicholson, "The Decalogue as the Direct Address of God," *VT* 27 (1977): 422–33 (in relation to Exod 20 only); Dozeman, *God on the Mountain*, 51–52; Blum, *Studien*, 45–51, 92–93 (although he attributes it to his KD).

the Book of the Covenant, as in verse 22 the second person plural reference as the object of God's speaking from heaven coheres with Exodus
20:1–17, which is also direct address from God to Israel.[56] This seems to
me to carry some weight. However, he goes further to argue that this
Dtr redactor is later than, and influenced by, Deuteronomy 4–5: this
explains the strong parallels, already noted between Exodus 20:22–23 and
Deuteronomy 4:36a, 15ff, the same sequence of the Decalogue and theophany in Exodus 20 and Deuteronomy 5, and the influence of P in Exod
20:11 which he sees as late Exilic/post-Exilic. Dozeman, also noting the
parallels with Deuteronomy 4 and 5, concludes that the whole of Exodus
20 is the work of his Dtr redaction, that represents a single process, but
also embraces Exodus 19:3b–5bc, 6b–8a (as well as Exod 19:8b–9a, 19).
He perceives this Dtr redaction as on the same level as Deuteronomy
5:1–6:3, but as earlier than Deut 4:1–40, which was added later to
Deuteronomy 5.[57] Blum attributes Exodus 20, along with the bulk of
Exodus 19 to his post-DtrH KD, whose hand he sees especially in Exodus
19:3b–8; 20:22, and therefore as later than Deuteronomy 4–5.[58]

What, then, can be concluded from all this? It seems to me that the
evidence from the text suggests that a redactor inserted Exodus 20:1–17,
separating Exodus 20:18–21 from its earlier context as following on from
Exodus 19:19. This is possibly the same redactor that was responsible for
Exodus 20:22–23 and the incorporation of the Book of the Covenant.
This redactor can be described as Dtr in some sense. However, I prefer
to reserve judgment with regard to the relative level of composition
between this Dtr redaction with either Deuteronomy 5 or Deuteronomy
4, as one or both of the latter could just as easily be later and influenced
by Exodus 20 than vice versa. The relationship between Exodus 19:3b–8
and Exodus 20, in particular verses 22–23, also must be left as an open
question. Are they to be seen as part of the same redaction, basically
forming the shape of Exodus 19–20 as a whole, or not? It could well be
the case that Exodus 19:3b–8 (if the very late elements in vv. 6bb–7a are
an integral part of it) represents a later redactional level than Exodus 20.

---

[56] Nicholson, "The Decalogue as the Direct Address of God."

[57] Dozeman, *God on the Mountain*, 38–71, especially 51–52, 57, 70.

[58] Van Seters (*The Life of Moses*, 271–82) argues that his J text, that includes Exodus
20:18–26 and 19:3b–8 (and also 19:2–3a, 9–11, 13b–19, but not Exodus 20:1–17, which
he sees as Priestly redaction) is post-Deuteronomy 4–5 with which he does a detailed
comparison.

It remains to examine the theophany material in Exodus 19:9–25; 20:18–21, the bulk of which at least is earlier than the Dtr redaction(s). Here we enter more deeply into the realm of speculation.

Clearly in these verses there are tensions and discrepancies. Over and above Moses' repeated trips up and down the mountain (Exod 19:3a, 14, 20, 25; 20:21), there are three main tensions. First, on the one hand, although seemingly allowed to approach or even go up the mountain (e.g., Exod 19:13b, 17), the people themselves choose to keep their distance from it (Exod 20:18, 21); and, on the other, the people are repeatedly warned by God through Moses not to go up the mountain or even to touch it (Exod 19:12–13, 21, 23, 24). Second, the way in which God approaches the mountain along with the associated theophanic phenomena varies: on the one hand, God is described as "coming" (*bô'*) in a "cloud" (*'ānān*) on the mountain along with associated storm imagery of thunder and lightning, as well as the sound of the trumpet (Exod 19:9, 16aβb, 19; 20:18, 20); on the other, God is described as "coming down" (*yārad*) upon Mount Sinai in association with volcanic imagery of fire, smoke, and quaking (Exod 19:11, 18, 20). Finally, there are differences in the process by which Moses assumes the role of mediator of God's words for the people: on the one hand, Moses only becomes the mediator gradually and at the request of the people (Exod 19:9, 19; 20:19–21), on the other, Moses is portrayed as the mediator of God's words to the people from the beginning (Exod 19:10–15, 21–25).

On the basis of these tensions and discrepancies, as well as the criterion of coherence, it is possible at least to make some sort of a case, albeit with reservations, for discerning two different literary strands here. These would comprise: Exodus 19:9a, 13b, 16aβb–17, 19; 20:18–21;[59] and Exodus 19:10–13a, 14–15, 16aα, 18(20–25).[60]

Exodus 19:9a, 13b, 16aβb–17, 19; 20:18–21 displays a certain coherence as well as the use of consistent motifs and images. In a divine speech, Moses is told of God's intention to come in a cloud so that the people may overhear him speaking to Moses as an affirmation of Moses' authority

---

[59] Possibly also Exodus 19:3a, given 19:17.

[60] Possibly also Exodus 19:2b, although this could belong to either. Exodus 19:20–25, as is generally recognized, is a later addition, as will be discussed shortly. This division into written sources is basically in line with E and J, respectively, as outlined by Noth (*A History of Pentateuchal Traditions*, 31, 36), except that Noth ascribes Exodus 19:9a to part of the later Dtr addition of 19:3bff.

that will enable the people to trust him (Exod 19:9a), and that when the trumpet sounds the people may go up the mountain (Exod 19:13b). Accordingly, there is a theophany, comprising a cloud on the mountain along with storm imagery of thunder and lightning and the sound of a trumpet, causing the people, located in the camp, to tremble (Exod 19:16aβb); and so Moses brings the people out of the camp to the foot of the mountain (Exod 19:17). God's intention, stated in verse 9a, is unfolded with a dialogue between God and Moses, accompanied by the sound of the trumpet (Exod 19:19). In light of this theophany with its storm imagery, the trembling of the people is repeated, leading them to go no further but to stand at a distance rather than going up on the mountain (Exod 20:18). In fulfillment of God's intention in speaking with Moses, that the people will trust Moses (Exod 19:9a), the people do just that, by asking Moses to mediate God's words (Exod 20:19). Moses' response, then, picks up on the motif of the trembling of the people (Exod 19:16; 20:18), exhorting them not to fear, and explaining that God has come so that they will fear God (Exod 20:20), which is precisely what has occurred. Accordingly, Moses takes up his role as mediator for the people who stay at a distance (Exod 20:21). Admittedly, there are unevennesses within this, such as the different terminology for "trumpet" as *yōbēl* in Exodus 19:13b and as *šōpār* in Exodus 19:16b, 19; 20:18, the use of YHWH in 19:9a in contrast to the use of God (*Elohim*) throughout the rest of the verses, and the mention of smoke along with the storm imagery in Exodus 20:18. These unevennesses are not insuperable. The imagery of smoke in Exodus 20:18 may be redactional, that is, part of the process of combining the two literary strands. The discrepancy regarding the divine name is only important if this literary strand is aligned with an E source, the existence of which I am yet to be convinced.

Exodus 19:10–13a, 14–15, 16aα, 18, (20–25), which does use the divine name YHWH throughout, displays a certain coherence and consistency in the use of imagery and motifs that contrast with those just outlined. It also begins with a divine speech to Moses. It comprises instructions to consecrate the people involving them washing their clothes, and having them prepare for the third day when YHWH will descend upon Mount Sinai in their sight (vv. 10–11). The people, however, are not to go up the mountain or even touch it or they will die (vv. 12–13). Accordingly, Moses consecrates the people, who wash their clothes, and tells them to prepare for the third day (vv. 14–15). Consequently, on the third day, in fulfillment of the divine intention stated in verse 11, Mount Sinai is wrapped in smoke and quaking because YHWH has descended on it in fire: theophany here is accompanied by volcanic imagery (v. 18). So far the coherency in the account is clear. However, the question could be raised as to whether the motifs of the (cultic) cleanliness of the people (vv. 10–11, 14–15), though consistently and coherently linked with Yahweh's descent on Mount Sinai associated with volcanic imagery on the third day (vv. 11b, 16aα, 18), is entirely coherent with being forbidden to go up, or even touch the mountain (vv. 12–13a): perhaps, even, this preparation involving consecration is really more in line with the motif identified in the other strand where they are allowed to go up the mountain (v. 13b), closer to the theophany. This represents a potential difficulty. However, perhaps verses 12–13a have been secondarily inserted, especially given that these verses represent a speech within a speech and there is no reference to them in Moses' carrying out of the divine instructions in verses 14–15.[61] Alternatively, the forbidding of the people to touch the mountain can be seen as reinforcing and extending the need for the (cultic) purity of the people to even witness the theophany, as with YHWH's descent on the mountain it becomes so holy that it is fatally dangerous even to those who are clean. That Exodus 19:20–25 is a later addition is more certain. Verse 20, although repeating the motif of YHWH's descent on Mount Sinai, is not coherent with verse 18, as it reports it as if for the first time.[62] Moses' ascent in verse 20 and his descent in verse 25 form an inclusio. Verses 21–24 repeat the instructions in verses 12–13a, but in different wording, including singling out the priests (who must consecrate themselves rather than be consecrated by Moses, cf. v. 10) from the people in general; verse 23 even refers back explicitly to verse 12 with a summary statement of the gist of verses 12–13a. All this suggests that verses 20–25 are a later expansion, commenting on verses 12–13a in particular.

In conclusion, this proposal of two literary strands here, and their delineation, is at best tentative, given the conflicting evidence, of coherence and consistency in motifs and imagery within each alongside inherent unevennesses. Van Seters' observation that in other texts describing theophanies (e.g., Ps 18:8–16; Nah 1:3–5; Hab 3:3–15), as well as Ugaritic and

---

[61] Dozeman (*God on the Mountain*, 23 note 13, 99, 100), who attributes verses 12ab–13a to a later redaction level (his P redaction).

[62] See Childs, *Exodus*, 349.

Mesopotamian parallels, there is a mix of storm and volcanic imagery also tends to increase the tentativeness of the hypothesis outlined here, although I have argued, not on the basis of the different theophanic imagery alone, but as they occur in combination with other consistently used motifs.[63] In addition, whether or not these literary strands can be aligned with the traditional sources E and J respectively would take us even further into the realm of speculation. In order to determine this, coherence between each and the wider context, especially in Exodus 24: 32–34 would need to be established, something that must necessarily lie outside the scope of this brief discussion. However, the lack of consistency between these strands in relation to the divine name (see especially Exod 19:9a) tends to suggest otherwise.

When the issue of the redactional combination of our tentative literary strands is examined, it is possible to perceive a certain rationale which, moreover, explains some of the major inconsistencies in the text of Exodus 19:9–25; 20:18–21. It would appear that a redactor combined the initial divine speeches of both strands by bracketing that of the second strand (Exod 19:10–13a) with that of the first strand (Exod 19:9a, 13b).[64] This explains the illogical juxtaposition of verses 12–13a, in which the people are forbidden to go up, or touch, the mountain, with verse 13b, in which permission is given to the people to go up the mountain. Following Moses' carrying out of the instructions (vv. 14–15), the redactor appears to have used a similar technique to combine the accounts of theophany in each strand: again the material of the second strand (v. 18) is bracketed by that of the first strand (vv. 16aβ–17, 19), with the effect that the quaking of the people and that of the mountain are now juxtaposed.[65] The addition to the second strand in Exodus 19:20–25 has been placed after verse 19, in close proximity to verse 18, thus interrupting the coherent link in the first strand between Exodus 19:19 and 20:18–21, perhaps leading the redactor to add smoke to the storm imagery in Exodus 20:18 in an attempt conflate the theophanies of the two strands by way of summary.

Where, then, have these tentative ruminations taken us? At the earliest level of Exodus 19:9–25; 20:18–21,[66] it is possible that two literary strands

---

[63] See Van Seters, *The Life of Moses*, 254–70.

[64] Exodus 19:19b, which repeats verse 8b, does not follow logically from verse 9a and is out of place: it is generally seen as a gloss.

[65] Logically, the notice of the third day from the second strand was placed first (v. 16aα).

[66] And probably Exodus 19:2b–3a.

describing theophany and Moses' role within this have been combined rather mechanically by a redactor to accommodate the perspective and sequence of each, sometimes at the expense of coherence. Later, a Dtr redactor (or redactors) of some description inserted Exodus 20:1–17, thus separating Exodus 20:18–21 from the rest of the theophany material in Exodus 19, and composed Exodus 20:22–23 as an introduction to the laws of the Book of the Covenant (Exod 20:24–26ff) probably as a means of incorporating these laws into the Sinai context. The result was that the giving of the law, both the Decalogue and the Book of the Covenant, became the goal of the theophany, with the Decalogue (Ex 20:1–17) being spoken directly by God, and the remaining laws (Exod 20:24–26ff) being mediated to the people through Moses (Exod 20:18–23). A Dtr redactor, possibly at a later date, inserted Exodus 19:3b–8, as a proleptic summary in covenant terms of the whole shape of Exodus 19–24, thus providing a lens through which these chapters are to be interpreted. Finally, the P itinerary in Exodus 19:1–2a was added still later, along perhaps with fragments of P redaction for example in Exodus 20:11, possibly as part of a move by a redactor to incorporate this Dtr redacted material into P as a continuous source structured by means of such itineraries.

SELECT BIBLIOGRAPHY

Barton, John. "Source Criticism." Pages 162–65 in vol. 6 of *Anchor Bible Dictionary*. Edited by D. N. Freedman. 6 vols. New York: Doubleday, 1992.
———. "Redaction Criticism." Pages 644–47 in vol. 5 of *Anchor Bible Dictionary*. Edited by D. N. Freedman. 6 vols. New York: Doubleday, 1992.
Boorer, Suzanne. *The Promise of the Land as Oath: A Key to the Formation of the Pentateuch*. Pages 5–33. BZAW 205; Berlin: de Gruyter, 1992.
Childs, Brevard S. *Exodus: A Commentary*. London: SCM, 1974.
Clements, Ronald E. *One Hundred Years of Old Testament Interpretation*. Philadelphia: Westminster, 1976.
Dozeman, Thomas B. *God on the Mountain: A Study of Redaction Theology and Canon in Exodus 19–24*. Atlanta: Scholars Press, 1989.
———, and Konrad Schmid, eds. *A Farewell to the Yahwist? The Composition of the Pentateuch in Recent European Interpretation*. Atlanta: Society of Biblical Literature, 2006.
Hayes, John H. *An Introduction to Old Testament Study*. Nashville: Abingdon, 1979.
Hyatt, J. P. *Exodus*. Grand Rapids: Eerdmans, 1980. Repr., London: Marshall, Morgan & Scott, 1971.
Knierim, Rolf. "Criticism of Literary Features, Forms, Tradition and Redaction." Pages 123–65 in *The Hebrew Bible and Its Modern Interpreters*. Edited by Douglas A. Knight and Gene M. Tucker. Chico, CA: Scholars Press, 1985.

Nicholson, E. W. *The Pentateuch in the Twentieth Century: The Legacy of Julius Wellhausen.* Oxford: Oxford University Press, 1998.

Noth, Martin. *Exodus: A Commentary.* Philadelphia: Westminster, 1962.

———. *A History of Pentateuchal Traditions.* Translated by Bernhard W. Anderson. Englewood Cliffs, NJ: Prentice Hall, 1972.

Propp, William H. *Exodus 1–18; Exodus 19–40.* New York: Doubleday, 1999, 2006.

Rad, Gerhard von. "The Form-Critical Problem of the Hexateuch." Pages 1–78 in *The Problem of the Hexateuch and Other Essays.* London: SCM, 1984.

Rendtorff, Rolf. *The Problem of the Process of Transmission of the Pentateuch.* Translated by J. J. Scullion. Sheffield: JSOT, 1990.

Steck, Odil. *Old Testament Exegesis: A Guide to the Methodology.* 2nd ed. Translated by J. D. Noyalski. Atlanta: Scholars Press, 1998.

Van Seters, John. *The Life of Moses: The Yahwist as Historian in Exodus.* Louisville, KY: Westminster/John Knox, 1994.

Westermann, Claus. *Genesis 1–11.* Pages 575–84. London: SPCK, 1984.

4

↓

Liberation Criticism

JORGE PIXLEY

Liberation criticism begins with the hermeneutical insight that biblical interpretation is always affected by the experience and social location of the reader. For example, the description of Jesus as a *kyrios* or *dominus* by the early Christians meant that the Roman Caesar could not share this title. Thus the earliest Christians were unwilling to acknowledge the lordship of the Caesars and were, in fact, ready to die for their insistence that only Jesus Christ was their Lord. Yet by the time of the European Middle Ages, when Christians read in the Bible that Jesus was a *kyrios* or *dominus*, they understood this in terms of the feudal lord who owned the lands they tilled. The political and social structure of life in the Middle Ages influenced the meaning of the text, so that at the time of the conquest of the New World it was the kings of Spain and Portugal that were the lords and the language of lordship for Jesus Christ no longer had the same relevance as it did for the earliest Christians. At most, Christ was a lord in the image of the king of Spain or Portugal. This one example illustrates that the Bible is always read from our social context.

Liberation criticism is grounded in the experience of oppression, which necessarily affects the reading of the Bible. When life becomes intolerable because of an oppressive force, the lordship of Jesus Christ, who said that the Gospel he preached was for the poor, becomes a liberating message. A central hermeneutical principle of liberation criticism is that the Gospel preached by Jesus is meant to be relevant to life in this world, which means that it is a call to struggle for the liberation of the oppressed. This does not say what course that struggle will take. The manner of the struggle and its strategy must be a subject of discussion in the church where social analysis is placed alongside the study of the

Bible. Karl Barth dramatized this with the call to have the Bible in one hand and the newspaper in the other. And with this kind of liberating criticism, over against the liberal criticism of his professors, Barth led some churches and pastors to form the Confessing Church with the call to resist the government's call to be a German Church in service to the state. His was a liberation criticism, though he did not use this name for it. He did not read the Bible naively, nor believe that its myths and confessed history were to be taken at face value. It was the call to resist the state church during a time of oppression that guided his reading.

THE HISTORY AND METHODOLOGY
OF LIBERATION CRITICISM

The history of liberation criticism is closely tied to the reading of the Bible in Latin America, where it emerged in the modern era as a method of interpretation in conjunction with liberation theology. For this reason the following historical summary will concentrate on social, hermeneutical, and theological developments in Latin America, while also branching out to illustrate the global impact of the liberation criticism in the contemporary world. The summary will separate into four parts: (1) the prehistory of liberation criticism; (2) liberation theology and liberation criticism in the twentieth century; (3) the impact of liberation criticism beyond Latin America; and (4) recent political developments that affect the liberation movement.

The Prehistory of Liberation Criticism in Latin America

The prehistory of liberation criticism begins in Santo Domingo, the first city that the European Christians established in the New World, then known as the Indies, today as America. Santo Domingo was on the island of Española, an island shared today by Haiti and the Dominican Republic. The Dominicans had a monastery in the city. In 1511 c.e. they were disturbed by what they feared was the mortal sin of the conquerors in their mistreatment of the natives of the island. During Advent they chose one of their number, Fray Antonio Montesinos, to preach the sermon on December 21. He began his message by warning that it would be offensive to many, before he took the role of John the Baptist in the desert and stated: "You are called to love these meek peoples. They are your neighbors and you are called to love them as you love yourselves. Not doing so, you are in mortal sin. Repent!"

This was a new and critical reading of a well-known text about the Baptist preaching a difficult message in the wilderness. It was not yet addressed to the oppressed peoples of the island and was not yet therefore liberation criticism. But it did signal the recognition by the Dominicans that their social situation was one of oppression, which called for repentance and resistance. In their seeing that this situation was addressed in the Bible, it marked the beginning of the prehistory of liberation criticism.

The best-known of the liberation readers of the Bible in the early years of the Conquest was Fray Bartolomé de Las Casas (1484–1566 C.E.), who had been ordained at the Dominican monastery in Santo Domingo. From there he went to Cuba, where in addition to his duties to preach he also became a holder of an "encomienda," a number of natives whose labor he enjoyed while bringing them to Christ. The encomienda system was a form of social oppression that was devised by the conquistadores. Spanish theologians had determined that the natives of the Indies were not slaves (essentially, á la Aristotle). On the other hand, the crown was obligated to Christianize the natives in exchange for which the popes recognized its dominion over the islands and lands newly discovered. Labor was beneath the dignity of the nobles who came to the Indies. The encomienda resolved the problem. In exchange for their labor they would teach them the Christian faith. Bartolomé became convicted of the social injustice of this sin upon reading Sirach 34:24–27:

> Like one who kills a son before his father's eyes
> Is the person who offers a sacrifice from the
> property of the poor.
> The bread of the needy is the life of the poor;
> Whoever deprives them of it is a murderer.
> To take away a neighbor's living is to commit murder;
> to deprive an employee of his wages is to shed blood.

Taking the words to heart, he delivered his "Indians" to the governor of Cuba and determined to fight the encomienda, which he did to the end of his days (1563 C.E.[?]).

The life of Las Casas was truly amazing. He can almost be called a practitioner of liberation criticism. Among his many accomplishments were his conviction and practice that the missionizing of the natives had to be done with the absence of military escorts. Three times in his life he set out to do this. The first was in Cumaná, now eastern Venezuela. This experiment was undermined when the conquerors of Española, having run out of natives (whom they had killed with their diseases and harsh labor), came to Cumaná seeking more. The second was in Nicaragua where he planned to missionize the river area that was the outlet of the Great Lake (Cocibolca) to the North Sea (the Caribbean). The governor refused to let him go to such a sensitive area without a military escort, so he did not go. The third effort was in Guatemala in the area later called Verapaz on the northern side of the country. This was an area populated by a savage people. Bartolomé went without soldiers and succeeded in Christianizing its people. His insistence on peaceful preaching assumed the biblical models of Jesus and of Paul, and qualifies as liberation criticism before anyone called it such.

Another forerunner of liberation criticism was Felipe Guaman Poma de Ayala (1536–1616 C.E.), a native Quechua from the Ayacucho region of Perú. His name already reveals a somewhat assimilated Quechua: Felipe and Ayala are "Christian" names; while Guaman Poma is Quechuan, meaning "eagle puma." Late in his life he wrote a letter to Philip III, king of Castile, Primer Nueva Coronica y Buen Gobierno, 1,180 pages with 398 drawings. Poma reveals in this "letter" that he is indeed a Christian and that he accepts the fact of Spanish rule, appealing to the king about the abuses of the local government officials. For our purposes the most interesting facts are the drawings of Indians, on the one hand, and governors and priests on the other. In a scene of the crucifixion, the Christ is unmistakably an Indian while the crucifiers are Spanish functionaries, civil and religious. The ambiguity of his position is clearly revealed as he addresses the Christian king for redress in the face of the oppression that his people suffered at the hands of the royal and church functionaries in the Viceroyalty of Peru.

A final note on the prehistory of liberation criticism concerns the armed uprising in Mexico that led to independence in 1810, in which church leaders organized acts of resistance and liberation against the government. This uprising was led by two priests: Fr. Miguel Hidalgo who launched the "grito" to initiate the uprising, and Fr. José Morelos who led the military phase of the struggle and was executed by the Spaniards.

Liberation Theology and Liberation Criticism in the Twentieth Century

The Cuban revolution, which succeeded in gaining power on January 1, 1959, raised hope in Latin America that U.S. domination of the region could be successfully challenged. This event was important for the emergence of liberation criticism in the late twentieth century, in which the story of the exodus from Egypt and Jesus' call of liberation to the poor became central hermeneutical and social principles. The Cuban revolution influenced student Christian groups and university chaplains throughout Latin America, who later became known as liberation theologians, such as Gustavo Gutiérrez in Perú, Hugo Assmann and Richard Shaul in Brazil, and Julio de Santa Ana in Uruguay. The social and political setting also influenced religious communities, which gave rise to ecumenical relations between Catholics and Protestants, initially in the universities in the 1950s before making its way into the broader church experience. The Cuban model of armed insurgents was also preferred and it seemed clear that cooperation between Marxist and Christian groups would be essential. With this background the exodus from Egypt was read as a liberation movement and Jesus' calls to the poor were emphasized in the student Bible study groups.

Then came the church revolution of the Second Vatican Council from 1962 to 1965, initiated by Pope John XXIII and concluded under the leadership of Pope Paul VI. It was a call for the Church to open windows to the modern world, an attempt to recognize regional bishops' conferences as autonomous bodies, and to give lay Christians a greater voice in Church matters. In a sense Latin America was already set on this course. A meeting of the bishops of Latin America had been held in Rio de Janeiro in 1955 under the presidency of Dom Helder Camara, bishop of Recife in the poor northeast territory of Brazil. In Cuernavaca, Don Sergio Méndez Arceo led the way in distributing cheap Bibles for the people of his diocese, the State of Morelos in Central Mexico. He guided his priests to form small study groups, later known as base communities, while also simplifying his cathedral by removing the many statues and focusing on Jesus and Mary. Don Samuel Ruiz in Chiapas focused on a pastoral ministry that recognized the native languages and customs of the people in his mainly Indian Chiapas. Don Leónidas Proaño in Riobamba in Ecuador undertook significant pastoral work among the native peoples and prepared the ground for today's excellent network of popular Bible study groups throughout Ecuador.

Following the Vatican meeting, the CELAM – the Latin American bishops conference established in 1955 – was called to a second continental meeting to be held in Medellín in 1968. This meeting was fundamental in various ways for liberation theology. It took the Christian Action strategy, "see, judge, act," seriously by not beginning with the established teachings of the church, but by devoting the first two days of the meeting entirely to examining the present social context in Latin America under the direction of sociologists, political scientists, and economists, and by attempting to build doctrinal statements and pastoral actions from it. The process legitimated the base communities.

These great Church meetings were not just events within the Roman Catholic Church. Protestant observers were participants both in Rome and at Medellín. The ecumenical opening that evolved from the ecumenical discourse changed the church climate in Latin America. In fact, the first book of liberation theology was actually written by Rubem Alves, then a Presbyterian pastor. It was his doctoral thesis written at Princeton and published in Montevideo in 1970 under the title *Cristianismo, ¿opio o instrumento de liberación?* (Editorial Tierra Nueva).[1]

Liberation theology acquired maturity in 1971 with the appearance of three major books: José Porfirio Miranda, *Marx y la Biblia* (Mexico: self-financed edition), Gustavo Gutiérrez, *Notas para una teología de la liberación* (Lima: CEP [the school directed by Fr. Gutiérrez]), and Hugo Assmann, *Opresión-liberación, Desafío a los cristianos* (Montevideo: Tierra Nueva [publisher financed by ISAL and the WCC]). These books were translated and published in English by Orbis Books. Even though Miranda resigned as a Jesuit in 1972, his book is the most important for understanding the relationship between liberation theology and

---

[1] The thesis had come out earlier in English as *A Theology of Human Hope* (Washington: Corpus Books, 1969). Alves's original title was "Liberation Theology" but the publisher thought that wouldn't sell.

liberation criticism, because of its focus on the Bible, especially the Exodus and the Prophets. He tries to demonstrate on the basis of biblical texts that the God of the Bible is a liberating God. He concentrated on the story of the Exodus, the Prophets, and the Psalms to prove that the poor just supplicant is exalted in biblical tradition and the wealthy unjust oppressor is condemned. Miranda shaped liberation theology and liberation criticism by arguing that Marxism and the Bible are in fundamental agreement. Miranda was a very competent biblical scholar, trained at the Gregorian University in Rome, the Jesuits' premier university, with a master's degree in Economics in Germany. But his attempt to "prove" his thesis on the basis of biblical texts was definitely a wrongheaded approach, so that Miranda can be accused of a fundamentalism of the "Left." Even though the biblical scholarship in the linguistic analyses of this book is impeccable, the method of seeking "proofs" to establish social and hermeneutical principles is no longer used in liberation criticism.

Both Assmann and Gutiérrez are more sophisticated in their use of the Bible, although less versed in the Hebrew and Greek of the Bible. Assmann's work is a careful analysis of the theological problems confronting Christians, who are involved in the struggle for liberation. In 1971 he laid out the program of liberation theology for the coming years. He would later participate in the miners' uprising in Bolivia, the Allende period in Chile, and then settle in Costa Rica where he founded the Department for Ecumenical Research (DEI), a major center for the training of pastoral agents and the publishing of books on theology and the social sciences, a cooperation that he saw as necessary in 1971. Gustavo Gutiérrez was a university chaplain and a local pastor in Lima and his works have always been based in critical biblical study. Over time, his 1971 book has proved more important than the other major works of 1971. It combines in an artful way the dogmatic texts that give a Christian theology legitimacy, the biblical texts that make theology accessible to the faith of the people, and the call to liberating social action that make theology and the Bible relevant to the current Latin American context. This is liberation theology at its best.

About this same time a Carmelite monk in Brazil with biblical training in Europe was organizing a broad network of CEBIs – Comunidades Eclesiales Bíblicas – which soon covered the whole map of Brazil. Carlos Mesters was a modest man who could move comfortably among Bible teachers; he often rode buses for two or three days to attend national study gatherings. At that time the Brazilian Catholic Church was led by bishops, who were committed to a national church on the model of Vatican II. These bishops were almost all supportive of the CEBIs in their dioceses. The political conditions were favorable. After its coup of March 1964, the Brazilian army installed a National Security State, the model of which soon dominated the landscape in Latin America. The result was social intimidation through the unrestrained use of imprisonment and torture against "enemies of the State." But the ideology of an established Christian civilization that supported the State made it difficult for the soldiers to repress the church. Recognizing this, the people fled to the church to seek protection. In response, the church and her bishops became open to resistance to the government and supportive of liberation. It was in this context that a vast network of Bible study groups arose, which were committed to liberation at the local level (e.g., schools, roads, clinics, water systems, electricity) and supportive of the Workers' Party (PT).

Fray Carlos provided biblical foundations to the movement of liberation. In the book, *Flor sem defesa, uma explicação da bíblia a partir do povo* (Petrópolis: Editora Vozes, 1983), he illustrated the hermeneutics of the CEBIs with a triangle, whose points were the Pre-Text, Text, and Con-Text. The Pre-Text was the current social, political, and economic situation, in which the reading was being undertaken. The Text was a study of the biblical text itself with the help of whatever biblical critical methodology was available. The Con-Text was the confessing community, the believers. This book was a powerful instrument and is still useful with small groups of poor people concerned to transform their social situation in the light of the Gospel.

Two important books appeared in the late 1970s in the area of biblical studies that were also relevant to liberation criticism. Chronologically, the first of these was Jorge Pixley's, *Reino de Dios* (Buenos Aires: La Aurora, 1977), a short book that asked the question: What makes the Gospel good news *for the poor?* The content of the book included a brief outline of a kingdom presided over by the God who had liberated Israel from slavery in Egypt. The book also linked the God of the exodus to the message of Jesus, which he implemented in a small community of his followers in Galilee. The argument was built on Martin Buber's *Königtum*

Gottes of 1932 (English, *Kingdom of God* [New York: Harper, 1973]) and more recent studies by George Mendenhall on the so-called conquest of Palestine, which he argued was an uprising from within the small kingdoms of the Canaanites on the plains of the land of Palestine.[2] In *The Tribes of Yahweh* (Maryknoll, NY: Orbis Books, 1979), Gottwald expanded Mendenhall's research on the religion of Yahwism with sociological arguments to support the uprising. This was definitely more convincing and was introduced into our teaching of the Bible in Latin America, filling out Pixley's book with more concrete research.

The next step in liberation criticism was the founding of a journal that incorporated its principles, which was accomplished when the *Revista de Interpretación Bíblica Latinoamericana* (RIBLA) first came out in 1988. It was to appear simultaneously in Spanish and Portuguese, which complicated the production but made it available to all of Latin America – except for some of the Caribbean islands. Let me quote from the presentation in the first issue:

This journal is situated. It is placed within the experiences of faith and the struggles of communities and churches. The Bible is being rescued by the people. The hurts, the utopias and the poetry of the poor were taken by the communities as decisive hermeneutical mediations for Bible reading in Latin America and the Caribbean. This journal has a cradle, the burdened lives of our people and their persistent resistance in the direction of an existence of justice and dignity. The communities of the poor thus inserted constitute the ferment for the whole of Biblical hermeneutics.

Milton Schwantes, a Brazilian from an immigrant Lutheran family, accurately portrays the intent of all of us who founded the journal. RIBLA has appeared regularly in both languages three times a year. Most of its authors are professors at Catholic and Protestant seminaries, universities and institutes, who are committed to listening to the poor. This we do in part by teaching and praying with poor people directly and in part by teaching and praying with their pastoral agents. As one would expect of such an enterprise, there are tensions between those who want to avoid the academic tradition of biblical interpretation and others who want to engage scholarly research and apply it to the struggles of poor people for liberation.

---

[2] George E. Mendenhall, "The Hebrew Conquest of Palestine," *BA* 25, 1962, 66–87.

The tension with regard to the mission of the journal highlights an important issue in liberation criticism, which is how to put the Bible into the hands of people whose education is most basic, in most cases no more than the third grade of elementary school, while also teaching them to read the Bible critically. There is an important distinction to be drawn here between Protestant-Evangelical churches and Catholic base communities with regard to this tension, even though in the villages there is often some communication between the two communities. Evangelical (the term is used for all Protestant and Pentecostal groups in Latin America) Christians received the Bible as soon as they joined the church. If they can't read it they are taught to read. For them the novelty of liberation criticism is in part the historical-critical approach to the biblical text, which is required in order to see its relevance for contemporary social issues. One must understand the social problems faced by the prophets, sages, and by Jesus in order to see that they have relevance for social problems of poor people today.

The situation for base communities is different. Catholic Christianity is centered on the mass, and in most Latin American parishes the Bible has played a very small role. It is easier for the small groups in a base community to understand their social struggle for liberation, than to understand the Bible, which is basically foreign to them. Pope Pius XII officially made the Bible accessible in vernacular languages in his 1943 encyclical *Divino afflante spiritu,* but it took time for translations to be made and put into the hands of the laity by the priests, who often were themselves illiterate in the Bible. Nevertheless, in spite of these serious difficulties, the base communities do not have to unlearn past ways of reading the Bible, as is often the case with Evangelical communities, when they embrace liberation criticism. For the Catholic base communities the first order of the day is to read the Bible and become familiar with it. Usually the main obstacle a teacher must face is the moral rejection of the brutality sanctioned by the biblical God. Canaanites are to be wiped out, including men, women, and children. How can this be?

In the journey, RIBLA, an effort is made to address both the issues of Evangelical churches and those of Catholic base communities. The success is hard to measure but both the Spanish and the Portuguese editions pay for themselves. In this commercial sense we feel justified.

Liberation Criticism and Related Forms of Criticism

Liberation theology and liberation criticism have branched out from Latin America to find expression in nearly all the continents of the world. In the United States, black theology and the biblical interpretation that accompanied it reached maturity with the production of books by James Cone. The approach to Latin American black theology has had a lesser impact on liberation criticism. Theirs is not a religion of the book, but a religion of communion with the ancestors and, occasionally, possession by them. To enter into their rites and to learn their doctrines requires a rigorous training and initiation in candomblé, the largest religious group. It also supposes the knowledge of the Yoruba language, which is the language of their rites. The Caribbean black world, though smaller, is less closed and more easily accessed. Marcos Villamán, a Dominican sociologist of religion, put together RIBLA 19. The authors include two bishops, one Catholic (Josè Marìa Pires) and one Methodist (Paulo Ayres Mattos), both Brazilian. There are many blacks in Brazil who are not within the candomblé religion. They are also represented in this issue by Silvia Regina de Lima Silva, a well-known Brazilian feminist. In addition to the black theology of liberation in the United States, there also emerged a liberation theology in the Min Jung movement in Korea, which merits comparison with liberation theology in Latin America. The Dalit theology in India is another Asian phenomenon that would require further examination.

The most important sister of liberation theology is feminism. An important feminist voice in Latin America is Elsa Tamez, a professor at the Latin American Biblical University in San José, Costa Rica. Tamez is both a biblical scholar and theologian.[3] She was important in the early development of our journal *RIBLA*. She comes from a Presbyterian family in Monterrey, Mexico, but married a Methodist from Colombia and has been a Protestant voice for the equality of women, based on exciting work in biblical interpretation.[4] Another Latin American feminist interpreter

---

[3] One of Tamez's early works on feminism was a series of interviews with Liberation theologians, male and female, on the place of women, *Teólogos de la liberación hablan sobre la mujer* (San José: DEI, 1986).

[4] She has focused on the figure of Hagar, Abraham's Egyptian slave and concubine, in many lectures and publications. More recently, she has written a commentary on the

is Ivone Gebara of Recife in Northeast Brazil.[5] Her most influential piece was an article in *Veja*, a popular journal sold near supermarket counters. In it she defended the right of women to resort to abortion, considering the fate of many to find their health destroyed by successive pregnancies and their care for many children. Living as she does in a slum area of her city, her experience is with poor women and it is for them that she speaks. As a consequence of the piece in *Veja*, she was sanctioned by the Vatican and penalized with a year of retraining in France, a year that she used to improve her philosophical knowledge, already a rich source for her work. Her writings show that she is a feminist philosopher of religion, and a most exciting one who recognizes the need to begin one's thinking with the concrete reality of the lives that women live in poor contexts. Women such as Elsa Tamez, Ivone Gebara, as well as María Clara Bingemer, Carmiña Nava, Nancy Cardoso Pereira, Tirsa Ventura, and many others are liberation critics and important participants in the movement of liberation theology.

Recent Religious and Political Developments that Influence the Liberation Movement

The most significant religious development since 1980 has been Pope John Paul's aggressive effort to roll back the reforms laid out in the Second Vatican Council. This has had two prongs. First, the recent papal privilege of naming bishops all around the world has tended to replace progressive bishops, who fostered base communities and CEBIs in their dioceses, with conservatives, who were judged less likely to do so. This has been felt everywhere, but especially in Brazil where the Episcopal conference was almost unanimously progressive. Today progressives are in the minority. Second, the pope ordered the redaction of a new code

Pastoral Epistles to prove a point that we scholars must produce guides to the "difficult books" of the Bible, entitled *Struggles for Power in Early Christianity: A Study of the First Letter of Timothy*. *When the Horizons Close: Rereading Ecclesiastes* is a magnificent commentary on Ecclesiastes, *The Amnesty of Grace: Justification by Faith from a Latin American Perspective*, her doctoral dissertation at the University of Lausanne, and a fine treatment of Paul's theology. *The Scandalous Message of James. Faith Without Works is Dead. Jesus and Courageous Women*, 2001. All of these works are translations of Spanish originals.
⁵ See her *Teología a ritmo de mujer* (Madrid: San Pablo, 1995), a translation of the Portuguese original.

of canon law which included very few of the recommendations of the bishops at Vatican II. Regional bishops' groups were stripped of the authority that Vatican II had recommended and made dependent on the Vatican. Along with these two major retrograde actions of John Paul II, a lesser but important development has been the attacks on the dogmatic correctness of the most prominent theologians, among them Leonardo Boff, Gustavo Gutiérrez, Jon Sobrino, Juan José Tamayo, and José Marìa Vigil. Among these, Tamayo, a Spaniard, is a layman and was little affected by this development. Boff resigned his priestly orders and now functions as a lay theologian. Gutiérrez quit as a diocesan priest and went through the novitiate to become a Dominican with the protection that an important religious order affords. The cases of Sobrino and Vigil are still pending. Sobrino is a Jesuit and a Vigil, a Claretian. He is also a very active participant in EATWOT, a world ecumenical organization of theologians upon which he depends. The result is that theologians must proceed now with a self-censorship that was not necessary in the recent past.

The implosion of the Soviet Union was also a major setback for the liberation movement in Latin America. The Cuban revolution was able to consolidate under the umbrella of the USSR, and this was the hope of most revolutionary movements in Latin America, even if, like the Sandinista revolution, they were not Marxist but only anti-imperialist.

On the other hand, there have been some hopeful developments, first of all the election of "Leftist" governments in many countries (e.g., Brazil, Uruguay, Chile, Venezuela, Bolivia, Nicaragua, Ecuador), in spite of the always active meddling of the U.S. embassies in local politics to favor "safe," middle-class candidates and parties. It is too early to say what the long-term consequence of this drift to the Left is going to be. The PT in Brazil now has its leader, Lula, as the president, but because the party continues to be a minority party, Lula must govern with ministers of key ministries, among them economy, who are of Rightist inclination. Venezuela's effort to form an anti-imperialist alliance, the ALBA, has so far not met with great success. So the long-term importance of this surprising development is still uncertain.

Finally, we must mention the annual World Social Forum held every year in January, originally and most often in Porto Alegre, Brazil. Here, progressive organizations, that are working at the most basic social level to organize women, peasants, fishers, and others, gather for discussion. It has proved surprisingly enduring (since 2001) for an organization that has resisted a top-down pyramidal organization. This meeting is very hopeful and does provide a context for many groups that practice liberation criticism in the interpretation of the Bible. For liberation criticism is more a movement of poor people that an academic program, though it has some support in the academy.

The academic aspect of liberation theology and liberation criticism of the Bible has also developed in recent years. The history of liberation criticism in Latin America will conclude with a brief summary of the most important work.

A fine book appeared in 1991, *Rostros indios de Dios* (Quito: Abya Yala, 1991), in which five Jesuit missionaries from Bolivia to Chihuahua, northern Mexico, explore the understanding of God among five different native peoples. Most interesting is the chapter of Ricardo Robles on the rarámuri-pagótuame who were discovered by Jesuits in the Tarahumara hills of Chihuahua in the sixteenth century. When the Jesuits were expelled these people were left on their own for a century. During this time the Holy Week pageant evolved in a most interesting way. The scribes and pharisees who are represented as those that crucified Jesus (there was no memory of Romans) were painted white, while Jesus and his disciples remained their natural dark colors.

The year 1992 was celebrated in circles of popular resistance as the anniversary of five hundred years of resistance and struggle. Congresses were held by the native peoples in Quezaltenango, Guatemala, and Riobamba, Ecuador. For liberation theology, the awareness of these long suppressed peoples was raised to a significant degree. Of course, this was not the first awareness. Pablo Suess in the Amazonia and Eleazar López Hernández in Mexico, among others, had long worked among these peoples and raised voices in their defense. The University of Rio Grande do Sul in southern Brazil had long studied the Guaraníes, whose presence covers a vast area of southern Brazil and Paraguay. A distinguished anthropologist, Bartomeu Meliá, spent years with them and guided research at the university that explored their life setting. Leónidas Proaño, bishop of Riobamba, Ecuador, had a long and successful pastorate with the Quichua people. Don Samuel Ruiz, the bishop of San

Cristóbal de Las Casas, Chiapas, established a great pastoral work in the native languages, using deacons that were natural leaders.

The Nicaraguan journal of theology called *XILOTL* devoted its issue 16 to "Espiritualidad indígena." Wuqub' Iq' (José Angel Zapeta) explores the theoretical bases for an "intertheological" dialogue. Iq' is a Maya from Guatemala and it is the Maya culture and theology to which he draws attention. First, cosmogony is most basic. Humans are not the center of nature but an integral part of nature. This is a perspective shared by all the native peoples of the New World. And it is a call to awareness for Christian theologians, including liberation theologians. Too often anthropocentrism has led us to a grossly distorted perspective on our world and on God. Mayas speak of Father Sun, Grandmother Moon, and Mother Earth. Any dialogue must begin by dealing respectfully with this perspective.

RIBLA devoted its issue 26 (1997) to the topic "La palabra se hizo India." Luz Jiménez, an Aymara from Bolivia, was editor of the issue. Among the eleven articles is one by Eleazar López Hernández, a long-standing leader of pastoral work among the natives of Mexico. It is a comparison of the peoples of the Bible and the Indian peoples of today. Diego Irarrázabal, a scholar and priest to the people of the high Andes between Puno and Cuzco, Perú, has an article on the interaction in the Andes with the Word of God. Severino Croatto, our scholarly master, has one on cultural symbolism and biblical hermeneutics. Altogether, this is a fine collection of work on the encounter between native peoples and the Bible.

Graciela Chamorro, a Paraguayan Baptist who married a Brazilian Lutheran and became a Lutheran pastor, has been a star researcher under Meliá in the songs and prophecies of the Tupí-Guaraní people. Guaraní is a national language of Paraguay and is taught in the public schools, so Chamorro grew up hearing some of these songs. Her dissertation gives insight into the spiritual life of this people, though the Bible is not a central focus.[6] The main impact on liberation theology and liberation criticism has been the inclusion within our horizon of the Christian groups who

---

[6] Graciela Chamorro, *A Espiritualidade Guarani: Uma Teologia Ameríndia da Palavra* (São Leopoldo: Sinodal, 1998).

are resisting the dominant culture and its oppression. Its theoretical importance has been in forcing an awareness of the importance of our insertion in the whole of nature and the responsibilities that go with that. Leonardo Boff, in this as in many other areas, has been a pioneer; he has devoted a lot of effort to master current biology and physical astronomy and this all is reflected in his master work, *Ecologia: grito da terra, grito dos pobres* (Rio de Janeiro: Leonardo Boff, 1996).

LIBERATION CRITICISM AND THE BOOK OF EXODUS

The story of the Exodus is foundational to liberation criticism. The departure from Egypt, the wilderness journey, and the entrance into the land of Canaan are one grand narrative. How are we to interpret this action that is guided by God? There are several possibilities, and a liberationist reading is one of them.

Exodus 1:1–7 presents the central characters of the narrative as the sons of Jacob, which would have to mean that the exodus was the departure of a foreign group to return to the land they had left in the time of their ancestor Jacob. Nevertheless, once the narrative starts they are called Hebrews, a term that is still debated, but which many scholars identify as the Habiru of the Amarna correspondence, who seem to be insurgents or at least outsiders like merchants. In Exodus 12:38 we are told that a "mixed multitude" (*'ēreb rab*) went with them into the desert. This seems to mean that the people who accept the covenant with God in the wilderness at Sinai include the children of Jacob as well as others, and that altogether they are known as Hebrews.

A central question for a liberation-critical reading of the story of the exodus is the motivation of the Hebrew people for leaving Egypt. Were they just escaping Egypt or were they rejecting kingship and the tributes it required, which they interpreted as slavery? If they were just escaping from a land that had become hostile to them they would be refugees, but not revolutionaries. If, however, they were establishing a different system of government that did not include kings or tributes, and were seeking to replace it with a form of social equality, then the exodus is a revolution. J. Severino Croatto (1930–2004), undeniably the premier biblical scholar in Latin America, wrote a small book, *Liberación y libertad. Pautas hermenéuticas* (Buenos Aires: Mundo Nuevo, 1973), in which he traced the exodus as a liberation theme throughout the Old and the New Testaments. This was an important start. Jorge Pixley (1937–) was the first among the liberation theologians to write a commentary on the book of Exodus, *Exodo, una lectura evangélica y popular* (México: Casa Unida de Publicaciones, 1983), in which the slavery in Egypt was interpreted as the social-political enslavement of a whole population to a system of economic tribute and the exodus as an attempt to establish a different type of society. The application of liberation criticism to the story of the Exodus underscored that the story was about a revolution and not simply an emigration.

The liberationist reading of Exodus by Pixley was critically evaluated by the well-known Jewish scholar Jon D. Levenson for two reasons.[7] First, he observed that although Pixley announced his intention to read the text as it stands in its final edition, the liberationist reading of the Exodus relies on a hypothetically reconstructed vision of the history of ancient Israel to provide the necessary social context. Second, he accused Pixley of taking the Exodus away from its legitimate owners, the people of Israel, and giving it to the poor. He is, therefore, anti-Semitic.

The first criticism concerning the reconstruction of history underscores the importance of social context for the application of liberation criticism, which includes four stages in the history of ancient Israel: first, there is the flight from Egypt of a mixed multitude of peasants under the leadership and inspiration of Moses, the prophet of YHWH. Second, the Exodus group arrives in the land of Canaan and bands with diverse groups of peasant rebels against the kings of the cities of Canaan. The result of this coalition is that YHWH, the God who had liberated the slaves of Egypt, was also adopted by the indigenous peasants who had undergone similar experiences in fleeing from their kings and in establishing societies free from tributes within the hill country. Third, Israelite kingship emerged under Saul and David. And, fourth, a hierocratic society emerged in the post-Exilic period that was led by the returned exiles from Babylon. Levenson is correct is pointing out that this history has very little documentary support, which raises the important question of

---

[7] "Liberation Theology and the Exodus," in *Jews, Christians, and the Theology of the Hebrew Scriptures* (Atlanta: Society of Biblical Literature, 2000), 215–30. This essay also appears as chapter 6 of Jon D. Levenson, *The Hebrew Bible, the Old Testament, and Historical Criticism* (Louisville, KY: Westminster/John Knox, 1993).

whether such historical reconstruction is legitimate for interpreting the
Exodus. The challenge for liberation criticism is to apply its reading of the
Exodus to the final form of the text as well as the critical reconstruction
of social history.

The second accusation of anti-Semitism really has to do with the
legitimacy of the Christian Bible, which incorporates whole books from
the *Tanakh* of the Jewish community. But it also has to do with whether the
story of the Exodus is read as a story of liberation from slavery or a story
of immigration to the promised land. Both motifs are present throughout
the book of Exodus in the Hebrew words, *yāṣa'*, "to go out," and, *'ālâ*,
"to go up." The Hebrew verb, *yāṣa'*, "to go out," interprets the Exodus
as an act of liberation from slavery. Exodus 13:3 provides an example,
when Moses instructs the Israelites at Mount Sinai on the meaning of the
exodus: "Remember this day on which you came out (*yāṣa'*) of Egypt, out
of the house of slavery, because the YHWH brought you out (*yāṣa'*) from
there by strength of hand." The Hebrew verb, *'ālâ*, "to go up," on the other
hand, interprets the Exodus within the larger context of immigration to
the promised land. Exodus 3:8 illustrates this interpretation when God
speaks to Moses through the burning bush: "I will come down to rescue
them (*nāṣal*) from the hand of Egypt and to lead them up (*'ālâ*) from
this land to a good and broad land, a land flowing with milk and honey,
the place of the Canaanites, the Amorites, the Perizzites, the Hittites,
and the Jebusites." The two interpretations of the Exodus are interwoven
throughout the book of Exodus (*yāṣa'* occurs in 11:6; 13:3, 4, 8; 14:8; 16:1,
4; and 20:2; and *'ālâ* occurs in 3:8, 17; 17:3; 32:1, 4, 7, 8, 23; 33:1), indicating
that the story is multivalent and that both perspectives are important
in the interpretation of the Exodus, the freedom from slavery and the
goal of the land of Canaan. Obviously, liberation criticism emphasizes
the motif of the freedom from slavery in reading the Exodus. Levenson
does the reverse, questioning the application of the Exodus motif to
the poor, because he emphasizes the motif of emigration from Egypt and
immigration to Canaan. Although this cannot be denied we who struggle
for liberation must read the text in terms of our needs today.

EXODUS 1–2

An initial reading of Exodus 1–2 reveals that these chapters deal with
oppression and liberation. The story begins by stating that a new king

arose in Egypt, who sought to deliberately oppress the "children of Israel" until they were subdued and debilitated. The motivation for the king's oppression was largely demographic. The large number of Israelites threatened him. Hence the king sought to reduce their number (Ex 1:8–14) and to debilitate the people until the only survivors were women without men. The "Hebrew midwives" refused to obey the king's orders and their resistance is the beginning of liberation (Exod 1:15–22). Exodus 2 continues the story of liberation with the stories of Moses' birth and youth; while the revelation of law in the wilderness provides a vision of a liberated community. Not to see oppression and liberation in the book of Exodus would be to refuse to read the text honestly. These chapters *are* about oppression and the resistance that is the first step of liberation.

A writer never knows who his or her readers will be. And yet, in a Cambridge University Press book, one can legitimately assume that readers will be persons who are well-to-do, mostly academics with more or less secure positions in universities somewhere in our globalized world. This is definitely not the audience in which the methodology of liberation criticism evolved, where the focus is on rather small groups who study the Bible together in remote villages or in compact slums in the inner city in places like Sâo Paulo or Mumbai. Here they share their considerable knowledge of their lives and their timid approach to the book they revere as God's Word. It is most unlikely this book will ever get into those crowded houses where these groups meet.

There is, hence, an artificiality about reading the Bible as liberation criticism in a book like this one. Still, it is good to be challenged by a reading that seems obvious to people who are suffering oppression. The goal of liberation criticism is for all readers, regardless of their social location, to catch a glimpse of who created these stories, perhaps in huts, and handed them on until eventually they were written down.

Liberation criticism encourages the reader to overcome two obstacles in interpreting the oppression and suffering in Exodus 1–2. The first obstacle in reading Exodus 1–2 is the difficulty that is often associated with our comfortable surroundings of seeing that our Scriptures deal with such a "political" subject as liberation of the poor. The second obstacle is also tied to our social setting and our history. It is what is meant by slavery in Egypt (*'ăbōdâ qāšâ*, "hard work," *mas*, "forced labor"). The slavery in Egypt is not what we know from our social memory, which is recorded in our history books as African slavery. What existed in Egypt is explained in Genesis 47, where a "wise" Joseph, the king's vizier, gathers all of the grain in the land. When seven years of famine come, Joseph sells the grain. But when the money is gone from Egypt Joseph takes all the fields and the very bodies of the Egyptians to be the king's. In the end, the king is the owner of all the land, all the cattle, and all the people in the land. But the slaves and the land are of no value to the king unless the slaves are put to work and the land is planted and animals cared for. So Joseph gives out seed to the people so that they may plant the land. At the time of the harvest, the king will take one-fifth for a sort of rent by which the peasants can continue to use the land on which they live. The exception is the priests. In this kind of society, and there are many societies built up in this manner (e.g., early China, India, Mesopotamia, Mexico), the king has the ability to dispose at will the lives of all his subjects. He is an earthly God. But in order to maintain his aura of divinity he needs to have pompous religious ceremonies performed. Priests are an absolute necessity, and they are employees of the crown, so to speak. Soldiers in the king's army are another special group who are more like employees than slaves. In any case, here in Genesis we get an anecdotal picture of what such a society was like. The oppression in Exodus must be read against the background of Genesis.

Exodus 1:1 begins, "These are the names (šĕmôt, the Hebrew name of the Book of Exodus) of the sons of Israel" and there follows a list of the twelve sons of Israel (Jacob). These sons become tribes as the story progresses in the wanderings in the wilderness. Here it serves as a way of connecting the book of Exodus with that of Genesis, showing that both are to be read together. It is not of first importance that the stories of the patriarchs and matriarchs of Israel do not relate actual events that happened. They are stories made up by popular poets and singers and passed along by others at people's gatherings. On the other hand, we cannot simply ignore the events as we can best reconstruct them from the documents. It is clear that the so-called tribes formed in the land of Canaan, and also that Judah was the last to form already at the outset of history, until the reign of Saul of Benjamin.[8] But here the list serves

---

[8] Roland de Vaux devoted much of his two-volume work, *Ancient Israel: Social Institutions* (New York: McGraw-Hill, 1965) and *Ancient Israel: Religious Institutions* (New York: McGraw-Hill, 1965) to the formation of the tribes, and clearly demonstrates the lateness of Judah.

to link the stories of the book of Exodus to those of the patriarchs in Genesis. It introduces as a chief character of the story the people (sons) of Israel. This is not a simple matter, as we shall see. Exodus 1:7 tells us that the Israelites were fruitful and multiplied, which, assuming that the Israelites were a foreign group living among the Egyptians, was a threat to Egyptian identity.

Exodus 1:8–13 presents the king's strategy for dealing with this population problem. This king had grandiose building plans for two new cities for which he required large amounts of common laborers. Because we have been told that all Egyptians were slaves this ought not to have been a problem. But in generalized slavery a wise king will not call on his people to work in construction during seed-time or harvest time, or state income would be seriously affected. However, here was a pool of foreign labor about whose fields he cared less. In fact, as he wanted to reduce them, decreasing their production would be helpful. They were to be put to the hardest construction work and kept away from their flocks and their fields so that when they got to their fields they had to work extra hard: "They embittered their lives with hard labor of clay and bricks plus all the work in the fields" (Exod 1:14). Hard labor can in fact kill a people. It is believed that it was the labor forced on the natives in the Caribbean and certainly in the mines of Perú and Bolivia that killed more of them than the Spaniard weapons. The strategy was then to put them to hard labor and thus reduce their population. This was oppression.

Until now the presumption has been that the sons of Israel were a separate group living in the land of Goshen provided by Joseph to his father and his brothers according to Genesis 45:10. Their fear is that, in case of war, they join the enemies of Egypt and "go up," (ʿālâ), the verb used to express emigration to the promised land. All the hard labor had been deliberately designed by the kings and his advisors (nitḥakkĕmâ lô, "let us act astutely with them," Exod 1:10) to break the spirit of the sons of Israel and perhaps kill some of them.

But it did not work, and so they turned to a new strategy of oppression in Exodus 1:15 and, with it, the perception of the people changed. As they turn to population control, the people are suddenly called "Hebrews" and no longer "sons of Israel." The expression Hebrews is used only thirty-three times in the Hebrew Bible, eleven of them in these opening chapters of Exodus. When it is used in Ezra and Nehemiah it has an ethnic connotation. But the expression is found in the Amarna correspondence between the Egyptian chancery and the Canaanite kinglets of the coastal areas in the fourteenth century B.C.E.[9] Here it refers to outsiders who may be of various kinds, traveling merchants, shepherds, and sometime rebellious groups. In any case, Hebrews are always seen as dangerous people. That appears to be its connotation here. Shiphrah and Puah, the two Hebrew midwives of this story, are indeed disobedient to the king's orders, the first sign of an imminent insurrection.

If we remember that all of the peasants of Egypt were slaves obliged to obey orders from the king's men and to pay tribute to the king on all of their produce, then the exodus appears likely to have been a rebellion of all the peasants that were ready to risk the extreme measure proposed by Moses, the prophet of YHWH. Exodus 12:38 informs us that a mixed crowd ('ēreb rab) went up with the sons of Israel. It was only by accepting the covenant with YHWH in Exodus 19–24 that all become the people of Israel.

The orders to the midwives are to kill the male children immediately upon birth. The females may be allowed to live. In some ways this seems counterproductive. The surviving babies will become the reproducers of the Hebrews when they grow up. But we know the king's fears of hostile warriors in the midst of the people, and in the light of that fear it makes sense to kill the males. In any case, the midwives refuse to carry out the king's orders. This resistance is the beginning that announces the coming revolt. This is valid for today. The first step of revolution is resistance, standing up to rules and dispositions that fail to recognize the dignity of ordinary folks. It is the African American people in Birmingham who walked because they refused to sit in the back of the bus. It is the native nations of Chiapas who refuse to be pushed around by the police and the army in their villages. It is the Nicaraguan people who spread tacks in the streets in 1979 to stop the military vehicles from circulating, during the final insurrection against the Somozas.

---

[9] This is the so-called 'apiru question. It has been extensively discussed in the scholarly literature, as the word appears in similar linguistic forms widely scattered in the ancient Near East. Introductions to this literature can be found in George E. Mendenhall, *The Tenth Generation: The Origins of the Biblical Tradition* (Baltimore: Johns Hopkins University Press, 1973), 122–41; and in Norman K. Gottwald, *The Tribes of Yahweh* (New York: Orbis Press, 1979), 401–09.

Another note about the midwives before we move on. The midwives refused to kill the baby boys because they "feared God (*'ĕlōhîm*)." This God is not yet the YHWH who will be revealed to Moses and who will directly guide the revolt to leave (*yāṣaʾ*) Egypt. But neither is it Pharaoh, the God-king of the land of Egypt. So by recognizing a different God than the one worshiped in Egypt the midwives are taking distance from Egypt. We face the same problem today. God is invoked by all rulers. President Bush feels that God ordered him to invade Iraq. The rulers of South Africa felt that God ordered apartheid. Hitler had a German church that worshiped the God who accompanied the soldiers who invaded Poland and then managed the death camps. The people have to learn to distinguish from the God of some of their rulers and bishops and the God who loves justice and wishes their dignity. The conflict of God passes right through all Christian churches. When rulers appeal to "God" we have to be suspicious. There are many idols posing as the true God, and the main distinction between the one and the other is that the idol demands human sacrifice, the true God gives life. This distinction is not easy to apply but in our Christian groups we must make the effort. We know the difference in principal between the true God who raises the prophet that is killed by the authorities who feel they are only carrying out their obligations and the God of Pilate and the high priests of Jerusalem who killed him. We must learn how to apply it to the God of our government and our church.

Exodus 2:1–10 tells of the compassion of a daughter of the king of Egypt for a male child of the Hebrews, one of a class that had been condemned to death by her father.

But the story of Moses, who is given over to fate, abandoned in an elaborate watertight ark on the waters of the Nile is also a familiar legend about the birth of a king. The man who is destined to become king is abandoned as a child, picked up by someone other than his mother so that he does not know his origin, and yet he will displace his true father and become king. This legend, with variants, is created for Sargon of Akkad in the third millennium B.C.E. and in Greece for Oedipus in the fifth century. In the context of the book of Exodus it reveals the role of Moses with respect to the Hebrews. Of course, Moses was a prophet and not a king, but he did govern the people during their forty years in the wilderness according to the story in the Torah.

The story fulfills another purpose. Moses was known to have come out of the king's palace in Egypt, in spite of devoting his life to the freedom of the rebellious peasants of Egypt. The legend serves to connect him to the people of Israel, the people who will emerge in Canaan from the rebellious peoples of many different kingships, including perhaps the ones who came from Egypt (to the extent that the exodus tells events that actually happened, a matter which we cannot know for sure).

It is said that the daughter of Pharaoh gave the name Moses to the boy she adopted, because she drew him out of the water. If the name were Hebrew it would be an active participle, "the one who draws." But it is more likely an Egyptian name, the same name that appears in Tutmoses, Ahmoses, and other royal Egyptian names. This confirms Moses' Egyptian origin. The story of the Israelite mother who put him in a basket in the river is a legend, important to link him to the people he will lead to liberty.

Exodus 2:11–15 tells of the doing of justice by this royal boy. If we believe that all the peasants of Egypt were enslaved, as we are told in Genesis 47, Moses, a prince, goes out of the palace and is indignant that a foreman is mistreating a peasant slave. After looking to see that the coast was clear, he killed the Egyptian, probably a royal employee on our understanding of Egyptian society. At first, it seemed that he had gotten away with it. But on a second excursion out of the palace he found out that this was not so, and realized he must flee for his life.

This little episode shows the character of Moses as a man of the upper class who sees, understands, and rejects the suffering of the people of Egypt. He thus proves to be a person whom God can trust to lead his people out of Egypt into freedom. Every successful revolution has some support and leadership from the upper classes who as classes do not support revolution. Karl Marx was the son of a Jewish convert and an intellectual with a doctorate from a German university. He became a pauper later in life because he spent his days in the library in London. To survive he depended on his friend Friedrich Engels, who was a business-man. Lenin was also an intellectual, even though he became the leader of the workers of Russia. Fidel Castro in Cuba was the son of owners of a hacienda and became a revolutionary leader as he studied law. The man who served with him in the Sierra Maestra, Ernesto "Che" Guevara was a physician, a graduate of a university in Buenos Aires. The oppressor class cannot be ignored if a revolution is to be successful. In Nicaragua the chaplain at the Jesuit University in the 1960s, Father Uriel Molina, a biblical scholar, trained university students from wealthy families in the love of the poor by bringing them into his parish to study the Bible and to know and love poor people. Moses is certainly not an exception. The radical position that despises the rich as hopeless is condemning itself to failure in the revolutionary work.

The incident at the well in Midian, the land to which Moses fled, according to the story, deepens our picture of the man. A well is a natural place for people to gather. Every family needs water. At the well each must wait his or her turn, and during the wait neighbors come to know each other. Moses discovered that some shepherds were bullying some young women, pushing themselves ahead in the line to draw water for their animals. Indignant, Moses drove them out of the way and drew water for the young women. Moses appeared to all as an Egyptian, and an Egyptian of the upper class, and this no doubt helped him succeed in getting the shepherds out of the way of the young women.

Eventually the king of Egypt died. But the slavery continued and the "children of Israel" raised their cries to God, because of their slavery ('ăbōdâ, literally "work"). The cries have to be directed to the same God as that of the midwives, where their God heard them and gave them families (Exod 1:21). The children of Israel make no specific petitions. Two things are said of God's response (Exod 2:25). He saw and he knew. Both of these are transitive verbs in Hebrew and in English; they require an object, which is not there. In the context it is clear that what God saw was their hard labor and oppression. What he may have known is more mysterious. Perhaps he knew the plans he had for Moses to lead them out of Egypt, the house of slavery. This knowledge leads directly into the revelation to Moses in the burning bush. There God tells Moses of his redemptive plans for the liberation of the children of Israel, the rebellious Hebrews. When people become aware of their oppression one of the things they do is to cry out to God. We pastors ought to encourage such crying out. But we should also help the oppressed people understand the nature of their oppression with the help of sociological and political studies of our countries. With the studies in one hand and the Bible in the other and with prayers in our mouths we become a formidable force of liberation.

EXODUS 19–20

Exodus 19:1 informs us that on the third month of their departure (*lĕṣē'ṯ*, from the verb, *yāṣa'*, the one used for liberation more than emigration) the Israelites arrived at the Sinai desert. In verse 2 we are told that they encamped at "the mountain." The setting is following by the statement, "and Moses went up to God," an indication that this is the same mountain of God where Moses received his orders from God in the bush that burned but was not consumed to lead the oppressed people in Egypt to liberation. There YHWH spoke to him and told him to remind the "children of Israel" how YHWH took them on wings of eagles out and brought them to himself: "If you obey my voice and keep my covenant you will be special among all the peoples of the earth" (Exod 19:5). This is the introduction of the revealed law that will take up the remainder of the book of Exodus and all of the book of Leviticus.

There is a certain tension about being the people of YHWH. The tension resides in their identity as the children of Israel by genealogy or by their observance of YHWH's laws and by keeping YHWH's covenant. We were told in Exodus 12:38 that there was a "mixed multitude" that came out of Egypt with the children of Israel. In my opinion, the text wants us to believe that it was here at Sinai in the making of the covenant that all become the special people of YHWH, which included both the descendants of Abraham, Isaac, and Jacob and the other peasants who joined them in their revolt against the king and his slave system.

Exodus 1:1–7 introduces the book with a recollection of the twelve sons of Israel who were to father the tribes once they settled in the land of Canaan. But the tribes only were constituted in the hills of Canaan. Judah and Ephraim have the names of two mountain ranges. Benjamin means "southerner," obviously with reference to the people who lived to its north. So there were no tribes of Israel in Egypt. This is read back into the story. The nonethnic "Hebrews" in some portions of the book recalls the nature of the people who were called by the prophet Moses to rise up against their slavery and leave this land of slavery.

It was to this mixed multitude that Moses descended to announce that YHWH offered a covenant by which they would be come a special people, a holy people – if they obeyed the laws that were to be revealed.

The elders of the people listened to Moses and all the people together said that all that YHWH had spoken they would obey (Exod 19:8). This means that for the text as we have it all of the laws that follow are the conditions that make this people holy and special to YHWH, regardless of whether or not they are literally descendants of Jacob-Israel. They now declare themselves children of Israel. We are reminded of how, in the United States, Thanksgiving Day is when all the people declare themselves descendants of the Puritans who arrived in New England in the early seventeenth century.

Exodus 20 shifts from the theme of YHWH's appearance and the establishment of covenant in Exodus 19 to the revelation of law. The shift in theme is abrupt. Suddenly, YHWH speaks directly to the assembled people with what we know as the Ten Commandments, or Ten Words in Jewish tradition. Exodus 20:2, the first Word in the Jewish structuring of the passage, is the most important for Liberation Criticism: "I am YHWH who brought you out (*hôṣē'tîkā*, from *yāṣa'* which means to take out of slavery) of the land of Egypt, from the house of slavery." In the very first moment of his speech YHWH defines who he is as God. This is to be understood in the first place as a rejection of Pharaoh, the God of power and slavery. The divine proclamation of liberation from oppression echoes through the biblical literature. It empowers the prophets who denounced Solomon (Ahijah the Shilonite, I Kgs 11:20ff), Ahab (Elijah, I Kgs 17), Joram (Elisha, II Kgs 9), and many others.

When Solomon built his grand temple in Jerusalem to YHWH, he conscripted labor exactly after the fashion of Pharaoh: "King Solomon conscripted labor (*mas*) out of all Israel; the levy numbered thirty thousand men. He sent them to the Lebanon, ten thousand a month in shifts; they would be a month in the Lebanon and two months at home; Adoniram was in charge of the forced labor" (I Kgs 5:13–14; HB 5:27–28). The reader of this passage is expected to ask herself, "Can the God of Solomon be the YHWH who led the people out of slavery in Egypt where they had the same sort of conscripted labor in construction of grand projects for the glory of the king?" The First Word of the Ten Commandments in Exodus 20 gives the key to distinguish the true God from false Gods. The true God gives freedom and life; false Gods, whatever their name, demand forced labor and death.

The Second Word is a corollary of the First. "You shall not have other Gods before me" (Exod 20:3). Surprisingly, this command is negative. It means that the Israelites could not have false Gods alongside of the true God. The Catholic Church replaces this with a positive command to love God, which is natural in a community that does not understand the appeal of false Gods, an appeal that persists in the twenty-first century but is no longer understood. This commandment is the flip side of the First Word. If YHWH is the God who gives freedom and life, the male head of a family rescued from slavery in Egypt shall recognize no other God. By giving the positive and then the negative side of the same matter the issue is clarified, as in the *sic et non* of the theology of Abelard, Thomas Aquinas and other late medieval theologians.

The Second Commandment (in the Reformed tradition, as for Philo and Josephus in the first century C.E.) forbids making graven or carved images of God, presumably the true God. In some traditions, notably the Jewish, the Lutheran, and the Roman Catholic, this prohibition is simply a clarification of the First Commandment and not an independent demand. But the story about the golden young bull in Exodus 32 and the exhortation against graven Gods in Deuteronomy 4 make clear why images of YHWH are forbidden. They are an effort to manipulate God and are hence unacceptable. If, as some scholars believe, the golden bull in Exodus 32 was to be placed on a long pole and lead the way for the people, it is clear what this substitution means. When the people of God no longer wait for the voice of God to give the orders to march but move their God on a stick at their will, they no longer understand a fundamental characteristic of God who leads and cannot be led.

The next commandment orders that the Sabbath be made holy through rest. Later, it will be sacrifices that make the Sabbath holy (Num 28:9–10) but here it is rest, rest for males and females, rest for servants, and rest for oxen and asses. How this fits into laws made for a liberated community of former slaves is clear. Though there may have personal slaves, mostly because of unpaid debts (Exod 21:2–11; 20–21), these must not be treated oppressively and must be given the Sabbath for rest. The motivation clause here is an *imitation Dei* considering that God rested on the seventh day after working for six days on the creation (Gen 2:2–3). The motivation clause in the Deuteronomic version of the same commandment (Deut 5:15) recalls the oppression, which you suffered in

Egypt as a reason for giving rest on the Sabbath. Either way, it is a sign of the refusal of the liberated people to become enslavers themselves.

The honor of father and mother in Exodus 20:12 is no doubt a way of solving the problem of the elderly. Their (adult) children must be responsible for them since there will be no state to assume this task among the liberated people.

The next five commandments are common to any well-ordered society. This list does not mention the penalties to be imposed on the person who murders, commits adultery, steals or bears false witness. Elsewhere in the Sinai law these are crimes that merit the death penalty. With regard to the prevalence of the death penalty it must be remembered that the liberated Israel will have no jails, which would require jailors paid by the state, and this people is being liberated precisely from the oppressing of the states (kings) of their day.

Coveting in the last one or two commandments, depending on how the ten are counted, is something only wealthy people can do. They have the means to take what they desire without using the force, which would be required for ordinary people. Examples of coveting are David's quasi-legal appropriation of the wife of Uriah (2 Samuel 11) and the rich people accused by Micah (Mic 2:1–3).

The commentary on Exodus 20 has sought to illustrate that the revelation of law is aimed at a liberated people, who have been freed from the oppression that happens in a tributary society such as the ones in Israel's environment.

CONCLUSION: LIBERATION CRITICISM
AND A BIBLICAL LIBERATION THEOLOGY

This chapter on liberation criticism has sought to demonstrate that for a biblical theology of the Christian Bible or the Hebrew Bible, the Exodus is the foundational tradition. Here the God of Israel – and of Jesus – reveals himself as a liberating God: "I am YHWH your God who brought you out of the land of Egypt, the house of slavery." Centuries later, when Israel is captive in Babylon, God promises deliverance through the Exilic prophet Isaiah – second Isaiah to scholars – creating a second Exodus. The theme of a second Exodus for the captives in Babylon is dominant in the biblical tradition and reinforces a liberation theology.

But liberation criticism, with its focus on the poor, has also underscored that the theme of liberation from Babylonian captivity is also deceptive. Liberation criticism has emphasized that most of the people, many of them poor peasants, stayed behind in Canaan, while others fled to Egypt, Amon, Moab, or other lands to escape the approaching Babylonians.

The fate of the poor in the Second Temple period is an important topic of interpretation in liberation criticism. It is this God who delivers the poor from slavery that is the God of the Bible of both Jews and Christians, who first revealed himself (herself) in the Exodus. The emphasis on the Exodus in liberation criticism has created tension with biblical theologies of creation, which has prompted critics of liberation criticism to ask: Did not God reveal himself in creation? Yes, of course God reveals him(her)self in creation.[10] In fact, we humans are an integral part of a vast array of being, rocks, rivers, otters, rats, fish, trees, stars, and much more. The native people of this New World would have reminded us of that long ago, had we listened. The creating God is a marvelous presence and we must resist the temptation to raise ourselves above our modest place in this whole in which God is with us in our particular space where one day we will be buried. But it is not yet a revelation of a God who rescues the poor from their oppressions. It is the God of the Exodus who listens to the poor and oppressed. The God of the Exodus reverberates through the biblical Psalms, as Miranda taught us, as well as through the Prophets and Jesus Christ, whose message was good news for the poor. In the exodus, the creator God is now revealed in the burning bush to Moses as a God who hears the cries of the needy. That is the God that Jesus Christ knew and about whom he preached and taught.

The Social Gospel in the United States at the opening of the twentieth century is in most ways a form of liberation theology. Read from the point of view of liberation criticism, however, the biblical interpretation that supported the Social Gospel, was deficient, because it assumed that the Prophets were the creators of a religion of justice. The Prophets were most certainly not creating any new religion, they were using the laws of

---

[10] Today we hesitate to use gender pronouns for God. Of course, God has no gender. But in the Hebrew Bible God is normally addressed as male, in spite of a few exceptional expressions that are feminine. In this chapter, the male is used because it concerns the Book of Exodus.

Moses to judge the evils of their times, including the sins of the kings. Nor did most of them, with the possible exception of Micah,[11] call on the people to rise up against their oppressors. Their message was one of condemnation of the oppressors, calling them to conversion. This is necessary, but certainly not sufficient for the liberation of the oppressed. The oppressed themselves must become aware of their oppression and organize to reject it. Under the guidance of Moses this is what happened in Egypt, at least on one version of the plagues, as well as the founding of the Passover, and the revelation of the laws in the Book of the Covenant.

The relation of the Exodus to the Prophets can better be explained in the terms of Severino Croatto's hermeneutics.[12] Croatto believed that the study of hermeneutics should begin with the study of the relationship of one text to another with the Bible. The Prophets often drew on the Books of Moses for a new reading that found meanings not present in the original. This is a perfectly legitimate process. Every act of reading is an act in the production of meaning. The written page has no meaning until somebody reads it, who is living in a situation in which he or she expects to find a message to address a current situation. And often the message will have a scant relationship to the original intention of the author of the text read. The hermeneutical presupposition of Croatto illustrates well the central principles of liberation criticism and the influence of this methodology in creating a contemporary biblical liberation theology.

---

[11] See the argument that Micah was a revolutionary who called on the peasants of Judah to rise up against their king, "Miqueas 2, 6–11: ¿Qué quiso silenciar la casa de Jacob?" *Revista Bíblica* 51 (1989), 143–63. There is an abridged version in English, "Micah – A Revolutionary," in *The Bible and the Politics of Exegesis Essays in Honor of Norman K. Gottwald on His Sixty-Fifth Birthday* (Cleveland: Pilgrim Press, 1991) 53–60.

[12] Croatto wrote three books on hermeneutics: *Hermenéutica bíblica: para una teoría de la lectura como producción de sentido* (Buenos Aires: La Aurora, 1984); an extensive revision of that book published with the same title in Buenos Aires by Editorial Lumen in 1994; and *Hermenéutica práctica: Los principios de la hermenéutica bíblica en ejemplos* (Quito: Centro Bíblico Verbo Divino, 2002). An English translation of the first of these: *Biblical Hermeneutics: Toward a Theory of Reading as the Production of Meaning* (Maryknoll, NY: Orbis Books, 1987). Orbis later translated the second of the above works. He wrote an extensive three-volume commentary on Isaiah, *Isaías: La palabra profética y su relectura hermenéutica* (vol. 1; Buenos Aires: La Aurora, 1989); *Isaías: La palabra profética y su relectura hermenéutica* (vol 2; Buenos Aires: Lumen, 1994); and *Imaginar el futuro. Estructura retórica y querigma del Tercer Isaías (Isaías 56–66)* (Buenos Aires: Lumen, 2004). These books would be very difficult to translate, and, so as far as I know, have only been translated into Portuguese, a language akin to Spanish.

LIBERATION CRITICISM BIBLIOGRAPHY

Andiñach, Pablo. *Comentario sobre Exodo*. Salamanca: Sígueme, 2006.

Cormie, Lee. *"Revolutions in Reading the Bible,"* in *The Bible and the Politics of Exegesis*, ed. David Jobling et al., pp. 173–193.

Croatto, José Severino. *Liberación y libertad. Pautas hermenéuticas*. Buenos Aires: Mundo Nuevo, 1973. English versión: *Exodus: A Hermeneutics of Freedom*. New York: Orbis Books, 1981.

————. *Hermenéutica bíblica*. Buenos Aires: La Aurora, 1984. English: *Biblical Hermeneutics: Toward a Theory of Reading as the Production of Meaning*. New York: Orbis Books, 1989.

Gottwald, Norman K. *The Tribes of Yahweh*. New York: Orbis Books, 1979.

————, and Horsley, Richard A., eds. *The Bible and Liberation: Political and Social Hermeneutics*. New York: Orbis Books, 1993.

Horsley, Richard A. *Jesus and the Spiral of Violence*. Minneapolis: Augsburg/Fortress, 1992.

————. *Paul and Empire*. Valley Forge: Trinity Press, 1997.

————. *The Liberation of Christmas: The Infancy Narratives in Social Context*. New York: Crossroad, 1989.

Jobling, David, Peggy L. Day, and Sheppard, Gerald T., eds. *The Bible and the Politics of Exegesis*. Cleveland: Pilgrim Press, 1991.

Mesters, Carlos. *Flor sem Defesa*. Petrópolis: Vozes, 1983.

Pixley, Jorge. *Exodo: Una lectura evangélica y popular*. México: Casa Unida de Publicaciones, 1983. English version: *On Exodus, A Liberationist Perspective*. New York: Orbis Books, 1987.

Tamez, Elsa. *The Amnesty of Grace*. Louisville: Abingdon Press, 1993.

————. *When the Horizons Close. Commentary on Ecclesiastes*. New York: Orbis Press, 2000.

————. *Struggles for Power in Early Christianity*. New York: Orbis Books, 2007.

5

Feminist Criticism

NAOMI STEINBERG

VARIETIES OF FEMINIST BIBLICAL CRITICISM

Feminist biblical criticism is a form of scholarly inquiry rooted in the awareness that sexism characterizes both the biblical text and the institutions that claim it and interpret it – both past and present. Attention to reading the biblical text self-consciously from the perspective of women is typically traced back to the work of Elizabeth Cady Stanton who spearheaded a group of nineteen colleagues in the production of *The Woman's Bible* in the 1890s. Although now controversial for its lack of racial and ethnic inclusion, in its time *The Woman's Bible* was a radical endeavor aimed to expose the power of the Bible to oppress women. *The Woman's Bible* is a good example of the long chain of writing that identifies the importance of women's experiences for biblical interpretation. However, using the experiences of women and other groups to augment men's biblical interpretation remained a largely moribund enterprise after the work of Stanton until the rise of the women's movement in North America in the 1960s.

There are multiple versions of feminist criticism in the biblical scholarship that began in the late twentieth century, shaped by the social location of the interpreter. We will highlight four significant developments in contemporary feminist criticism of the Bible: (1) the first wave of white North American feminism; (2) race, social class, and ethnicity based feminism; (3) gender-based feminism; and (4) theological feminism.

The First Wave of White North American Feminism

Out of the civil rights movement for racial equality came a challenge
by middle-class North American women to the androcentrism of the
Bible and its history of interpretation, as exemplified by Phyllis Trible's
"Depatriarchalizing in Biblical Interpretation." This groundbreaking
work probed "the problem" of women and their relationships to men in
the biblical text. Her study gave rise to the scholarship now referred to
by the umbrella term "feminist criticism."

At its start, feminist criticism was hardly comprehensive; it defies definition. It is fair to say, however, that the scholarship of the women's movement was intended to challenge traditional understanding of women and
their roles – both past and present. Specifically, a common concern of
this work was to scrutinize and reform constructions of reality that were
formerly thought to be "objective" truth but were, in fact, exposed as
reflections and biases of white, middle-class men, and other dominant
social groups. The recognition that men's perspectives had shaped earlier investigations of biblical data led to further analytical nuances in the
history of the development of feminist criticism at this time.

Subsequent efforts to study the Hebrew Bible from a feminist perspective made clear that women's interests are not universal. This insight has
led to a proliferation of approaches to the biblical text based on a concern for gender that sought to understand how notions of womanhood
are socially constructed. By the twenty-first century, feminism has come
to include other perspectives on the social location of the interpreter
beyond gender. Feminist criticism includes differences of race, social
class, ethnicity, gender orientation, and cultural imperialism that function as sources of oppressions. Thus, while feminist criticism began as
an attempt to redress the omission of women from the history of biblical
interpretation, it was soon recognized to address primarily the interests
of white, North American, middle-class, heterosexual women.

Race, Social Class, and Ethnicity Based Feminism

African American women challenged the uncritical awareness of early
feminist writing that failed to address differences in experience grounded
in race, class, and ethnicity. African American feminists celebrated their

unique identity separate from the experiences of white feminists, while at the same time emphasizing their solidarity with African American men based on their shared history of racism. As a distinct expression of this unique identity, the term "womanist" was coined to give voice to the perspectives of black feminists. The term comes from the preface of Alice Walker's *In Search of Our Mothers' Gardens*, where she writes: "[W]omanist is to feminist as purple is to lavender." By focusing on the intersection of race, social class, and gender, womanist scholars make clear that white middle-class women can simultaneously be dominated by men and can be dominators of other women and men. In *Just a Sister Away: A Womanist Vision of Women's Relationship in the Bible*, Renita Weems illustrates this point in her interpretation of Genesis 16 and 21, where Sarah is marginalized by gender, but still able to dominate Hagar.

The issues of race, social class, and ethnicity have branched out in feminist criticism to include a broad range of international perspectives of global feminist voices in the twenty-first century. Elsa Tamez exemplifies Latin American *mujerista* feminism in *Bible of the Oppressed*. Laura Donaldson gives expression to Native American feminism in *Decolonizing Feminism: Race, Gender, and Empire Building*. The readings expand further to include all the corners of the world from which women have interpreted biblical texts.

Gender Based Feminism

The theorizing about gender has led feminist critics to distinguish between "sex roles" and "gender roles." Sex roles refer to biological characteristics. Gender roles refer to behaviors assigned to each sex through socialization into a particular culture. The ability of women to bear children is a sex role. The meaning of motherhood is an example of gender roles. For example, debates about what it means to be "maternal" in contemporary western culture influence a woman's decision to be a stay-at-home mom rather than a career woman. The same cultural forces also influence the gender roles of men with regard to family and career. Thus, sex roles are genetically fixed, while gender roles vary from one culture to the next. As a result what is considered masculine in one society may be deemed feminine in another, or the meaning of femininity in one racial group may differ from the construction of femininity in another racial group, even within the same national boundaries.

Gender-based criticism explores the importance of socially constructed gender roles of both men and women within biblical literature. Ken Stone illustrates the critical study of male gender roles in "Gender Criticism: The Un-Manning of Abimelech." He writes: "Gender criticism analyzes critically the cultural notions and social processes that function . . . to differentiate 'men' from 'women' [and] to differentiate some men or male characteristics from other men or male characters."[1] As a result the construction of gender roles cannot be understood in strictly binary terms such as male versus female, or masculine versus feminine so that gender criticism includes a critique of heterosexuality as the standard for sexual behavior in males and females. Gender-based criticism of women in the Bible exposes the cultural biases in the evaluation of female characters that do not fit culturally defined roles, such as the generalizing of an evil woman as a seductress.

Theological Feminism

Feminism can also represent a theological approach to the biblical text. Feminists who identify with a religious tradition aim to expose the sexism of the biblical text, but they are not willing to abandon the Bible as the foundation of their religious faith. Theological feminists recognize that despite the Bible's important place in Western culture and religion, it is not a neutral text. The Bible is often closely associated with the dominant forms of male power, which affects the theology and spirituality of women. Consequently, theological feminism often intersects with the other forms of feminism discussed earlier to give theological voice to women who have been silenced by the biblical text. In addition, most theological feminists intend to bring about religious and social reform. Theological feminism takes different directions in Jewish, Protestant, and Catholic interpretation, as a reflection of the diverse lived experiences of the interpreters. The methodology of theological biblical feminism is often interdisciplinary, employing historical, literary, social-scientific,

---

[1] Ken Stone, "Gender Criticism: the Un-Manning of Abimelech," in *Judges and Method: New Approaches in Biblical Studies* (2nd ed; ed. Gale A. Yee; Minneapolis: Fortress Press, 2–7): 183.

and theological approaches to the text. In addition, theological feminists exhibit different interpretive strategies based on the perspective and the social location of the reader, which range from challenge, resistance, transformation, and liberation. A common aim of theological feminism, however, is to expose both the sexism of the biblical text and the male-centered focus of past interpretations, while also claiming a voice for women in the ongoing tradition of biblical interpretation.

A good example of a Jewish feminist theological reading of the biblical text is Judith Plaskow's *Standing Again at Sinai: Judaism from a Feminist Perspective.* Plaskow aims to find a place for liberating contemporary Jewish women despite the sexism of the ancient male writers of the biblical text. Katherine Dobb Sakenfeld voices the same concerns as a North American Christian in *Just Wives: Stories of Power and Survival in the Old Testament and Today.*

Summary

Feminist criticism critiques gender and power and lays bare a multiplicity of interpretations of texts. The overview illustrates the dynamic character of feminist biblical criticism and its variety of methodologies. It should be emphasized that the identity or social location of the interpreter does not always shape her politics. Not all women are feminists, and depending on his politics, a man can be a male-identified feminist. Thus, it is impossible to offer a single definition of feminism that would suit all those who employ this methodological strategy of interpretation, which is illustrated in the previous survey. Different understandings of feminist criticism come from the diverse social locations and politics of the feminist interpreters. These diverse perspectives result in different readings of the biblical text that should not be set in opposition to each other nor should one ask if one perspective is more legitimate than the next. To pit one reading against another as being "more legitimate" would be to return to the hierarchy of dominance that feminist criticism set out to dismantle.

What unites the array of perspectives above under the umbrella of feminist criticism of the Hebrew Bible is the self-conscious use of lived experiences as the vantage point for evaluating the biblical text and for critically assessing the history of interpretation. Thus a common feature of feminist criticism is the aim to undermine the tradition of androcentric biblical interpretation, which was often reinforced by the assumption that there is only one meaning to a text. The critical aim of feminist investigators is meant to make room for new readings that arise from lived experiences that were often excluded from the composition of the text and the authoritative history of interpretation. As one commentator remarks: "Feminist criticism is a political act whose aim is not simply to interpret the world but to change it by changing the consciousness of those who read and their relation to what they read."[2] The change of consciousness is particularly important to feminist criticism, because without it biblical texts will continue to be read from the androcentric perspectives of their authors. Even feminist readers will unconsciously identify with the male attitudes of the writers.

FEMINIST CRITICISM AND THE BOOK OF EXODUS

A starting point for understanding feminist criticisms of the Hebrew Bible in general, and of Exodus, in particular, is to ask questions about the perspective from which the biblical story is told and interpreted. Feminist interpreters agree that not only is the biblical text male-centered and the product of male authorship, but that past biblical scholarship is also androcentric, that is, male-centered. One avenue of feminist criticism that has attempted to counter past androcentrism has focused on female imagery for God and female imagery in general within the Hebrew Bible. Another is a focus on women's roles. These shifts in perspective challenge the official male gaze of the text and respond to it with feminist insights about women in ancient Israel.

Phyllis Trible is a Protestant feminist literary critic whose work exposes the sexism of Bible – but who also wants to remain within the community of scholars of faith. Her book *God and the Rhetoric of Sexuality* accomplishes the two goals by exploring the feminine imagery of God in the Hebrew Bible. Trible associates the Hebrew word for womb with the compassion of God because both the terms "womb" and "compassion" are from the same Hebrew root, *rhm*. For her, and other feminists,

---

[2] Judith Fetterley, *The Resisting Reader: A Feminist Approach to American Fiction* (Bloomington: Indiana University Press, 1978), viii.

this imagery reveals the maternal aspects of the God of Israel. Thus, in Exodus 34:6–7 God is said to be: "YHWH, YHWH, a God merciful (from the same root as womb) and gracious, slow to anger, and abounding in steadfast love and faithfulness, keeping steadfast love for thousands, forgiving iniquity and transgression and sin, but who will by no means clear the guilty, visiting the iniquity of father's upon the children and the children's children, to the third and the fourth generation." Feminist interpreters underscore that the liturgical confession is grounded in the feminine imagery of God.

Feminists also note the frequent references to water and life in Exodus and argue for an association between water and amniotic fluid. For example, in Exodus 2:3 Moses is placed in the water by his mother to save him; later in the same chapter, Zipporah, Moses' future wife, draws water at a well (Exod 2:15–17); while the waters of the Sea of Reeds (Exod 15) save the Israelites from the Egyptians pursuing them in the wilderness. In Exodus 16:1–35 and 17:1–7, when the people have no food or water in the wilderness, God feeds them as a mother would feed her hungry children. In addition, feminist biblical critics also interpret the experience of the liberation of the Israelites from Egypt as a metaphor for the birth of Israel, with God the liberator being understood as the mother who gives birth to Israel.

Further work of Trible's has focused on the character of Miriam[3] – despite the fact that in the Bible as we now have it, Miriam and other women are portrayed as secondary to the figure of Moses through whose agency Israel was liberated from slavery under the Pharaoh of Egypt. The secondary function of Miriam is evident in the literary design of Exodus 15, which contains two hymns of praise to YHWH in response to the deliverance of the Israelites from Egyptians slavery. Moses is the author of the central hymn of praise in Exodus 15:1–18, the Song of the Sea. Exodus 15:20–21 presents Miriam as the author and singer of another song, which presently functions in a secondary role in the text as a conclusion to the more prominent Song of the Sea, even though it may represent the more original hymn. The literary design suggests the loss of the role of women in ancient Israel in the formation of the Hebrew Bible. The feminist commentator Rita Burns summarizes the situation: "It can

3 Phyllis Trible, "Bring Miriam Out of the Shadows," BR 14 (1989): 14–25, 34.

be said that the primary characteristic of the biblical portrait of Miriam is that she was a leader in the wilderness. In addition, it can be said that, although the texts do not yield a single role designation of her leadership position, they do firmly reflect traditions which regarded Miriam as a cult official and as a mediator of God's word."[4]

The interpretation of Exodus 15:20–21 provides a window into the gender-segregated roles of women in the institutions of the Hebrew Bible, which contemporary feminists have sought to recover. According to this text, Miriam, along with a group of women, sang a victory song to Israelite warriors returning from battle. The text indicates that as the women sang they played musical instruments. Other examples of women musicians singing celebratory songs can be found in 1 Samuel 18:6; Jeremiah 31:4, as well as the related examples of Judges 11:34 and 5:1. Some feminist biblical scholars infer from these examples that there may have been training and practice sessions geared only to girls and women. This is the view of Carol Meyers, who writes:

Training and practice sessions mean that the women involved have frequent contact with their female peers. Such connections, which transcend household boundaries, afford women the opportunity to achieve status and recognition that is not dependent on the parameters set by male-oriented kinship patterns. Senior women who are experts in a professional activity exercise control over themselves and their cohort that affords them prestige and enables them to experience a sense of power rather than powerlessness, at least with respect to the dynamics of their female-gendered group. In their mentoring roles they exercise leadership. Moreover, professional women providing services that are both expected and needed by their community act autonomously and authoritatively.[5]

The tragic story of Jephthah's daughter (Judg 11) who is sacrificed by her father provides another example of women with musical instruments and song coming out to meet victorious warriors after battle. Moreover, the story of Jephthah and his daughter introduces the one and only example of an exclusively women's ritual in the Hebrew Bible (Judg 11:37). This fact moves us to two possible interpretations: (1) women's gender-segregated

[4] Rita Burns, *Has the Lord Indeed Spoken Only Through Moses: A Study of the Biblical Portrait of Miriam* (Atlanta: Scholars Press, 1987), 124.

[5] Carol Meyers, *Exodus* (New Cambridge Bible Commentary; Cambridge: Cambridge University Press, 2005), 118.

rituals in ancient Israel were rare; or (2) more, likely, women's rituals were not rare but they were of little interest to the male authors of the text.

Phyllis Bird, who like Phyllis Trible, maintains theological interest in the biblical text as one source of personal faith, argues that we must move beyond the male perspective in the text in order to form a picture of women's participation in the religion of ancient Israel. Thus, although we can no longer go back and speak to ancient Israelite women about their participation in religious life, we can shift our focus of study from the male perspective inscribed in the text to models from other cultures and use these models to reconstruct the religious lives of ancient Israelite women.

Feminist practices of recovering the lost experiences of women in ancient Israel find clear illustration in Bird's writings. For example, the ritual of Passover in Exodus 12 – with its concern for the preparation of the meal consumed – requires the work of women, who prepare the food. By introducing the work of food preparation into the discussion of religious participation, the feminist critic moves beyond male defined religion and allows other forms of religious life into our understanding of religious practice. Such interpretation brings out one of the essential roles of women in ancient Israel's religious life.

Bird, noting that the priesthood and religious system of worship in ancient Israel was organized and staffed by men, works to recover women's religious experiences by shifting the categories of analysis away from male constructed religion in which women play no part. For example, life-cycle events, such as birth, probably were the occasion for female-only celebration. Exodus 1 introduces the midwives who were expected to attend Israelite women when they gave birth. One can imagine, based on evidence from other societies, that the sex-segregated rituals of women presided over by the female midwives occurred on the occasion of a birth. However, because men were excluded from such rituals, the Bible omits record of women's participation in such events.

An overlooked example of women being written out of the biblical text is Exodus 4:24–26. One cannot deny that in the final form of the Hebrew Bible, only men – and typically only priests (who were men) – were sanctioned for ritual performance. But Exodus 4:24–26 preserves memory of at least one time when a woman circumcised a man. In this story, Zipporah, the wife of Moses, circumcises their son, who is named

Gershom in Exodus 2:22. Although the events recounted here are lost to us, the fact remains that Zipporah performs a ritual act otherwise reserved for men in the official story of the Hebrew Bible. At the time of this event, there were no priests at hand and the closeness of Zipporah to Moses (and God) is probably the point of the story, that is, ritual trumps gender. However, the gender exclusivity of the ritual of circumcision that introduces only baby boys into the covenant between God and Israel troubles feminists. The question of whether or not women were considered true members of the covenant community will surface again below when we turn to Exodus 19–20, which formalizes the covenant between God and the Israelites after they fled Egypt and arrive at the base of the mountain of God.

Feminists can use the story of Zipporah in Exodus 4:24–26 as the jumping off point for conjecture that in the history of early Israel, before the Hebrew Bible text became the product of male authors, women may have had more ritual activities than the text now preserves. Feminist scholars discuss the evidence for how the roles of women in Israel were eclipsed by men in the editing of the final formation of the Bible. Feminist critics can only begin to recover data by shifting their understanding of what constitutes religious practices to categories beyond the male experiences preserved in the biblical text and by integrating dimensions of life that include women's lives and differentiated religious situations. Such an approach involves nothing less than a complete shift away from men's understanding – both past and present – of defining what constitutes religious life in ancient Israel.

Let us now see how a shift from past androcentric perspectives to more recent feminist readings of Exodus 1–2 and 19–20 allows for a reevaluation of the issues raised in these texts. We suggest that there are alternative modes for reconstructing meaning in these familiar texts than past scholarship has allowed.

EXODUS 1–2

Our first step is to review the content of Exodus 1–2. The opening verses of Exodus 1 tie the circumstances described at the beginning of this book to the events and characters recounted at the conclusion of the preceding book of Genesis. Although the Israelites enjoyed favor with the Egyptians at the end of Genesis, due to the successful economic planning for famine designed by Joseph, we learn in Exodus 1:1 that "a Pharaoh arose who did not know Joseph." Thus, the fate of the Israelites under Egyptian rule shifts from the importance of Joseph recounted in Genesis to the enslavement of the Israelites in the story of the Exodus. We begin reading Exodus with questions of the repercussions signaled by this abrupt change in leadership for the Israelites in Egypt.

Our next step is to review how traditional biblical scholarship answers these questions. Although Moses does not appear until Exodus 2, the events in chapter 1 shape the circumstances that account for the fate of Moses. Specifically, Pharaoh, in his fear that the Israelites will become too numerous for the Egyptians to manage through enslavement (vv. 8–10), issues a decree designed to institute Israelite population control: all newborn Israelite boys are to be killed at birth. Girl babies are allowed to live (vv. 15–16), presumably based on the stereotypical thinking that strength is a physical attribute and that only males are strong enough to fight back against the Egyptians. However, one baby escapes this plan; he is saved by his mother and raised by the daughter of the Pharaoh, who issued the decree for the death of Israelite baby boys. This rescued child marries a daughter of the priest of Midian and grows up to be the human liberator of the Israelites from Egyptian bondage. Thus, Exodus 1–2 is traditionally labeled "the story of the birth of Moses." Some scholars link the story of the birth of Moses to other ancient texts regarding the birth of a hero figure whose very start in life could have jeopardized his future chances to liberate his people, for example, the stories of the birth of Sargon of Akkad,[6] and Oedipus. In these legends a future hero is left to die suggesting that the liberator must first be liberated.

Our next step is to explore how biblical feminist scholarship has expanded our reading of these two chapters in Exodus and challenged past analyses of these texts. The interpretation will separate into two parts. The first section will explore debates among feminist biblical critics in evaluating the primary role of the women as either mothers or care-givers of children. The second section will review feminist interpretations of the named women characters in Exodus 1–2.

[6] The legend of the birth of Sargon can be found in *Ancient Near Eastern Texts Relating to the Old Testament*, 3rd ed. (ed. James B. Pritchard; Princeton: Princeton University Press, 1969), 119.

Feminist Interpretations of Motherhood

In her 1994 article "Second Thoughts about Secondary Characters: Women in Exodus 1:8–2:10," Cheryl Exum reexamines the stories of the women of Exodus 1–2 that she first studied almost a decade earlier in a work entitled, "'You Shall Let Every Daughter Live': A Study of Exodus 1:8–2:10." Exum's aim is to "step outside the text's ideology and consider what androcentric agenda these narratives promote." Exum argues that Exodus 1–2 relegates women to their traditional family roles, which led to her conclusion that the text fails to liberate women today.[7] She asserts that motherhood brings status and honor to women in a patriarchal cultural and that when women desire and fulfill this role they are embracing male norms for women.

Esther Fuchs analyzes Exodus 1–2 from her perspective as a Jewish-feminist educated in Israel.[8] She writes of how the dominant male perspective on these texts educated her to see these chapters with only a focus on the importance of Moses. The sexism of modern interpretation reinforces the sexism of the ancient text to obliterate the women in the texts. Thus, Fuchs is in sympathy with Exum's reevaluation of these chapters and agrees that the texts reinforce male ideology on women as mothers. Fuchs remarks: "The mother-figures who are further from the male object of concern are presented in more positive terms than the mother-figures who are closer and more directly involved in his [Moses'] rescue."[9] Fuchs understanding of male ideology leads to the conclusion, that "the biblical narrator both promotes and undercuts the status of mother-figures; they are valued, but they must not emerge as too important."[10] By associating women with marriage and children, that is, the private sphere, the women fulfill roles of secondary importance for the male narrator, according to Fuchs, and are disassociated with public roles leading to the departure from Egypt and the wanderings in the wilderness.

---

[7] J. Cheryl Exum, "Second Thoughts about Secondary Characters: Women in Exodus 1:8–2:10," in *A Feminist Companion to Exodus to Deuteronomy* (ed. Athalya Brenner; Sheffield: Sheffield Academic Press, 1994), 79.

[8] Esther Fuchs, "A Jewish-Feminist Reading of Exodus 1–2," *Jews, Christians, and the Theology of the Hebrew Scriptures* (eds. Alice Ogden Bellis and Joel S. Kaminsky; Symposium 8. Atlanta: Society of Biblical Literature, 2000), 307–26.

[9] Ibid., 311.

[10] Ibid., 311.

Contemporary feminists, such as Exum and Fuchs, are interested in the social location of women's and men's roles as an indicator of the importance of women in society. Their perspective on women in the biblical text is based on the near universal existence of sexually segregated roles for women. The dichotomy that results from segregated roles is one of private/domestic versus public/political spheres of activities. This model presumes that women universally operate in the private/domestic domain and men in the public/political. A further assumption of the social location approach in feminist critique is that the only really important type of power in society is formal political power, which is limited to the activities of men. The distinction between public and private domains means: "Women will seem to be oppressed or lacking in value and status to the extent that they are confined to domestic activities, cut off from other women and the social world of men."[11] Some feminists argue that women are universally relegated to this less valued sphere in this model of social dualism because of the fact that they are the sex responsible for childbearing and childrearing. According to this perspective, all women in all societies are involved in these activities, which are all-consuming. Being confined to the domestic arena, women are denied the opportunities to participate in the public arena where the official power of a society is wielded and hierarchy is determined. Men, by dominating in the extra-domestic sphere, the public sphere, are the ones given social recognition. Therefore, the argument continues, the public sphere always outranks the private sphere in importance. Some feminist criticism aims to expose the realities of women's putative secondary importance in society based on this model of social structure.

Sherry Ortner provides a different analysis of the same private/domestic distinction, which has been foundational for much feminist criticism.[12] Central to Ortner's critique of sexism in society is her hypothesis of a universal cultural dichotomy between "nature" and "culture." In this model, culture is assumed to be superior to nature and to transcend it. Guided by a theory of sexual differentiation based on the supposed

---

[11] M. Z. Rosaldo, "Woman, Culture, and Society: A Theoretical Overview," *Woman, Culture, and Society* (ed. M. Z. Rosaldo and L. Lamphere; Stanford: Stanford University Press, 1974), 41.

[12] S. B. Ortner, "Is Female to Male as Nature is to Culture," *Woman, Culture, and Society* (ed. M. Z. Rosaldo and L. Lamphere; Stanford: Stanford University Press, 1974), 67–87.

physiological constraints of bearing and raising children, Ortner investigates the relationship between the cultural view of women as inferior to men and the actualities of gender role action. In general, asserts Ortner, women's biological function as child bearers, social role in mothering, and feminine personality provide the societal rationale for viewing women as more closely associated with the world of nature than men. The reason women are identified with nature, and transcended by the cultural realm in which men are said to be located, is that:

Woman's physiology, more involved more of the time with "species of life"; woman's association with the structurally subordinate domestic context, charged with the crucial function of transforming animal-like infants into cultured beings; "woman's psyche," appropriately molded to mothering functions by her own socialization and tending toward greater personalism and less mediated models of relating – all these factors make woman appear to be more rooted more directly and deeply in nature.[13]

Women, concludes Ortner, are differentiated from men in a hierarchical sense that results not only from their biological characteristics, but from the cultural evaluation of these distinctions, which stems from men but is also embraced subsequently by women. As Ortner sees it, the subordination of women to men is founded on circular reasoning: women are identified with the realm of nature and thus thought to be inferior to the cultural world with which men are identified; then, women's roles become institutionalized in a pattern that excludes them from the world of men and thus perpetuates the dichotomy between women and men, and nature and culture. In other words, the domination by men and secondary value placed on women's roles is predicated on cultural consensus of the transcendence of culture over nature and of men over women. For some feminists, the closeness of women to nature explains the secondary roles of women in the Bible in general, and in Exodus 1–2 in particular.

On this separation of public and private spheres as a universal problem, one critic writes: "When the authors give the public sphere primacy, they accept modern and male definitions of cultural importance; when they suggest that true equality will result only when men enter the domestic sphere, they accept the proposition that an activity can only

13 Ibid., 84.

have value if men take part in it."[14] Carol Meyers's extensive research on preindustrialized agrarian societies in *Discovering Eve: Ancient Israelite Women in Context* reveals a world in which the boundaries between the public and private are far less differentiated than they are in our contemporary society. The rural environment and the need to farm in order to survive speak to the family-based social world in early Israel that required both women and men to contribute to family survival. Thus, for some feminists the heavy emphasis on the dichotomy of the public and privates spheres, as applied to ancient Israel, is a projection of contemporary Western ideology onto an ancient society where it has no place. The distinction between the private/domestic arena of women and the public/political area of men may be more a function of our highly differentiated society than a universal reality. Although the story of the Hebrew midwives and their dealings with the unnamed Pharaoh of Egypt illustrates the strict separation between the private sphere of the world of women giving birth and the public sphere of the world of men, it also makes clear the interconnection of these spheres.

The controversy among feminists regarding the significance of the separation between public and private spheres extends into feminist analyses of the role of mother and other related family-based roles in the Hebrew Bible. As a result, the negative evaluation of the domestic role of women in Exodus 1–2 by Exum and Fuchs is reevaluated by African American feminist interpretation. The intersection of gender and race and the history of African Americans leads black feminist Patricia Hill Collins and other womanist critics to write of the importance of motherhood in the African American community as a source of power and a network of resistance against oppression for women.[15] In her analyses of "Black Women and Motherhood," Collins reexamines the roles of African American women in the family in different historical periods. Rather than arguing that social restraints, and particularly racism, kept African American women out of the workplace and confined them to roles as mothers and caretakers, she maintains that women's gender roles in the African American community must be understood in light of class

---

[14] L. A. Tilly, "The Social Sciences and the Study of Women: A Review Article," *Comparative Studies in Society and History* 20 (1978), 169.

[15] Patricia Hill Collins, *Black Feminist Thought: Knowledge, Consciousness, and the Politics of Empowerment* (New York and London: Routledge, 1990), 115–37.

and race issues in the United States. Thus, she rejects the cultural model used by white middle-class elite women, who judge a woman's worth is determined by her participation in the labor force. She deems it to be ethnocentric for evaluating the significance of motherhood in North America. To apply a universalistic approach fails to differentiate family structures that include racial and class issues.

Collins provides an "Afrocentric Feminist analysis of Black motherhood"[16] that attends to the diverse functions women fill in the African American family and the importance of these roles for the survival of the family and the individuals who comprise it. Motherhood can be a source of power, recognition, and the base for political activism. Collins challenges white feminist analyses by arguing that "the particular form that Black women's relationships with one another, children, community, and self actually take depends upon on how this dialectical relationship between the severity of oppression facing African American women and our actions in resisting that oppression is expressed."[17] Her perspective allows African American women to reclaim their own history and to express contradictory understandings of African American women in family relationships in diverse historical periods, while also undermining stereotypes of black women as either the mammy or the matriarch. The different perspective results in a more positive evaluation of the domestic role of the women in Exodus 1–2.

Feminist Interpretations of the Women Characters in Exodus 1–2

Feminist critics are also attentive to women characters whose names are preserved in the record of the Hebrew Bible. In a story where most of the male characters go unnamed – that is, the Pharaoh of Exodus 1, the father of the baby boy in Exodus 2, and the priest of Midian (Exod 2:16, although he is identified by the name Reuel in 2:18) – it is striking that the midwives Shiprah and Puah are identified by name (Exod 1:15). The Hebrew text is, however, ambiguous in referring to them as Hebrew midwives: it is unclear whether these two women are Egyptians who

---

[16] Ibid., 115.
[17] Ibid., 119.

function as midwives to the Hebrew women when the Israelite women give birth, or midwives of Hebrew origin.

Exodus 2:1–10 recounts the birth story of Moses. It depends on the actions of several women to defy Pharaoh's orders, yet these women – in contrast to the midwives Shiprah and Puah in Exodus 1 – are anonymous in the story. They are never explicitly named. In the larger context of the ensuing events, commentators define these women through the men in their lives – even though one of these "men" is only an infant in chapter 2. Chapter 2 introduces Moses' unnamed mother (2:2), Moses' sister (2:4), and Pharaoh's daughter (2:5).

In subsequent biblical texts, Moses' mother is identified by the name Yochebed (Exod 6:20; Num 26:59), Moses' sister is named Miriam (Num 26:59, 1 Chron 6:3) but Pharaoh's daughter, who names Moses, is never named. Neither Moses' mother nor his sister's names appear in Exodus 2. Moreover, Moses' biological father is unnamed in the story, although he is identified by the name Amram in Exodus 6:20 and Numbers 26:59 where Moses, Aaron, and Miriam are listed as siblings – as they are in 1 Chronicles 6:3. The father in whose house Moses grows up, that is, the Pharaoh, is also unnamed. The only explicit designation is the tribal reference to the Levites as the genealogical link of Moses' parents. It is important to notice that Moses himself is not named specifically until the final verse of this unit, verse 10.

Feminist biblical critics remark that Exodus 2 begins with a marriage and moves immediately to the birth of a son. These events would lead the reader to think that this baby is the firstborn child of the couple. The birth of the sister of the baby boy, later identified as Miriam, is never recounted. Emphasis on the birth of the son, rather than the daughter, may reflect the importance of sons in ancient Israel for the continuation of the patrilineage, the line of inheritance, from fathers to sons. It may also reflect the context – the son has to be saved, not the daughter. The silence surrounding the birth of the daughter indicates that the authors do not care about the details of her birth.

Feminist scholar, Siebert-Hommes, shifts the focus away from the sons to draw attention to the active roles of daughters in Exodus 1–2. She notes that the traditional number of Israelite sons is twelve; yet Exodus 1–2 celebrate twelve daughters: the two Hebrew midwives, the mother and the sister of Moses, the daughter of Pharaoh and the seven daughters of Jethro (Exod 3:1; as noted earlier, he is named Reuel in Exod 2:18) the priest of Midian. She states further that the sister of Moses and the daughter of Pharaoh take on active roles in the story. They are the agents who make it possible for Moses to live, whose leadership is tied to the emergence of the Israelites as a nation.[18]

Although there is much information that goes unstated in Exodus 1–2, what is clear from the perspective of feminist critics is that while Moses may be the "hero" in the text as we now have it – and as we have been taught to read it by male interpreters – the actions of women Exodus 1–2 are nothing short of heroic based on the courage that many of them display in defying male authority – and that of the ultimate male authority in ancient Egypt, the Pharaoh himself. In order better to understand the dynamics of the interactions between Pharaoh and the women in Exodus 1–2, we turn now to terminology from the social sciences.

In the social sciences, power, authority, and influence are distinguished from each other. *Power*, according to the sociologist Max Weber, "is the probability that one actor within a social relationship will be in a position to carry out his own will despite resistance, regardless of the basis on which this probability rests."[19] When power is grounded in socially sanctioned rights, that is, social legitimacy, it is defined as *authority*. Authority "is the aspect of a status in a system of social organization . . . by virtue of which the incumbent is put in a position legitimately to make decisions which are binding not only on himself but on the collectivity."[20] Lastly, *influence*, a form of persuasion, depends not on sanctions but on an actor's ability to convince another person to change their mind.[21]

The terms, power, authority, and influence often appear in feminist literature to describe the world of ancient Israel. The political issues surrounding the feminist movement in the late 1960s often informs the

---

[18] Jopie, Siebert-Hommes, "But if she be a Daughter . . . She May Live! 'Daughters' and 'Sons' in Exodus 1–2," in *A Feminist Companion to Exodus to Deuteronomy* (ed. Athalya Brenner; Sheffield: Sheffield Academic Press, 1994): 62–74.

[19] Max Weber, *The Theory of Social and Economic Organization* (trans. A. M. Henderson and Talcott Parsons; New York: Oxford University Press, 1947), 152.

[20] Talcott Parsons, "On the Concept of Power," *Proceedings of the American Philosophical Society* 107 (1963): 232–62.

[21] Ibid., "On the Concept of Influence," *Public Opinion Quarterly* 27 (1963): 37–62.

interpretation of these important terms. In particular, some feminists suggest that the insight gained from contemporary social and political experience of women allows feminist interpreters to go beyond tradition biases, in which women were viewed as victims. New insight into the social function of power, authority, and influence allow, instead, for a view of women as agents in their own lives – regardless of what social structures of male oppression might exist. With this approach, feminists gain new insights into the midwives, Shiprah and Puah, and the secret negotiations between the women in the adoption of Moses as agents who control events around them by exercising power through words.

The lie of the midwives to Pharaoh about the dangerous fertility of the Hebrew women and the secret negotiations between the daughter of Pharaoh and Moses' sister and mother in Exodus 2 could be categorized as a form of gossip. Within the framework of feminist interpretation gossip – pejoratively understood as "women's words" in Western society – can be analyzed as a political act, a form of power, by virtue of its being a form of dissemination of information. Gossip is a strategy of behavior designed to bring pressure, based on self-interest, which intends to change people's minds. From this perspective, women who gossip are agents of change through the words they exchange with others – be they women or men. But why do conversations between women deserve the label of gossip? Who is judging the power issues when women speak to other women? Rather than labeling women's words as gossip, we might instead understand them as acts of resistance or aggression. The words of women are, from some feminist points of view, intended to disrupt or subvert male power structures. Women working together can be understood as an attempt to subvert power and resist circumstances that exploit women or what women disapprove of. The midwives unnerving of Pharaoh through their lie and the clandestine adoption of Moses by the daughter of Pharaoh, who negotiates in secret with other women for the baby's care, are examples of the ability of women's words to resist and subvert men's actions. Pharaoh may be the authority figure in Exodus but the women are the individuals who exert power over him and in the end subvert his plans.

Shiprah and Puah also represent other forms of power, authority, and influence in Exodus 1–2 through action, rather than words. They defy Pharaoh's command by allowing newborn boy babies to live. When questioned about this, the women lie to Pharaoh – with a lie that he cannot substantiate or deny, because childbirth occurs in the realm of women, thus not allowing him access to it in a timely manner – and assert that the Hebrew women are so strong that they are able to give birth before the midwives arrive. Thus, according to them, the Hebrew midwives do not have access to these babies.

From a feminist perspective, the midwives model the courage of women to subvert the oppression represented by Pharaoh. The midwives, whether Hebrew or Egyptian, are tricksters who thwart the evil command of Pharaoh. Had Pharaoh known their cunning, writes Phyllis Trible, he would have commanded all infant females to be killed.[22] "Their clever response to Pharaoh," writes Renita Weems, "is not a lie, they simply do not tell the whole truth . . . a conventional weapon of the powerless, especially women in the Old Testament."[23] Not only are they clever, the midwives also embody the theme of birth in the book of Exodus, according to Drorah O'Donnell Setel: "They are the first to assist in the birth of the Israelite nation."[24]

The lie told underscores the irony of Pharaoh's decree to kill baby boys based on his fear of their strength. According to Shiprah and Puah, not only are Hebrew women strong, but they are stronger than Egyptian women – who require the help of midwives when giving birth (v. 19). One commentator notes: "Just as the Hebrews had succeeded in increasing when the Egyptians were seeking their diminishment, so the midwives had succeeded in preserving the Hebrew males when the Pharaoh was seeking their elimination."[25] For their refusal to aid in Pharaoh's plan, God rewards Shiprah and Puah with children of their own (vv. 20–21). Notes feminist critic Carol Meyers of the midwives: "Perhaps childless themselves, they are now given 'families' (v. 21). The Hebrew word translated 'families' actually means 'house' or 'households.' As such, in this female-centered text, the identifications of households are with

[22] Phyllis Trible, "Depatriarchalizing in Biblical Interpretation," *JAAR* 41 (1973): 34.
[23] Renita D. Weems, "The Hebrew Women Are Not Like the Egyptian Women: The Ideology of Race, Gender and Sexual Reproduction in Exodus 1," *Semeia* 59 (1992): 29.
[24] Drorah O'Donnell Setel, "Exodus," in *The Women's Bible Commentary* (eds. C. A. Newsom and S. H. Ringe; Louisville, KY: Westminster John Knox, 1992), 30.
[25] Alice. L. Laffey, *An Introduction to the Old Testament: A Feminist Perspective* (Philadelphia: Fortress Press, 1988), 47.

women, as in several other female-centered texts, rather than with men."[26]

The story documents the roles of women as midwives and highlights the importance of childbirth. The role of midwife is here professionalized and indicates technical training in these women-only jobs. That we have no knowledge of what training was involved reflects the male authorship of the text and the fact that men were denied access to the exclusively female world of childbirth. Exodus 2 also affords information on the profession of wet-nurse and child-rearing practices. The text suggests that women normally suckled their own children but that women of elite status sought out nursing mothers to breastfeed their infants. The socioeconomic ability to pay for the services of a wet-nurse would limit the number of families able to afford lactating women, but the evidence in Exodus indicates that women would be paid for this service.

The African American biblical scholar Renita Weems offers a womanist interpretation of these texts in "The Hebrew Women Are Not Like the Egyptian Women: The Ideology of Race, Gender and Sexual Reproduction in Exodus 1." Her reading of the first chapter of Exodus explores the ideology of difference between Egyptians and Israelites and between men and women established by the words of Pharaoh – who distinguishes male power from female weakness in his decree to kill male babies – and in the words of the Hebrew midwives – who emphasize the difference between Hebrews and Egyptians in saying that the former give birth more quickly than the latter. Although Weems notes that Exodus 1 pokes fun at these stereotypes, and specifically at Pharaoh's assumptions about male power, she notes that the story ultimately upholds ideological differences between men and women and Egyptians and Hebrews. In the context of struggles for racial and gender equality today, Weems holds up this story as an example of how uncritical reading of the biblical text, that is, failure to explore the ideology of difference, contributes to contemporary discrimination based on race and gender.

Thus, we see that different feminist interpreters bring different perspectives to the text and that there can be tensions between their interpretations based on the social locations of the interpreters and on their

---

[26] Carol Meyers, *Exodus*, 37.

understanding of whether contemporary feminist issues should be super-
imposed on ancient texts. Although their assessments differ from each
other, some common ground between all of these scholars leads to the
conclusion: "Still, the most important story in the Hebrew Bible begins
with women determining events. It begins with God using the weak
and the lowly to overcome the strong. It begins with women who act
courageously, defying oppression. It begins with women who are life-
affirming, women who are wise and resourceful in tough situations.
Without these women, there would be no Moses to liberate the Hebrews
from bondage."[27]

EXODUS 19–20

After their escape from Egypt and the period of wilderness wandering, the
Israelites stand at the foot of Mt. Sinai, where, through the mediation of
Moses, they are poised to enter into a formal covenant relationship with
Yahweh. At Sinai the people receive instructions from Moses on how to
prepare themselves for the coming revelation of God. The central themes
in the modern history of research of Exodus 19–20 include the preparation
of the people for the appearance of Yahweh and the revelation of law.
Feminist biblical critics have raised the question of the role of women
within each of these themes.

The Preparation for Theophany

The preparation of the people for the appearance of Yahweh on Mount
Sinai is recounted in Exodus 19:10–15, when God tells Moses to secure the
mountain and to purify the people. Although these instructions initially
appear to be inclusive of women and men– in Exodus 19:10 the order
is for all the people to stay pure – the specific charge in verse 15 is that
preparation for the upcoming revelation of God involves staying away
from women for three days. Thus, in its present form, the text appears
to be addressed to the men, who are ordered not to go "near" a woman
before the Sinai revelation. The prohibition against approaching women

---

[27] Alice Ogden Bellis, *Helpmates, Harlots, and Heroes: Women's Stories in the Hebrew Bible*
(Louisville, KY: Westminster/John Knox Press, 1984), 101.

for purposes of sexual intercourse presumably has its roots in ancient Israelite religious ideas of purity. Women are considered impure (Lev 15:19–24) by virtue of the discharge of menstruation, as well as after sexual intercourse (Lev 15:18). Men as well are impure after sexual intercourse (Lev 15:16–18). These injunctions uphold the biblical perspective that maintains a separation between clean/pure and unclean/impure and serve as indicators of the distinction between the two spheres that has to do with bodily discharges (Lev 15) – understood to cause pollution to the individual and to God.

The injunction in Exodus 19:15 troubles feminist interpreters, because it appears to make women invisible in the covenant community. The command of Moses is specifically addressed only to males: "Prepare for the third day; do not go near a woman." The injunction of Moses follows the legislation of Leviticus 15:16–18, which specifies that bodily emissions, for example, the ejaculation of semen in sexual intercourse, render an individual ritually impure. In this context, a man who had sexual intercourse would be prohibited from approaching the base of Mt. Sinai where God would descend to give the divine law. The impurity of the women from sexual intercourse appears to be of no concern for the author of Exodus 19:15, even though the book of Leviticus contains sexual laws for both the man and the woman. The narrow focus on the injunction in Exodus 19:15 clearly presents the situation from the male point of view. The text reflects a community of Israelite men but does not address the experiences of women assembled in the wilderness after the exodus from Egypt. The Jewish feminist Judith Baskin writes of Exodus 19:10–11:

It is striking that *God's* instructions to Moses are addressed to the whole community. It is *Moses* who changes them, who glosses God's message, who assumes that the instructions are meant for only half the people. Thus, at this early stage in Jewish history, Moses filters and interprets God's command through a patriarchal lens. . . . They show how Jewish tradition has repeatedly excluded women, but also the way in which that exclusion must be understood as a *distortion* of revelation.[28]

---

[28] Judith R. Baskin, "Contemporary Reflection," *The Torah: A Women's Commentary* (ed. Tamara Eskenazi; New York: Union of Reform Judaism Press, 2008), 423.

The assumption among feminist biblical critics is that the injunction to men to abstain from sex in Exodus 19:15 represents a male interpretation of the purity laws of the Hebrew Bible. Feminist interpreters point out that the washing of clothes in Exodus 19:10 and 14 is just as important in fulfilling the requirement to stay pure as abstaining from sex. The reason is that the washing of clothes is probably connected with the impurity of discharges that may be in the clothing. The washing of clothes in ancient Israel, moreover, was the work of women, not men. Thus, feminist interpreters would not only criticize the narrow focus on males in the injunction to abstain from sex in verse 15, they would also argue that the ritual of purification actually required the participation of women, which is only partially obscured by the male perspective that dominates the present form of Exodus 19.

The Revelation of Law

The Ten Commandments in Exodus 20:1–17 have also undergone interpretation by feminist biblical criticism. Feminist interpreters debate whether the Ten Commandments were addressed to only males, or whether they were also intended for females. That the laws are (in Hebrew) masculine, singular imperatives suggest to some the androcentric perspective of the laws. In the grammar of biblical Hebrew, the masculine form is used as long as there is one male in the group; it is the form used even if there are women included in the verb – thus it can be interpreted as gender inclusive. That the text intends to include women finds some support in the fact that one cannot understand the commandment to keep the Sabbath (Exod 20:8–11) as being solely addressed to men. The commandment specifies that neither sons nor daughters, neither manservants nor maidservants are to work on the Sabbath.

Feminist critics agree that the Ten Commandments (Exod 20:1–17) and the laws in the subsequent legislation reflect the ideology of (elite) men. Women are assumed in the commandments, though typically not directly addressed. Exodus 20:12 enjoins the Israelites to honor both father and mother, while Exodus 20:14 prohibits adultery. The latter refers to the violation of another man's wife. When one man has sexual intercourse with another man's wife, he violates the property of another individual. The commandment against adultery in Exodus 20:14 is addressed to men and is presented with the Israelite understanding that a man who has sexual relations with a betrothed or married woman is violating the rights of another man. This is based on the Israelite concern for paternity and inheritance from one generation of men to another, that is, if a man has sexual intercourse with another man's wife, should she become pregnant it will be impossible to determine who the father of the child is – jeopardizing both the patrilineage, the family line traced through the father, and the rights to property through the patrilineage. Also the command against coveting in Exodus 20:17 specifies that a man's wife is part of his household.

The law against adultery in Exodus 20:24 and coveting in Exodus 20:17 indicate the dominance of the male in ancient Israelite culture at the time of the writing of the Ten Commandments. A controversy that has arisen in feminist biblical scholarship concerns the appropriateness of the term "patriarchal" when analyzing the laws of the Ten Commandments as compared to the concept of the "patrilineage." Although many scholars have expressed their perspectives on this topic, and most would agree that patriarchy refers to a system of male domination over women, how this oppression is understood varies. To illustrate the controversy, we focus on the perspectives of Carol Meyers[29] and Cheryl Exum.[30] Both would agree that the Hebrew Bible in its final canonical form is androcentric, that is, male centered, but the two feminist scholars strongly disagree on whether or not to apply the label patriarchal to the texts.

Technically speaking, patriarchy is a form of family organization in which the head of the household is the father and he holds absolute authority within the family. Exum argues that the Hebrew Bible is patriarchal, because it reveals a world characterized by the dominance of the father in the family and assumes an attitude of the oppression of women by men. Meyers contends that such perspectives result from the imposition of contemporary thinking onto an ancient society, and do not reflect the world within the biblical text. Meyers maintains that what feminists label as patriarchy should be termed "patrilineal" – a word that characterizes group organization in biblical times around the lineage of the

---

[29] Carol Meyers, *Discovering Eve: Ancient Israelite Women in Context* (New York: Oxford University Press, 1988), 24–46.

[30] Cheryl Exum, "Feminist Criticism," in *Judges and Method: New Approaches in Biblical Studies* (2nd ed., ed. Gale A. Yee; Minneapolis: Fortress Press, 2007), 65–66.

father and lineage property rights. Meyers bases her analysis on patterns of social organization in biblical times. Thus, it is important to recognize that there is terminological imprecision – even conflict – among feminist critics of the Hebrew Bible on the term patriarchy. All feminist critics do not agree with each other. Inherent in the controversy is the appropriateness of contemporary categories of gender equality for interpreting ancient Israelite society. The debate illustrates that gender roles in one culture may not have the same meaning in another.

Feminist social scientific study has also explored the relationship between hierarchical legal structures and the position of women in society. The research suggests that the nature of male control based on the rule of the father over the family, which is likely the setting of the Ten Commandments, changes over the course of Israelite history. The family setting of the laws in the book of Exodus, including both the Decalogue in Exodus 20 and the Book of the Covenant in Exodus 21–23, gives way to a more centralized legal structure in the later law of the book of Deuteronomy. Feminist biblical interpreters suggest that as a centralized government developed in biblical Israel, women lost power and status within the society. The reason for this is that the legal situation prior to the political centralization of the monarchy (tenth century B.C.E.) depended on the execution of justice by the adult males of the nuclear family. With the onset of the monarchy, the authority of the father was eclipsed and power shifted to the control of the local elders, who were organized through the local group larger than the boundaries of the nuclear family unit. Through the politics of governmental centralization women lost autonomy as hierarchical systems of justice subverted earlier legal structures and took power out of the hands of the family and shifted it into authorities organized removed from the nuclear family.[31]

Thus, despite the perspective on women in Exodus 19–20 and the arguments about the patriarchal nature of this literature, some have argued for more equality between men and women in the Ten Commandments and in the Book of the Covenant, than in the laws of Deuteronomy. The reason is that the Ten Commandments and the Book of the Covenant

---

[31] Naomi Steinberg, "The Deuteronomic Law Code and the Politics of State Centralization," *The Bible and the Politics of Exegesis: Essays in Honor of Norman K. Gottwald on His Sixty-Fifth Birthday* (eds. D. Jobling, P. Day, and G. Sheppard; Cleveland: Pilgrim Press, 1991), 166.

reflect the family based system of law, as compared to the later laws in Deuteronomy, where the development of a hierarchical monarchy replaced the earlier family based systems of law.

The law of rape in Exodus 22:16–17 and Deuteronomy 22:28–29 illustrates the difference. Deuteronomy 22:28–29 legislates that a man who has raped an unbetrothed woman must marry her. The rapist pays a bride-price to the father of the woman, and he may never divorce her. In this case, a woman who has been raped is forced to be married to her rapist and can never be divorced from him. By contrast, in the earlier version of this legislation in Exodus 22:16–17, the father of the woman decides whether the two will be married. Whether or not the father approves of the marriage, the rapist must pay the father the marriage present due for a virgin.

The law in Deuteronomy takes decisions out of the hands of the father and makes categorical imperatives reinforced by the larger community. As a result the woman has no chance of influencing her own future by appealing to the kindness of her father. Despite the modern-day perspective that might interpret women as property in Exodus 21:16–17, because her father is compensated for the loss of her virginity, in the Exodus law there is the possibility of choice regarding the woman's future. There is no chance for choice in Deuteronomy where male elites in the community control the administration of justice. The comparison suggests that the earlier law of the Book of the Covenant grants greater freedoms to women than does the later legislation in Deuteronomy. Thus, despite surface appearances of the circumscribed role of women in comparison to the rights of men, the law of Exodus better protects women against absolute male authority than Deuteronomy does.

CONCLUSION

We conclude this introduction to feminist criticism of the Hebrew Bible with a reminder that this essay has illustrated the multiple possibilities for new interpretations of old texts, which result from the fresh perspectives of feminist biblical critics. Despite differences in interpretation, which arise in part from debates over the relevance of contemporary social issues for analyzing ancient biblical texts, feminist investigators are unified in the goal to break down gender stereotypes in the interpretation of the

Hebrew Bible. What is most important in the scholarship that is reviewed in this chapter is not the adjective "feminist" in the label attached to this work, but the resultant insights into the biblical texts that emerge from the research.

FURTHER READING

General

Anderson, Janice Capel. "Mapping Feminist Biblical Criticism: The American Scene, 1983–1990. In *Critical Review of Books in Religion: 1991*, edited by Jap Epp, pp. 21–44. Atlanta: Scholars Press, 1991.

Bass, Dorothy C. "Women's Studies and Biblical Studies: An Historical Perspective." JSOTt 22 (1982): 6–12.

Bellis, Alice Ogden. *Helpmates, Harlots, and Heroes: Women's Stories in the Hebrew Bible.* Louisville, KY: Westminster/John Knox Press, 1984.

Bird, Phyllis A. *Missing Persons and Mistaken Identities. Women and Gender in Ancient Israel.* Overtures to Biblical Theology. Minneapolis: Fortress Press, 1997.

———, et al., ed. *Reading the Bible as Women: Perspectives from Asia, Africa, and Latin America.* Semeia 78. Atlanta: Scholars Press, 1997.

Brenner, Athalya. "Who's Afraid of Feminist Criticism? Who's Afraid of Biblical Humor? The Case of the Obtuse Foreign Ruler in the Hebrew Bible." *Journal for the Study of the Old Testament* 63 (1994): 38–55.

Collins, Patricia Hill. *Black Feminist Thought: Knowledge, Consciousness, and the Politics of Empowerment.* New York and London: Routledge, 1990.

Day, Peggy L., ed. *Gender and Difference in Ancient Israel.* Minneapolis: Fortress, 1989.

Donaldson, Laura E. *Decolonizing Feminisms: Race, Gender, and Empire Building.* Chapel Hill: University of North Carolina Press, 1992.

Dube, Musa W., ed. *Other Ways of Reading: African Women and the Bible.* Global Perspectives on Biblical Scholarship 2. Atlanta: Society of Biblical Literature, 2001.

Eskenazi, Tamara, ed. *The Torah: A Women's Commentary.* New York: Union of Reform Judaism Press, 2008.

Exum, J. Cheryl. "Feminist Criticism." In *Judges and Method: New Approaches in Biblical Studies.* 2nd ed., edited by Gale A. Yee, pp. 65–88. Minneapolis: Fortress Press, 2007.

Hackett, JoAnn. "Women's Studies and the Hebrew Bible." In *The Future of Biblical Studies: The Hebrew Bible*, edited by Richard E. Friedman and Hugh G. M. Williamson, pp. 141–64. Atlanta: Scholars Press, 1987.

Laffey, Alice L. *An Introduction to the Old Testament: A Feminist Perspective.* Philadelphia: Fortress Press, 1988.

Lerner, Gerda. *The Creation of Patriarchy.* Oxford: Oxford University, 1986.

Meyers, Carol. *Discovering Eve: Ancient Israelite Women in Context.* New York: Oxford University Press, 1988.

Plaskow, Judith. *Standing Again at Sinai: Judaism from a Feminist Perspective.* San Francisco: Harper & Row, 1991.

Sakenfeld, Katherine Dobb. "Feminist Uses of Biblical Materials." In *Feminist Interpretation of the Bible.* Ed. Letty M. Russell, pp. 55–64. Philadelphia: Westminster, 1985.

———. *Just Wives? Stories of Power and Survival in the Old Testament and Today.* Louisville, KY: Westminster John Knox Press, 2003.

Stanton, Elizabeth Cady, ed. *The Woman's Bible.* 2 vols. New York: European Publishing Company, 1895–1898.

Stone, Ken. "Gender Criticism: The Un-Manning of Abimelech." In *Judges and Method. New Approaches in Biblical Studies.* 2nd ed., edited by Gale A. Yee, pp. 183–201. Minneapolis: Fortress Press, 2007.

Tamez, Elsa, *Bible of the Oppressed.* Maryknoll, NY: Orbis, 1986.

Trible, Phyllis. "Depatriarchalizing in Biblical Interpretation." *JAAR* 41 (1973) 30–48.

———. *God and the Rhetoric of Sexuality.* Overtures to Biblical Theology. Philadelphia: Fortress Press, 1978.

———. *Texts of Terror. Literary-Feminist Readings of Biblical Narratives.* Overtures to Biblical Theology. Philadelphia: Fortress Press, 1984.

Weems, Renita J. *Just A Sister Away: A Womanist Vision of Women's Relationships in the Bible.* San Diego, CA: LuraMedia, 1988.

Williams, Delores S. "The Color of Feminism: Or Speaking the Black Woman's Tongue." *Journal of Religious Thought* 43 (1986): 42–57.

———. *Sisters in the Wilderness: The Challenge of Womanist God-Talk.* Maryknoll, NY: Orbis Books, 1993.

Feminist Criticism of Exodus

Burns, Rita. *Has the Lord Indeed Spoken Only Through Moses: A Study of the Biblical Portrait of Miriam.* Atlanta: Scholars Press, 1987.

Clines, David J. A. "The Ten Commandments, Reading from Left to Right." In *Words Remembered. Essays in Honour of John F.A. Sawyer,* edited by Jon Davies, Graham Harvey and Wilfred G. E. Watson, pp. 97–112. JSOTSup 195. Sheffield: Sheffield Academic Press, 1995.

Exum, J. Cheryl. "'You Shall Let Every Daughter Live': A Study of Exodus 1:8–2:10." *Semeia* 28 (1983) 63–82. Reprinted in *A Feminist Companion to Exodus to Deuteronomy,* edited by Athalya Brenner, pp. 37–61. Sheffield: Sheffield Academic Press, 1994.

———. "Second Thoughts about Secondary Characters: Women in Exodus 1:8–2:10." In *A Feminist Companion to Exodus to Deuteronomy,* edited by Athalya Brenner, pp. 75–87. Sheffield: Sheffield Academic Press, 1994.

Fuchs, Esther. "A Jewish-Feminist Reading of Exodus 1–2." In *Jews, Christians, and the Theology of the Hebrew Scriptures,* edited by Alice Ogden Bellis and Joel S. Kaminsky, pp. 307–26. Symposium 8. Atlanta: Society of Biblical Literature, 2000.

Meyers, Carol. *Exodus.* The New Cambridge Bible Commentary. Cambridge: Cambridge University Press, 2005.

Setel, Drorah O'Donnell. "Exodus." In *The Women's Bible Commentary,* edited by Carol Newsom and Sharon H. Ringe, pp. 26–35. Louisville, KY: Westminster/John Knox Press, 1992.

'Siebert-Hommes, Jopie. "But If She Be a Daughter . . . She May Live! 'Daughters' and 'Sons' in Exodus 1–2." In *A Feminist Companion to Exodus to Deuteronomy*, edited by Athalya Brenner, pp. 62–74. Sheffield: Sheffield Academic Press, 1994.

Trible, Phyllis. "Bring Miriam Out of the Shadows," *BR* 5 (1989): 13–25, 34.

Weems, Renita J. "The Hebrew Women Are Not like the Egyptian Women: The Ideology of Race, Gender and Sexual Reproduction in Exodus 1." In *Ideological Criticism of Biblical Texts*, edited by David Jobling and Tina Pippin. *Semeia* 59 (1992): 25–34.

6

↓

Postcolonial Biblical Criticism

GALE A. YEE

Accessible on the Web is a humorous map depicting "The World According to America."[1] The United States was, of course, at the center of this map. Mexico was a tiny orange splotch, inhabited by "smelly people with big hats." Red blobs representing Cuba, China, and Russia were labeled "Commies," with the helpful definition that "Commies are our enemies they must be destroyed." The whole continent of "Yurop" was reduced to a small island. Latin America and Africa became purple smudges that contained "No civilisation [sic]. People eat each other here." The Arctic Circle was merely a cold place where Santa lives.

The modern Western empires of Britain, Spain, France, and Portugal regarded the Asian, African, and Latin American colonies that they seized and exploited in similar ways as this map. Postcolonial theorist Edward Said identified the Western representation and so-called knowledge about non-Western countries, for example, "People eat each other here," as Orientalism.[2] Similar to the distortions and denigrations of Mexico, "Yurop," and other places in "The World According to America," non-Western lands, cultures, and peoples were depicted by the West as the inferior Other: ignorant, dangerous, morally corrupt, and savage. Under the pretext of bringing "civilization" to their colonies, Western imperial nations rationalized their brutal conquest and predatory extraction of their colonies' natural and human resources. It is the conflicted unequal relations between colonizer and colonized that are the focus of postcolonial studies as an academic endeavor.

---

[1] http://www.msxnet.org/humour/world-according-to-america.png.
[2] Edward W. Said, *Orientalism. With Afterword* (1978; repr., New York: Vintage Books, 1994).

POSTCOLONIAL CRITICISM AND POSTCOLONIAL THEORY

As with many of the newer exegetical methods adopted by biblical scholars, such as narrative criticism, structuralism, and deconstruction, postcolonial[3] studies emerged in the field of literature. Specifically, from the 1950s onward commonwealth literature described the writings in English produced in settler countries, such as New Zealand and Australia, and in nations, such as India and Africa, with histories of Western colonialism. Studies in commonwealth literature laid the foundation for different developments of postcolonial studies. Moore-Gilbert helpfully distinguishes between postcolonial criticism and postcolonial theory. *Postcolonial criticism* is a group of reading strategies examining economic, cultural, and political relations of domination and subordination between nations, races, and cultures with histories of colonial and neocolonial[4] rule. Postcolonial critics would include C. R. James, Aimé Césaire, Albert Memmi, and Franz Fanon, whose analyses were often informed by Marxist theory. *Postcolonial theory*, on the other hand, is particularly influenced by the French theorists Jacques Derrida, Jacques Lacan, and Michel Foucault. The big names in postcolonial theory, deemed the "Holy Trinity" by one scholar, are Edward Said, Gayatri Chakravorty Spivak, and Homi Bhabha.[5]

It is the incursion of this "high" French theory into postcolonial studies that has produced the most heated debates in the academic guild. In a piercing review of Spivak's *A Critique of Post-Colonial Reason*, Terry Eagleton wryly observes that a secret handbook for postcolonial critics must prescribe a rule that one should "Be as obscurantist as you can decently get away with."[6] Deciphering the dense and tortuous prose of

---

[3] Nowadays, scholars prefer the unhyphenated form of "postcolonial" rather than the hyphenated "post-colonial," which suggests a temporal or ideological discontinuity from colonial times. The beliefs, practices, and structures of oppressive colonial systems do not completely disappear when the colonizers leave a country. See Anne McClintock, "The Angel of Progress: Pitfalls of the Term 'Post-Colonialism'," *Social Text* 31/32 (1992): 84–98 and Ella Shohat, "Notes on the 'Post-Colonial'," *Social Text* 31/32 (1992): 99–113.

[4] Neocolonialism refers to the replication of colonial rule and exploitation by an indigenous elite brought to power in a newly independent nation that has thrown off its Western colonizer.

[5] Bart Moore-Gilbert, *Postcolonial Theory: Contexts, Practices, Politics* (London and New York: Verso, 1997), 1–33. The term "Holy Trinity" was applied by Robert J. C. Young, *Colonial Desire: Hybridity in Theory, Culture and Race* (Routledge, 1995), 163.

[6] Terry Eagleton, "In the Gaudy Supermarket," *London Review of Book* 21, no. 10 (1999). Online: http://www.lrb.co.uk/v21/n10/print/eagle01_.html.

theorists, like Spivak and Bhabha, can be quite challenging for even the most sophisticated reader, becoming occasions for critique and parody. Bhabha was the runner-up in the 1998 Bad Writing Contest sponsored by the journal *Philosophy and Literature*.[7] Spivak was undoubtedly the target for the character Lavatri Alltheorie, a certain diasporic Indian academic, described as a "Post-modern theoretician, boa deconstructor, discourse analyst, post-structuralist critic, feminist historian of subalternity, colonialism and gender" in Rukun Advani's novel *Beethoven among the Cows*.[8] Russell Jacoby declares, "While post-colonial studies claims to be subversive and profound, the politics tends to be banal; the language jargonized; the radical one-upmanship infantile; the self-obsession tiresome; and the theory bloated."[9]

Nevertheless, by adding the category of imperial/colonial relations into the analysis of the biblical text, postcolonial criticism *and* theory become important methodological tools for interpreting the Bible, which was compiled and produced primarily under imperial auspices. According to Said, *imperialism* is the "practice, the theory, and the attitudes of a dominating metropolitan center ruling a distant territory," while *colonialism* "almost always a consequence of imperialism, is the implanting of settlements on a distant territory."[10]

Because of Israel's strategic position at the crossroads of ancient superpowers, the empires in the Mediterranean basin, such as Egypt, Assyria, Babylonia, Persia, Greece, and Rome, exerted their often harsh imperial control over Israel's territories at different times during its long history. Postcolonial biblical criticism therefore analyzes the factors of economic and cultural expansion, domination, and exploitation as major forces in the production of the biblical texts under the colonial rule of different empires in antiquity. It seeks to determine the range and nature of Israel's relations with the empires that governed them, from passive assent, collusion, and/or resistance. It endeavors to uncover the subaltern or marginalized lives and voices that suffered under imperial rule. It

---

[7] http://www.denisdutton.com/bad_writing.htm.

[8] Cited in Sugirtharajah, R. S., "A Postcolonial Exploration of Collusion and Construction in Biblical Interpretation," in *The Postcolonial Bible* (ed. Sugirtharajah, R. S.; Sheffield: Sheffield Academic Press, 1998), 113.

[9] Russell Jacoby, "Marginal Returns. The Trouble with Post-Colonial Theory," *Lingua Franca* 5, no. Sept./Oct. (1995): 37.

[10] Edward W. Said, *Culture and Imperialism* (New York: Vintage Books, 1993), 9. See also Ania Loomba, *Colonialism/Post-Colonialism* (New York: Routledge, 1998), 1–19.

investigates the reception history of both the oppressive use of the Bible in the interests of Western imperialism and colonial expansion and its liberative use to oppose these interests. Just as feminist and liberation criticisms in this volume highlight gender and economic class, respectively, postcolonial criticism foregrounds the unequal and exploitative relations between the imperial and the colonial in ancient and modern times.[11]

Stephen D. Moore provides a convenient list of phenomena relevant to biblical studies that overlap with postcolonial criticism and theory:

imperialism, Orientalism, universalism, expansionism, exploration, invasion, enslavement, settlement, resistance, revolt, terrorism, nationalism, nativism, negritude, assimilation, creolization, hybridization, colonial mimicry, the subaltern, marginalization, migration, diasporization, decolonization, globalization and neo-colonialism – all intersected by the ubiquitous determinants of language, gender, race, ethnicity, and class.[12]

I will discuss some of the less familiar items on this list that have been incorporated already in postcolonial biblical studies, and which are pertinent for my later examination of Exodus 1–2 and 19–20 and their reception history.

Orientalism

In his groundbreaking work, *Orientalism*, Said investigates how European powers constructed a literary and cultural universe divided between the Occident and the Orient, between the West and the Rest, between "us" versus "them." This binary opposition between colonizer and colonized was asymmetrical, with official power residing in the former. It assigned all positive attributes of racial, moral, intellectual, cultural, and technological superiority to the West, and all deficits in these areas to the Rest. Orientalism branded the Orient as static, foreign, seductive, and dangerous. It is not surprising therefore that the Orient was often

[11] For a thorough discussion of the various definitions of postcolonial criticism with respect to biblical studies, see Fernando F. Segovia, "Mapping the Postcolonial Optic in Biblical Criticism: Meaning and Scope," in *Postcolonial Biblical Criticism: Interdisciplinary Intersections* (eds. Stephen D. Moore, and Fernando F. Segovia; London and New York: T & T Clark International, 2005), 23–78.
[12] Stephen D. Moore, "Postcolonialism," in *Handbook of Postmodern Biblical Interpretation* (ed. A. K. M. Adam; St. Louis: Chalice Press, 2000), 185–86.

typified metaphorically as feminine, while the West was cast as masculine. And like women in male fantasy, the lands of the Orient were thus ripe for conquest, domestication, and exploitation.[13] Orientalism permeated all areas of Western scholarship in the humanities and social sciences, implicating even the study of biblical languages and literature.[14]

Said's work has been criticized for making sweeping judgments about the long history of Western discourse, totalizing the dichotomy between Orient and Occident into a fixed and static East/West divide. Said did not account in *Orientalism* for the various historical expressions of political and cultural resistance against colonization, depriving colonized peoples of their agency and voice. Moreover, he did not consider the advocates of anticolonial resistance within the West itself, leveling all Europeans as racist, imperialistic, and totally ethnocentric.[15] Although Said was aware of the feminization of the East in male Western discourse, he did not examine the discourse of Western women and their attitudes and positions as colonials, which may have differed from colonial men. Nor did Said include colonized women in relation to their own menfolk and to their male and female colonizers. By overlooking agency among the colonized, Said inadvertently privileges and empowers the Orientalism that he tries to dismantle.[16]

Stereotyping, Mimicry, and Hybridity

These critiques of Said set the stage for postcolonial theory to wrestle with the question of agency among the colonized. One of the major features of colonial relations is the racial stereotyping of the colonized by their colonizers as the inferior Other. In his major work, *Location of Culture*,[17] Homi Bhabha explores the psychosocial dynamics of stereotyping through his understanding of the basic *ambivalence* or contradictions at the heart of colonial relations of dominance and subordination.

[13] Said, *Orientalism*, 182–90.
[14] Ibid., 17–18, 74–77, 134–7.
[15] Ibid., 204.
[16] For an extended critique of Said's work, see Moore-Gilbert, *Postcolonial Theory*, 34–73. Also, John McLeod, *Beginning Postcolonialism* (Manchester and New York: Manchester University Press, 2000), 46–50.
[17] Homi K. Bhabha, *The Location of Culture. With a New Preface by the Author* (London and New York: Routledge, 1994).

According to Bhabha, the colonizer constructs racist stereotypes in order
to justify its conquest and rule, depicting "the colonized as a social reality
which is at once an 'other' and yet entirely knowable and visible."[18] The
colonizer attempts to create a colonial object that is completely different
from itself, with respect to intelligence, moral superiority and so forth,
yet remains still "knowable" and recognizable.

Stereotyping is not the setting up of a false image which becomes the scape-
goat of discriminatory practices. It is a much more ambivalent text of projection and introjection, metaphoric and metonymic strategies, displacement,
over-determination, guilt, aggressivity; the masking and splitting of 'official'
and phantasmatic knowledges to construct the positionalities and opposi-
tionalities of racist discourse.[19]

On the one hand, stereotypes make the Other familiar and knowable:
"Africans are all cannibals." "The Indians are lazy and shiftless." "The
Chinese are dishonest." On the other hand, stereotypes are meant to distance the colonizer from the colonized as different, since to acknowledge
any similarity with the peoples they rule would challenge the colonial
order. In order to maintain that distance, their colonizers must in all their
dealings with their subjects continually repeat and sustain the fiction of
these racist stereotypes, producing an anxiety that their dominance is
not as stable as it seems.

As a form of splitting and multiple belief, the stereotype requires, for its successful signification, a continual and repetitive chain of other stereotypes.
The process by which the metaphoric "masking" is inscribed on a lack which
must then be concealed gives the stereotype both its fixity and its phantasmatic quality – the *same old* stories of the Negro's animality, the Coolie's
inscrutability or the stupidity of the Irish must be told (compulsively) again
and afresh, and are differently gratifying and terrifying each time.[20]

It is this ambivalence and anxiety on the part of the colonizers that opens
a space for agency which can be exploited by the colonized.

   One must reassess Rudyard Kipling's imperial declaration "East is East,
and West is West, and never the twain shall meet," in light of Bhabha's
theories on mimicry and hybridity. Here, the borders between the Orient

[18]   Ibid., 101.
[19]   Ibid., 117.
[20]   Ibid., pp. 110–11.

and the Occident, which Said seemingly regarded as entrenched, become fractured and blurred. Where East and West do meet and overlap opens up a space for resistance against colonial discourse. As a springboard to the discussion, let us first consider Thomas Macaulay's "Minute on Indian Education," arguing in 1835 for the education of an indigenous class to assist Britain's colonial rule in India:

It is impossible for us, with our limited means, to attempt to educate the body of the people. We must at present do our best to form a class who may be interpreters between us and the millions whom we govern; a class of persons, Indian in blood and colour, but English in taste, in opinions, in morals, and in intellect. To that class we may leave it to refine the vernacular dialects of the country, to enrich those dialects with terms of science borrowed from the Western nomenclature, and to render them by degrees fit vehicles for conveying knowledge to the great mass of the population.[21]

Colonizers want to create an educated class of "mimic men" to assist them in their dominance over the people. Building upon his insight into the ambivalence at the heart of colonial relations, Bhabha describes colonial mimicry as "the desire for a reformed, recognizable Other, *as a subject of a difference that is almost the same, but not quite.*"[22] Colonizers want their subjects to be similar to them in matters of taste, opinions, morals and intellect, *but* in no way identical. Otherwise, the hierarchical barriers separating the superior Us versus the inferior Them would topple. This "ironic compromise" however allows for the unintended possibility for the mimicry of the colonized to slip into mockery and threat: "mimicry is at once resemblance and menace."[23] The trappings of the colonizers, their language, customs, traditions, and so forth, can become tools by which the colonized can create their own challenges to colonial identity and authority. The image Bhabha effectively uses to describe this phenomenon is a photographic negative, which reverses the image it mirrors in a distorted or displaced manner that estranges it from the original.[24] In essence, the colonized subject returns the colonizer's gaze, threatening the "narcissistic demand of colonial authority": "The *menace* of mimicry

[21] Macaulay in Bill Ashcroft, Gareth Griffiths, and Helen Tiffin, eds., *The Post-Colonial Studies Reader* (New York: Routledge, 1995), 430.
[22] Bhabha, *Location of Culture,* 122, *italics* in the text.
[23] Ibid., 123.
[24] Ibid., 157.

is its *double* vision which in disclosing the ambivalence of colonial discourse also disrupts it authority."[25] We will see shortly how stereotypes,
mimicry, and mockery can profitably illumine Exodus 1–2.

Along with ambivalence and mimicry, the third Bhabhian concept that
disrupts the colonizer/colonized binary and allows for agency among the
oppressed is *hybridity*. For Bhabha, the identities of both colonizer and
colonized are never completely "pure," even though colonial discourse
devotes considerable energy to generating ideologies and institutions
that prescribe essential differences between the two. Both cultures react
and interact in a continual interdependent process of mixing in what
Bhabha calls a "third space." Here in this liminal interstice, the identities
of both systems become fluid, partaking of each other in ways that
undermine and destabilize former beliefs and practices that determine
colonial status and orders of precedence.[26] It is through these in-between
spaces, the contact zones where East and West overlap, that the colonized
can disrupt, challenge, and intimidate the colonizer's efforts to construct
a national script dictating their subordinate place within it. "Hybridity
represents that ambivalent 'turn' of the discriminated subject into the
terrifying, exorbitant object of paranoid classification – a disturbing
questioning of the images and presences of authority."[27] An obvious
example of resistance emerging from hybridity in India is the use of
spoken and written English among the colonized natives to challenge
the oppressive rule of the British colonizing classes. In "Signs Taken for
Wonders," Bhabha demonstrates how native Indians appropriated the
Bible, meant to be a British propaganda tool, and subverted its teachings
in ways that were not foreseen by their colonizers.[28]

Bhabha's theories are valuable in reminding us of the interconnect-
edness or relationality between the colonizer and colonized. Although
the power differential between them is considerable, the two are not
independent of each other, and therefore their identities are continually

---

[25] Ibid., 126, *italics* in the text.
[26] Homi K. Bhabha, "The Third Space: Interview with Homi Bhabha," in *Identity:
Community, Culture, and Difference* (ed. Jonathan Rutherford; London: Lawrence
and Wishart, 1990), 211 (207–221). Online: http://www.wsp-kultur.uni-bremen.de/
summerschool/download%20ss%202006/The%20Third%20Space.%20Interview%20
with%20Homi%20Bhabha.pdf. Also, Bhabha, *Location of Culture*, 53–5.
[27] Bhabha, *Location of Culture*, 162.
[28] Ibid., 145–74.

unstable and in constant flux. Bhabha's theories, however, are not with-out their problems. Mimicry seems to function among the colonized pri-marily at the level of the unconscious, and therefore cannot become the basis for a conscious program of resistance against colonial oppression.[29] Hybridity assumes that nonhybrid cultures exist, which has not been demonstrated. If all cultures are characterized in some way by hybridity and liminality, Bhabha's theory of hybridity can lose its conceptual force. Moreover, hybridity and mimicry can work on behalf of the dominant.[30] Consider Macaulay's call for an educated class of Indians who will mediate between the British colonizers and the Indian masses. We will encounter a similar situation with the returning exiles to Yehud (Judah), who become agents for the Persian empire, enabling Persia's exploitation of the colony and profiting from it.

Critiques of Postcolonial Theory

A major criticism, not simply of Bhabha, but of postcolonial *theory* in general, is its inability to deal with the world of global capitalism in its adoption of the French theories of Derrida and Foucault. Instead of viewing language as a medium that reflects reality, these theories argue that reality is actually an "effect" of language and the world is primarily a *textual* product. However, the world is more than a fragmentary "text" or "discourse." By staying at the level of discourse analysis, these theories overlook the material ways in which economic and social conditions remain a fundamental reality and have a major say in how we live our lives. In short, they often disregard the issue of class in their analyses.[31] They reject master-narratives such as Marxism, which have played a significant

---

[29] Moore-Gilbert, *Postcolonial Theory*, 133.

[30] Ibid.

[31] This is particularly the complaint of Aijaz Ahmad, *In Theory: Classes, Nations, Litera-ture* (London: Verso, 1992) and Benita Parry, *Postcolonial Studies: A Materialist Critique* (London: Routledge, 2004) against postcolonial theory. See also the critique of biblical scholars on this anti-Marxist propensity in postcolonial theory: Roland Boer, "Marx, Postcolonialism, and the Bible," in *Postcolonial Biblical Criticism: Interdisciplinary Inter-sections* (eds. Stephen D. Moore, and Fernando F. Segovia; London and New York: T & T Clark International, 2005), 166–83; and David Jobling, "Very Limited Ideological Options: Marxism and Biblical Studies in Postcolonial Scenes," in *Postcolonial Bibli-cal Criticism: Interdisciplinary Intersections* (eds. Stephen D. Moore, and Fernando F. Segovia; London and New York: T & T Clark International, 2005), 184–201.

role in anticolonial and antiracist struggles, at the very moment when such oppositional discourses are needed to contend with economic and social inequalities and exploitation in a world of global capital.

By throwing the cover of culture over material relationships, as if the one had little to do with the other, such a [Postcolonialist] focus diverts the task of criticism from the criticism of capitalism to the criticism of Eurocentric ideology, which helps disguise its own ideological limitation but also, ironically, provides an alibi for inequality, exploitation, and oppression in their modern guises under capitalist relationships.[32]

Besides the category of class, Bhabha, like Said, has been guilty of skirting the issue of gender in his analysis. The literature on the feminist analysis of gender in postcolonial studies is extensive, rich, and impossible to cover in this brief overview.[33] Let us build on the chapter of feminist criticism in this volume. In contrast to white middle-class Western women, colonized women experience multiple oppressions, two

[32] Arif Dirlik, "The Postcolonial Aura: Third World Criticism in the Age of Global Capitalism," in *Dangerous Liaisons: Gender, Nation, and Postcolonial Perspectives* (eds. Anne McClintock, Aamir Mufti, and Ella Shohat; Minneapolis: University of Minnesota Press, 1997), 515–16.

[33] A good place to start for theory is Reina Lewis and Sara Mills, eds., *Feminist Postcolonial Theory: A Reader* (Edinburgh: Edinburgh University Press, 2003). I have profited from Anne McClintock, *Imperial Leather. Race, Gender, and Sexuality in the Colonial Contest* (New York: Routledge, 1995); Ann Laura Stoler, *Carnal Knowledge and Imperial Power: Race and the Intimate in Colonial Rule* (Berkeley, CA: University of California Press, 2002); Anne McClintock, Aamir Mufti, and Ella Shohat, eds., *Dangerous Liaisons: Gender, Nation, & Postcolonial Perspectives* (Minneapolis: University of Minnesota, 1997); Uma Narayan, *Dislocating Cultures: Identities, Traditions, and Third World Feminism* (New York and London: Routledge, 1997); Rey Chow, *The Protestant Ethnic & the Spirit of Capitalism* (New York: Columbia University Press, 2002); Laura E. Donaldson, *Decolonizing Feminisms: Race, Gender, & Empire Building* (Chapel Hill & London: University of North Carolina Press, 1992); Revathi Krishnaswamy, *Effeminism: The Economy of Colonial Desire* (Ann Arbor: University of Michigan Press, 1998); Meyda Yegenoglu, *Colonial Fantasies: Towards a Feminist Reading of Orientalism* (New York: Cambridge University Press, 1998); Chandra Talpade Mohanty, *Feminism Without Borders: Decolonizing Theory, Practicing Solidarity* (Durham, NC: Duke University Press, 2003), which includes her important essay, "Under Western Eyes: Feminist Scholarship and Colonial Discourses" as well as a response to it sixteen years later. One of the foremost feminist postcolonial theorists is Gayatri Spivak, especially her essay, "Can the Subaltern Speak?," in *Colonial Discourse and Post-Colonial Theory: A Reader* (eds. Patrick Williams, and Laura Chrisman; New York: Columbia University Press, 1994), 66–111 (1988), not easy reading but important. Also, Gayatri Chakravorty Spivak, *In Other Worlds: Essays in Cultural Politics* (New York and London: Routledge, 1988).

under the racism and classicism of colonialism, the third under the sexism of patriarchy. These oppressions are exhibited in their material lives as the wives of colonized men who have their own nativist forms of sexist beliefs and practices, and as the domestic and oftentimes sexual servants of colonial men and women with their arrogant attitudes of superiority and dominance.

These subjugations are manifested in ideological representations of colonized women by the West. In art, for example, a popular colonial fantasy of Orientalist painters of the Middle East are the harem and baths, where supposedly indolent carnal women primp and beautify themselves for the sexual whims of one man. No European males had firsthand experience of the harem or witnessed naked female voluptuaries in Turkish baths, but that did not stop them from depicting a place of erotic availability. Those who claimed to have gained entry into a harem or bath were no doubt gullibly taken in by their "dragoman" (guide) to a bordello.[34] Much more sinister are the Orientalist depictions of slave markets, in which nude females are erotically posed,[35] belying the unspeakable conditions female slaves endured. The "real" lives of these women under both colonization and patriarchy become invisible in these representations. Middle Eastern women are not the only victims of the colonial gaze. Sander Gilman analyzes the trope of the sexualized African and other dark-skinned woman in nineteenth-century European art, who are often portrayed as servants or slaves to the lighter colored women in the harem, bath, or brothel. Particularly notorious was the prurient exhibition of the Hottentot Venus with her exaggerated buttocks and genitalia.[36] These Orientalist stereotypes of non-Western women

---

[34] Joan DelPlato, *Multiple Wives, Multiple Pleasures: Representing the Harem, 1800–1875* (Madison, NJ: Fairleigh Dickinson University Press, 2002). Christine Peltre, *Orientalism in Art* (trans. John Goodman; New York: Abbeville Press, 1998), pp. 46–47, 87, 126, 200–01, 202, 210–11; 187; and the plates in Reina Lewis, *Gendering Orientalism: Race, Femininity and Representation* (Gender, Racism, Ethnicity; London and New York: Routledge, 1996); Rana Kabbani, *Imperial Fictions: Europe's Myths of Orient* (rev. and exp. ed.; London: Pandora, 1994).

[35] For example, Jean Léon Gerome, "Selling Slaves in Rome," 1886 and his "Slave Market," 1866. Also Edwin Long's "Babylonian Marriage Market," 1875.

[36] Sander L. Gilman, "Black Bodies, White Bodies: Toward an Iconography of Female Sexuality in Late Nineteeth-Century Art, Medicine, and Literature," *Critical Inquiry* 12, no. 1 (1985): 204–42.

"body forth two ideological assumptions about power: one about men's power over women; the other about white men's superiority to, hence justifiable control over, inferior, darker races."[37] Such racialized gender stereotypes are linked to and imbedded in projects of on-going racial and economic domination.

Postcolonial Studies and Biblical Studies

Since the late 1990s, biblical scholars have taken up the insights and tools of both postcolonial criticism and theory, primarily in the field of New Testament,[38] although scholars of the Hebrew Bible are catching up.[39] Two volumes of the journal *Semeia* and a volume of *Biblical Interpretation* were devoted to postcolonial analyses of the Bible.[40] Stephen Moore provides an excellent annotated bibliography, not only of postcolonial biblical

[37] Linda Nochlin, "The Imaginary Orient," *Art in America* 71, no. 5 (1983): 125.
[38] See Sugirtharajah, Segovia, Moore, Kwok, and Dube in the Bibliography for this chapter.
[39] See Boer, Brett, Kim, McKinlay, Runions, and Whitelam in the Bibliography for this chapter. Significant articles and essays adopting Postcolonial methods in Hebrew Bible include Jon L. Berquist, "Postcolonialism and Imperial Motives for Canonization," *Semeia* 75 (1996): 15–35; Mark G. Brett, "Genocide in Deuteronomy: Postcolonial Variations on Mimetic Desire," in *Seeing Signals, Reading Signs: The Art of Exegesis. Studies in Honour of Antony F. Campbell, SJ for His Seventieth Birthday* (eds. Mark A. O'Brien, and Howard N. Wallace; London & New York: T & T Clark/Continuum, 2004), 75–89; Laura E. Donaldson, "The Sign of Orpah: Reading Ruth Through Native Eyes," in *Ruth and Esther. A Feminist Companion to the Bible* (ed. Athalya Brenner; Second Series ed.; Sheffield: Sheffield Academic Press, 1999), 131–44; Jin Hee Han, "Homi K. Bhabha and the Mixed Blessing of Hybridity in Biblical Hermeneutics," *The Bible and Critical Theory* 1, no. 4 (2005): 37.1–37.12; Katherine Doob Sakenfeld, "Postcolonial Perspectives on Premonarchic Women," in *To Break Every Yoke: Essays in Honor of Marvin L. Chaney* (eds. Robert B. Coote, and Norman K. Gottwald; Sheffield: Sheffield Phoenix Press, 2007), 188–199; Daniel Smith-Christopher, "Ezekiel on Fanon's Couch: A Postcolonialist Dialogue with David Halperin's *Seeking Ezekiel*," in *Peace and Justice Shall Embrace. Power and Theopolitics in the Bible: Essays in Honor of Millard Lind* (eds. Ted Grimsrud, and Loren L. Johns; Telford, PA: Pandora, 1999), 108–44; Gerald West, "Finding a Place Among the Posts for Post-Colonial Criticism in Biblical Studies in South Africa," *OTE* 10 (1997): 322–42; and the postcolonial analyses on Ezekiel 23 and Proverbs 7 in Gale A. Yee, *Poor Banished Children of Eve: Woman As Evil in the Hebrew Bible* (Minneapolis, MN: Fortress, 2003), 111–58.
[40] Laura E. Donaldson, ed., *Postcolonialism and Scriptural Reading* (*Semeia* 75; Atlanta: Society of Biblical Literature, 1996); Roland Boer, ed., *A Vanishing Mediator? The Presence/Absence of the Bible in Postcolonialism* (*Semeia* 88; Atlanta: Society of Biblical Literature, 2001); Archie C. C. Lee, "Returning to China: Biblical Interpretation in Postcolonial Hong Kong," *BibInt* 7, no. 2 (1999): 156–73, with responses by Philip Chia, Pui-Lan Kwok, Katherine Doob Sakenfeld, and Fernando Segovia, with a rejoinder by Lee.

criticism but also of some of the major works in postcolonial studies.[41] The postcolonial analysis of the Bible emerged particularly with the insertion and challenge of voices from the so-called Third World in the academic guild, many of whom interpreted the biblical text from out of their postcolonial or neocolonial contexts. With their shared concern for the preferential option for the poor, postcolonial biblical criticism is sympathetic to the liberation hermeneutics which influenced much of these contextual interpretations that is described by Professor Pixley in the volume. However, it goes beyond the focus on the economic poor of liberation hermeneutics to embrace those marginalized by gender, sexuality, race, ethnicity, culture, colonialism, and religion, particularly indigenous groups which the Christianity of the colonizers oppressed and tried to rub out.

Postcolonial criticism falls under the general category of ideological criticism, whose various approaches highlight and theorize the inequities of power in different types of relations. For example, feminist criticism addresses gender disparities. Liberation criticism focuses on economic and class differentials. Minority criticism explores the categories of race and ethnicity. Sexuality and sexual orientation are spotlighted by queer criticism. The special focus of postcolonial biblical criticism is the power relations and disparities between empire and colony, between center and periphery. The particular focus of the different criticisms does not mean that the other categories of analysis are ignored. In fact, the "isms" of racism, classism, sexism, and colonialism interconnect, implicate, and reinforce each other in a cruel web of domination. Because of its emphasis on imperial/colonial relations and its multifaceted attentiveness to matters such as gender, race, and class, postcolonial biblical criticism must incorporate these other critical approaches to accomplish its task.

Fernando Segovia helpfully outlines three focal points of postcolonial biblical criticism.[42] The first is that of the *biblical text itself*. Throughout the course of its history, ancient Israel had various and often antagonistic relations with different empires of southwest Asia, also known from

[41] Stephen D. Moore, *Empire and Apocalypse: Postcolonialism and the New Testament* (Bible in the Modern World 12; Sheffield: Sheffield Phoenix Press, 2006), 124–51.
[42] Fernando F. Segovia, "Biblical Criticism and Postcolonial Studies: Toward a Postcolonial Optic," in *The Postcolonial Bible* (ed. R. S. Sugirtharajah; Sheffield: Sheffield Academic Press, 1998), 156–63.

a colonialist Eurocentric perspective as "the ancient Near East." These empires include Egypt, Assyria, Babylonia, Persia, Greece, and (for the New Testament) Rome. Their socioeconomic and cultural domination of Israel makes it an excellent subject for postcolonial scrutiny. The stories of the Hebrew Bible narrate Israel enduring the different structures of imperial control in the course of its history, each with its particular brand of oppressive rule. Certain questions occupy the critic at this stage. Keeping in mind the long traditioning process in which the texts may pass through different imperial contexts, a critic can ask:

- What is the material and economic context of the colonies and how does it affect the production of the text and its ideologies under colonialism?
- What groups produced these texts under this imperial setting?
- What is the relation of these groups to others and to the center?
- How does the text reflect imperial concerns?
- Whose interests does the text serve: the center or the periphery?
- How does the text depict the nation of Israel as a people?
- Who or what threatens the identity of Israel and how is it dealt with?
- What are the subaltern voices suppressed by the text?
- What are the rationales provided in the biblical story for conquest, domination, exile, diaspora, and return that exhibit imperial control?
- How does the text collude with empire? How does the text resist empire?
- Are there instances of hybridity and mimicry in colonial Israel?
- What are the stereotypes of the inferior Other in the text (gender, racial, religious, etc.) and how do they function with respect to imperial domination?
- How does the text deal with difference, real or imaginary?

The second dimension of postcolonial criticism involves *the reception history (history of interpretation) of the biblical text* in the context of the imperial tradition of the West. This history stretches from the early stages of European conquest and expansion in the fifteenth century, continuing through the high imperialism of the end of the nineteenth to the middle of the twentieth, up to the present neocolonial period of global capitalism. Western economic and political expansion heavily involved a religious and cultural colonialism, in which the Bible was a major component in the evangelization of Asia, Africa, and the Americas, in many ways legitimizing the suffering and destruction of indigenous peoples.[43] Thus accompanying the center/periphery binary are the dualities of believer/unbeliever, true God/idol, religious/idolatrous, educated/ignorant, and civilized/savage, in which religious and cultural differences in colonies are derided and/or abolished. At this stage, a postcolonial biblical critic investigates the myriad textual (re)interpretations of the biblical text that may support or resist the workings of empire. These may be found in sermons, laws, chronicles, diaries, political and religious tracts, colonial myths and histories, and many other forms of Western textual discourse. Questions posed at this level are:

- Who wrote these (re)interpretations and how are their authors mapped according to gender, race, ethnicity, religion, occupation, and so forth?
- How has the Bible been used to religiously sanction the conquest and seizure of lands in the interests of imperial expansionism?
- Are colonized or indigenous peoples equated with the enemies of Israel? If so, what roles do gender, race, and class play in the characterization of the colonized or indigenous?
- Are there voices utilizing the Bible to resist this expansionism and colonization?
- How are Western biblical scholars themselves implicated during this phase in interpreting the Bible from the standpoints of Western expansions and attitudes of superiority?

Given the Bible's pervasive presence and influence in colonial discourse, there is a relative absence of investigations on the Bible's role in colonialism in both postcolonial criticism and theory.[44] Thus, postcolonial studies of the biblical text and its reception history offer many rich opportunities for the scholar.

---

[43] Michael Prior, CM., *The Bible and Colonialism: A Moral Critique* (The Biblical Seminar 48; Sheffield: Sheffield Academic Press, 1997); R. S. Sugirtharajah, "Charting the Aftermath: A Review of Postcolonial Criticism," in *The Postcolonial Biblical Reader* (ed. R. S. Sugirtharajah; Malden, MA: Blackwell, 2006) (2001).

[44] This is the complaint of Roland Boer, "Home Is Always Elsewhere: Exodus, Exile and the Howling Wilderness Waste," in Last Stop Before Antarctica: The Bible and Postcolonialism in Australia (2nd ed.; Atlanta: Society of Biblical Literature, 2008), 81–107, who tries to rectify this lacuna with his edited volume, *Vanishing Mediator?* (*Semeia* 88; Atlanta: Society of Biblical Literature, 2001).

The third level examined by postcolonial biblical critics is that of *real "flesh and blood" readers of the Bible* and their global contexts (Western and non-Western). As already noted, interpreters from the so-called Third World have confronted the dominant Western hold on biblical interpretation and have issued their own readings from the margins that disturb and challenge the center. These readers are joined by Western women and sympathetic men, and male and female racial and ethnic minorities in the West in destabilizing and deconstructing traditional Eurocentric biblical scholarship. At this phase, postcolonial biblical criticism turns a metacritical and even self-critical eye on the different groups of readers of the Bible, scrutinizing their particular standpoints or social locations that exert significant influences on the task of biblical interpretation, such as gender, race, class, colonial status. For example, how do traditional (male) readers of the West view themselves with regard to the relationship between empire and margins, the West and the Rest, Christendom and outsiders, mission and conversion, who goes to heaven and who goes to hell? How do Western women position themselves on these issues, or non-Western male and female readers, along with those from racial and ethnic minorities in the West? These multidimensional critical questions of ideology, culture, and power in a world dominated by global capitalism will occupy the postcolonial biblical critic for some time to come.

Postcolonial biblical criticism thus situates the Bible in a larger global context: "the geopolitical relationship between center and periphery, the imperial and the colonial, whether in antiquity or modernity or postmodernity."[45] At the level of the texts themselves, this context is the larger world of the different ancient empires that impinged upon that small strip of land known as ancient Israel in their conquest and colonial administration. In their different ways, these empires exerted major controls on both the socioeconomic conditions of all sectors of Israelite society, from the male and female peasantry up to the elite, and the cultural production of its public national myth, the Hebrew Bible. Postcolonial biblical criticism also investigates how different stories of ancient Israel, such as its slavery, liberation, and subsequent conquest

---

[45] Fernando F. Segovia, *Decolonizing Biblical Studies: A View From the Margins* (Maryknoll, NY: Orbis, 2000), 140.

of Canaan, became paradigms legitimating Western expansion and conquest in Asia, Africa, and the Americas. It then attends to contemporary readers and readings of the biblical text and the ways in which they support, collude with, or resist the current global state of affairs, in which the West continues its domination of the Rest in its neocolonial economic exploitation of its natural and human resources and its cultural hegemony.

POSTCOLONIAL ANALYSIS AND THE BOOK OF EXODUS

The book of Exodus describes Israel's bondage in Egypt and the birth of Moses, the hero of the Exodus, who leads the people to Sinai where they enter into a covenantal relationship with their God YHWH. Because of the limitations of this chapter, I will primarily be focusing on the first phase of a postcolonial biblical study, viz. that of the biblical text itself, although I will make some remarks on the reception history of the Exodus/Sinai story. Because a postcolonial analysis investigates the geopolitical relations between dominant and subordinate, we must first deal with the historicity of the Exodus event itself. Were the Hebrews enslaved by an Egyptian pharaoh and did they leave Egypt *en masse* as the Exodus story relates? Some of these matters were discussed in the chapters on genre criticism and source and redaction criticism in this volume. Here you learned that the stories of the Exodus have undergone a long process of transmission, making the question – What really happened? – very difficult to answer. Archaeological evidence also casts grave doubts on the historicity of the biblical story.[46] Furthermore, from a postcolonial perspective, the Exodus/Sinai account cannot be studied in isolation. This narrative is inseparable from the larger story of Israel's "conquest" of Canaan, and indeed from a large portion of the Hebrew Bible that interacts with the story of the Exodus. The compilation of these traditions most likely took place in late Exilic or post-Exilic times, when Israel was a colony under Babylonian and Persian rule.

According to Norman Gottwald, one can examine the Exodus story from the perspective of four consecutive social "horizons" or "moments,"

---

[46] See the essays by Dever and Weinstein in Ernest S. Frerichs and Leonard H. Lesko, eds., *Exodus: The Egyptian Evidence* (Winona Lake, IN: Eisenbrauns, 1997), 67–86, 87–103.

that relate to the different sources and textual levels of the narrative.[47] "Horizon no. 1 is that of the hypothetical participants in the events reports";[48] "Horizon no. 2 is that of the Israelite social revolutionaries and religious confederates in the highlands of Canaan in the twelfth and eleventh centuries";[49] "Horizon no. 3 is that of Israelite traditionalists in monarchic times to conceive Israel of the exodus experience as an essentially national entity in transit toward its secure establishment as a state of Canaan";[50] "Horizon no. 4 is that of the late Exilic and post-Exilic restorers of Judah as a religious and cultural community that had lost its political independence."[51] Traces of the earlier horizons are perceivable in the later ones. In the long formation of the biblical tradition, Gottwald theorizes that in the early formation of the exodus story, hostile relations with Egypt and Egyptian representatives *in Canaan* were "gathered up" into the paradigm of a single mass captivity *in Egypt*, and, similarly, all the successes of Israelites in eluding Egyptian–Canaanite–Philistine control *in Canaan* were condensed and projected into the paradigm of a single mass deliverance *from Egypt*.[52] The way these coalesced traditions are utilized in Horizon no. 4 will have considerable importance in a postcolonial analysis, because it is the stage that gave rise to the canonical text as we have it in the Torah/Pentateuch.

The Persian Imperium and Canonization

Biblical scholarship has been shifting toward dating the compilation of the Torah (Pentateuch) and Prophets during Israel's time as the Persian colony Yehud between the late sixth to the fourth centuries B.C.E. This does not mean that there were no collections of earlier traditions, but rather that the canonization of the text as we presently have it began under the colonial rule of Persia and in significant ways authorized by

---

[47] Norman K. Gottwald, "The Exodus As Event and Process: A Test Case in the Biblical Grounding of Liberation Theology," in *The Future of Liberation Theology: Essays in Honor of Gustavo Gutiérrez* (eds. Marc H. Ellis, and Otto Maduro; Maryknoll, NY: Orbis Books, 1989), 250–60.

[48] Ibid., 254.

[49] Ibid., 255.

[50] Ibid., 256–57.

[51] Ibid., 257.

[52] Norman K. Gottwald, *The Politics of Ancient Israel* (Louisville, KY: Westminster John Knox Press, 2000), 167.

it.[53] A postcolonial analysis of Exodus must therefore investigate Yehud's colonial relations with the Persian Empire and Persia's imperial role in the formation of the biblical text.

The first question to ask is the nature of the material and economic context of Yehud as a colony under Persian rule and the power groups involved in governing it. The economy of Yehud was essentially village-based agrarian, cultivating three lucrative cash crops for export: grain, wine, and oil.[54] Jerusalem was the provincial capital that housed the colony's ruling elite. This elite was largely comprised of priestly and political immigrants and their scribes from Babylon, who had probably served in the Babylonian cult or royal court and now enjoyed Persian support. Many had descended from Judean aristocrats, priests, upper-class landowners, and so on who had been exiled to Babylonia years earlier. In many ways, these Jewish elites functioned as Persian imperial agents. In Bhabhian terms, they were "mimic men" in some ways, mediating between the imperial center and the indigenous natives living in the land when the exiles returned. Many of these natives descended from those not exiled during the Babylonian conquests who were considered "the poorest of the land" (2 Kgs 14:14; 25:12; Jer 39:10). They comprised the bulk of the population of Yehud, as the peasants who cultivated the land. Under the rule of the minority elite at the top of the social structure, they were excessively burdened with paying three sets of taxes: a tribute tax, a poll tax, and a land tax.[55]

The survival of empires depends on how effectively and efficiently they are able to extract material resources from their colonies that will compensate for administrative and military expenses for the colony, and also contribute to the deep coffers in the imperial center. Yehud experienced a heavy twofold extraction. The three taxes that were squeezed

---

[53] Berquist, "Postcolonial and Imperial Motives," 15–35. See also Peter Frei's "Persian Imperial Authorization: A Summary," in *Persia and Torah. The Theory of Imperial Authorization of the Pentateuch* (ed. James W. Watts; Atlanta: Society of Biblical Literature, 2001), 3–40, as well as the responses to it. Also Philip R. Davies, *Scribes and Schools: The Canonization of the Hebrew Scriptures* (LAI; Louisville, KY: Westminster John Knox Press, 1998). Richard A. Horsley, "The Origins of the Hebrew Scriptures in Imperial Relations," in *Orality, Literacy, and Colonialism in Antiquity* (ed. Draper, Jonathan A.; Atlanta: Society of Biblical Literature, 2004), 107–34.

[54] The following is a summary of Yee, *Poor Banished Children of Eve*, 137–43.

[55] Joachim Schaper, "The Jerusalem Temple As an Instrument of the Achaemenid Fiscal Administration." *VT* 45 (1995): 528–39.

from the peasants first passed through the hands of Persia's agents, the Jerusalem Jewish elite. After taking their cut to support the local temple and governmental bureaucracy, these "mimic men" then submitted their quotas to the Persian treasury. This two-tiered mode of colonial extraction undoubtedly placed an additional burden on Yehud's already impoverished peasantry, in that it supported the lavish lifestyles of two sets of elites – one foreign and the other domestic. If Nehemiah 5 is any indication, economic abuses of the elite against the natives came to a head during the latter part of the fifth century under Artaxerxes I: "Now there was a great outcry of the people and of their wives against their Jewish kin" (Neh 5:1). Significant is that the peoples' complaint is lodged against their own "Jewish kin" in this colony, a case in which the "mimic men" collude with their Persian colonizers in oppressing the natives. The narrative continues describing the drastic measures the natives had to take to repay their debts to their elite Jewish landlords: mortgaging their land if they owned any; taking out loans at high interest to pay imperial taxes; selling sons and daughters into slavery and risking the rape of their daughters by their creditors in doing so (Neh 5:2–5).

The empire not only exploited its colonies economically with the support of its colonial agents, but also intruded in their ideological and cultural production. The Persian king Darius (522–486 B.C.E.) enacted several political strategies designed to unify his empire. He constructed temples throughout his kingdom which encroached on the religious life of his colonies, making him well liked and supported. These temples performed an ideological function in stabilizing a society when their cult personnel were loyal to the empire. They also had an important economic function by increasing employment and strengthening the collection of levies and tribute for imperial purposes. It was Darius who facilitated the building of the Second Temple in Jerusalem through Zerubbabel (Ezra 3, 6). The personnel of this temple acted as the interface between the tax-paying population of Judah and the Persian government. Because they profited from revenues collected by the temple, these Jewish cult functionaries insured that religious/ideological interests of the temple coincided with the economic interests of the empire.[56]

One of the ideological missions or goals that empires arrogate to themselves is to function as a pedagogue, teaching their colonies the

[56] Ibid., p. 537.

ways of "civilization." In another policy to unite and stabilize his empire, Darius allowed local elites in Persian colonies in Babylonia and Egypt (and perhaps others) to codify and standardize their earlier narrative and legal traditions, but within the interests of imperial control. Berquist infers that a similar collection and codification occurred with ancient Israelite traditions in Yehud:

If this conjecture is right, then the Pentateuch is a strange document, both internal and external at the same time. It is internal in that it represents the old Israelite traditions that had formed monarchic identity and had become the cultural basis for Yehud's own existence, but the Pentateuch is also external in that its final form represents Persia's imposition of a text upon Yehud. Persia not only promulgated a law for Yehud to obey but presented a story that defined who Yehud was. This external definition rhetorically limited Yehud's own self-understanding and kept it within certain ideological confines.[57]

In very real ways, the Pentateuch, compiled during the Persian period and in which our Exodus texts are situated, can be considered a product of colonial hybridity. The religious and political elites governing Yehud were themselves hybrids. They were ethnically Jewish but also Persian agents. They thus had a curious social location, sharing the ethos of the colonizer and colonized simultaneously. In the colony, their status was of the highest order; they were the privileged few. But in the empire itself, they were merely civil servants. Although the source of their power in the colony came from the center, they shared an ethnicity and a strong past history with the natives of the land. The canonical text, which their priestly scribes produced, is thus a hybrid, codifying the ancient stories and laws of Israel, which provided a deep sense of ethnic identity, but also advanced the interests of the Persian imperium. Facilitating the empire's role as pedagogue, Torah and (Former) Prophets "explained" the colonial situation in Yehud, and why it needed the civilizing enlightenment and rule that the empire provided. We will see these ambivalences and tensions in this hybrid nature as we examine the text of the book of Exodus more closely. I will first analyze Exodus 1–2, paying particular attention to the enslavement of the Hebrews and female resistance. I will then develop my interpretation to include the broader literary context of the story of the exodus (Exod 1–2) and the codification of Israelite law (Exod

---

[57] Jon L. Berquist, *Judaism in Persia's Shadow: A Social and Historical Approach* (Minneapolis: Fortress Press, 1995), 138–39.

19–20) as the larger national myth found in Torah and the Prophets, the first two sections of the Hebrew canon.

EXODUS 1–2: STEREOTYPING, WOMEN, AND RESISTANCE

Although the canon was created to serve the needs of the Persian Empire and its Jewish enablers in Yehud, it was not a completely consistent and coherent exposition of imperial objectives. Because it is a compilation of a long traditioning process, it is a bricolage of voices, viewpoints, geographies, classes, and ideologies. Although the voices of empire are distinctly heard in the canonical setting of Exodus 1–2 and 19–20, voices of resistance are also apparent. The hybridity that is so characteristic of the colonizer/colonized relationship makes a deconstruction of imperial ideology possible so that subaltern voices may emerge.

The Postcolonial interpreter faces this bricolage with sensitivity to the ideological use of these different texts. First the interpreter must transcend the contemporary imperializing ideologies to allow the text to deconstruct, but then the interpreter is faced with the variety of voices within the text. Again, Postcolonialism provides a space in which to choose voices to construct interpretations that may have decolonizing effects in the contemporary world.[58]

As was seen in Pixley's chapter on liberation criticism in this volume, the Exodus traditions have been taken up in famous causes of liberation, as in the cases African American slaves in the antebellum South or peasant base communities in Latin America. Steinberg's feminist criticism chapter in this volume highlights the importance of women in the Exodus story, without whose agency the hero of the Exodus would not have survived. These counter voices are already ingrained in the text. Let us build on these two analyses by looking at Exodus 1–2 through postcolonial eyes.

One of the most notable insights of Homi Bhabha is the inherent ambivalence in the colonizer/colonized relationship, which is embedded in the split or fracture in the text's meaning. The biblical text produced under such circumstances can therefore be both liberative and oppressive, depending on the context in which it is used. The Exodus story has primarily been enlisted in causes of liberation. And yet, there is a darker side of the Exodus story in which the victim becomes the victimizer, and

---

[58] Berquist, "Postcolonial and Imperial Motives," 29.

the oppressed mutates into the oppressor. A text produced in an imperial context can be used to benefit the empire's material extraction and
ideological hegemony, but this domination is not absolute. The opposite
is also true. Because the text is a hybridic mixture, anticolonial voices
of resistance submerged in the text have the potential to deconstruct its
dominant meaning.

Berquist argues that the canon manifests a particular interest in Egypt
that was Persia's main rival at its western borders during its earlier years.
As imperial pedagogue, Persia directs Yehud to "fix its gaze upon Egypt,
the great oppressor who remains a constant threat morally if not mil-
itarily. By gazing upon Egypt with animosity, the text refocuses Yehudite social vision and obscures the domination that Persia plays in the
present."[59] Let us speculate then on how Egypt is portrayed in Exodus
1–2 from both Persian imperial and Yehudite colonial perspectives, which
will exhibit both imperialist interests and anticolonial resistance.

Egypt was under the control of Persian imperialism at different times
in its history. However, being a mighty kingdom itself at the outer-
most corner of the empire made Egypt a persistent threat to the Persian
center.[60] Depictions of Egypt, its pharaoh, and its people in Exodus 1–2
are highly stereotypical and humorous.[61] Manfred Pfister's comment on
laughter can also apply to the colonial context of Persia and Egypt:

Laughter is always caught up in the kinds of distinctions between centre
and margins every society employs to establish and stabilise its identity: in
one society, the predominant form of laughter can be that which aims from
the site of the ideological or power centre at what is to be marginalised or
excluded altogether; in another, the most significant form of laughter can
arise from the margins, challenging and subverting the established ortho-
doxies, authorities and hierarchies.[62]

As noted earlier in the discussion on Bhabha, stereotypes reflect the
anxiety at the heart of colonial relations. The constant repetition of
stereotypes mirrors the colonizer's uncertainty and fear regarding the

[59] Ibid., 24–25.
[60] Alan B. Lloyd, "Egypt, History of: Persian Period (Dyn. 27–31)," *ABD* 2 (1992): 364–67;
      Berquist, *Judaism in Persia's Shadow*, 45–49, 53–58, 61–62, 91–93, 108–11.
[61] J. William Whedbee, "Liberation and Laughter: Exodus and Esther As Two Comedies of
      Deliverance," in *The Bible and the Comic Vision* (Cambridge and New York: Cambridge
      University, 1998), 129–71.
[62] Cited in Susanne Reichl and Mark Stein, "Introduction," in *Cheeky Fictions: Laughter
      and the Postcolonial* (Amsterdam and New York: Rodopi, 2005), 9.

fixed identity of the colonized as subordinate. In the case of Egypt/Persia
relations, the fear is that Egypt will throw off its shackles and threaten
Persian supremacy. For Yehud, it is also the very real fear that Egypt
will encroach upon its borders. Given that two ethnic superpowers are
involved in this colonial conflict with Yehud caught in between, it is not
unthinkable that the stereotyping of Egypt be considered an ethnic slur
or joke.[63] Ethnic jokes mock groups who are peripheral to the central or
dominant group or who are seen by them as ambiguous.[64] Stereotypical
ethnic slurs and jokes are based upon contradictions that make the Other
"knowable" but still maintain its difference and distance. They poke fun
at the racialized object, while simultaneously reinforcing the identity of
the joke-teller as superior, as the joke is constantly retold.

Exodus 1–2 exhibits a range of binaries that comically exploits and
plays on the differences between the Egyptians and their Hebrew slaves.
The master/slave binary highlights socioeconomic class disparities. The
Egyptian/Hebrew binary takes advantage of racial/ethnic differences. The
binary between male babies and female babies exploits gender differences.

The contrasts between Egyptian women and Hebrew women manipulate gender and racial differences. The opposition between pharaoh and
midwives profits from gender, race, and class dissimilarities. The overriding binary governing the two groups across gender, race, and class
differences is the stupid/clever one, as we shall see.

We learn in Exodus 1 that a new king arose in Egypt who did not know
Joseph. He lays out before his subjects a series of hypothetical scenarios
should the birthrate of the Israelites continue: "Look, the Israelite people
are more numerous and more powerful than we. Come, let us deal
shrewdly with them, or they will increase and, in the event of war, join
our enemies and fight against us and escape from the land" (Exod 1:9–
10). There is no justification for these accusations against the Israelites.
They simply provide an excuse to enslave them. However, from a Persian

---

[63] Cf. Johnny Miles, "'Who Are You Calling "Stupid'?" Ethnocentric Humour and Identity
     Construct in the Colonial Discourse of Judges 3.12–30," *The Bible and Critical Theory*
     4, no. 1 (2008): 04.1–04.16; David Jobling and Catherine Rose, "Reading As a Philistine:
     The Ancient and Modern History of a Cultural Slur," in *Ethnicity & the Bible* (ed. Mark
     G. Brett; Leiden: E. J. Brill, 1996), 381–417.
[64] Christie Davies, "Ethnic Jokes, Moral Values and Social Boundaries," *The British Journal
     of Sociology* 33, no. 3 (1982): 384 (pp. 383–403). Ferdinand Deist, "Boundaries and
     Humour: A Case Study From the Ancient Near East," *Scrip* 63 (1997): 415–24.

perspective, these scenarios epitomize the real fears that the Persians have of the inhabitants of their Egyptian colony itself. They are anxious that the Egyptians will become more numerous and powerful and that they will make alliances with the enemies of Persia, threatening war and escaping their control. The pharaoh's command to set taskmasters over the Israelites and put them to forced labor will resonate with Persia's own desires to keep Egypt under their imperial thumb.

The word for "shrewdly" in pharaoh's injunction to his people, *niṭhakkĕmâ*, is related to the Hebrew word for "wisdom," *ḥokmâ*. However, instead of being wise in their dealings with the Israelites, the overriding characterization of the pharaoh and the Egyptians is "stupidity" or "foolishness," a heavily sardonic depiction since Egyptian wisdom was celebrated throughout southwest Asia. (cf. 1 Kgs 4:30). Their "shrewd" plan to oppress the Israelites with forced labor backfires. "The more they were oppressed, the more they multiplied and spread, so that the Egyptians came to dread the Israelites" (Exod 1:12). Rather than learning from their mistakes, the Egyptians intensify their subjugation: "The Egyptians became ruthless in imposing tasks on the Israelites, and made their lives bitter with hard service in mortar and brick and in every kind of field labor. They were ruthless in all the tasks that they imposed on them" (Exod 1:13–14). And yet these brutal policies still didn't work.

So, in yet another stupid move, the great male Egyptian pharaoh asks two seemingly powerless female Hebrew midwives to help him keep his kingdom safe.[65] He mistakenly orders them to kill the wrong gender and age group. If he really wants to reduce the Hebrew population, he should be killing off (or sterilizing) women of child-bearing age. The security of his great empire rests ironically on these two women, Shiphrah and Puah (Exod 1:15). Notice that the midwives are named in the narrative, while our great and powerful pharaoh is not. Pharaoh asks for their aid only after his other harsh measures failed to stem the birthrate. The comedy here relies on the fact that the mighty pharaoh has to turn to lower-class women to maintain the stability of the nation, after his testosterone-filled methods fail. Midwives by profession are women who help bring life into the world. They are commanded by pharaoh to do

---

[65] The ethnicity of these midwives is not clear. While the Masoretic text understood the midwives to be Hebrew, the unpointed text is ambiguous. My analysis presumes that the midwives are Hebrews.

something totally against their profession: bring death to the new lives that are born. Pharaoh asks professional life givers to become death-dealers.

Pharaoh is very selective about whom he wants killed. He wants only male babies killed. Presumably females do not pose a threat to him. However, Pharaoh gets undone by these two female midwives when they save the male children. When he sees that male Hebrew babies are still being born, he confronts the midwives in Exodus 1:18: "Why have you done this, and allowed the boys to live?" Midwives declare, "Because the Hebrew women are not like the Egyptian women; for they are vigorous and give birth before the midwife comes to them" (Exod 1:19). The midwives deceive the Pharaoh by exploiting and playing upon the stereotypical racial/ethnic prejudices held by the Pharaoh and the Egyptians themselves. In a wonderful example of colonial mimicry becoming mockery,[66] the midwives turn the Pharaoh's biases and slurs about racial differences to their own advantage. The Hebrews are different from Egyptians anyway, so even in giving birth Hebrew women are different than Egyptian women.[67] The midwives are the wise ones in this episode, directly contrasting pharaoh's stupidity.

So at this point Pharaoh tries another command. "Every boy that is born to the Hebrews you shall throw into the Nile, but you shall let every girl live" (Exod 1:22). Pharaoh still does not get it. He still thinks that females do not pose a threat to his kingdom. However, in the very next story, a brave Hebrew mother hides her newborn son in a basket and flows him down the river. The baby is rescued by the Pharaoh's own daughter and the baby grows up in Pharaoh's court right under his own nose. Pharaoh gets undone again by a woman, this time his own daughter, who saves the future savior of Israel (Exod 2:1–10). The caricature of the Pharaoh and the Egyptians continues through the plague stories, in which the Pharaoh's pride and stubbornness bring a series of calamities to the land, and ultimately tragedy to his family and his people in the

---

[66] Bhabha, *Location of Culture*, 123: "It is from this area between mimicry and mockery, where the reforming, civilizing mission (of the colonizer) is threatened by the displacing gaze of its disciplinary double, that my instances of colonial imitation come."

[67] Renita J. Weems, "The Hebrew Women Are Not Like the Egyptian Women: The Ideology of Race, Gender and Sexual Reproduction in Exodus 1," *Semeia* 59 (1992): 25–34.

death of the firstborn (Exod 7–12). The Persians would have relished this cartoon of Pharaoh and Egypt as consummately stupid, as well as the black humor in seeing their dangerous enemy suffering under the plagues, humiliated and ultimately defeated. The ancient traditions of their colony Yehud would have fed into Persia's own attitudes regarding their superiority and control over their vast empire that extended as far west as Egypt itself!

Steinberg's feminist analysis in this volume of Exodus 1–2 has undoubtedly highlighted the positive as well as the negative interpretations of the roles and portrayals of the different women in this text. Shiphrah and Puah, Moses' mother and sister, and Pharaoh's daughter all in their own ways resist the tyranny of empire, and yet ultimately serve the male interests embedded in the narrative.[68] Let us see how postcolonial criticism can deal with the presentation of women in these stories, which requires that we situate their adventures in the larger biblical story. Since it concerns the formation and identity of the nation of Israel, one that is currently under colonization, Exodus 1–2 subsumes gender under a nationalist and survivalist struggle.[69] Its perspectives are therefore largely male and represent the political and ideological interests of both the Persian Empire and Yehud.

Nira Yuval-Davis and Floya Anthias outline the five different ways in which women have been positioned in nationalist discourses:[70]

a. as biological reproducers of members of ethnic collectivities;
b. as reproducers of the boundaries of ethnic/national groups;
c. as participating centrally in the ideological reproduction of the collectivity and as transmitters of its culture;

---

[68] See, for example, how J. Cheryl Exum, "Second Thoughts About Secondary Characters: Women in Exodus 1.8–2.10," in *A Feminist Companion to Exodus to Deuteronomy* (ed. Athalya Brenner; Sheffield: Sheffield Academic Press, 1994), 75–87 reassesses her earlier article from a more negative perspective: J. Cheryl Exum, "'You Shall Let Every Daughter Live': A Study of Exodus 1.8–2.10," in *A Feminist Companion to Exodus to Deuteronomy* (ed. Athalya Brenner; Sheffield: Sheffield Academic Press, 1994), 37–61. Repr. from *Semeia* 28 (1993).

[69] This is also Mosala's argument regarding the Book of Esther: Itumeleng J. Mosala, "The Implications of the Text of Esther for African Women's Struggles for Liberation in South Africa," in *The Postcolonial Biblical Reader* (ed. R. S. Sugirtharajah; Malden, MA: Blackwell Publishers, 2006), 134–41. Repr. from *Semeia* 59 (1992).

[70] Nira Yuval-Davis and Floya Anthias, "Introduction," in *Woman-Nation-State* (New York: St. Martin's Press, 1989), 7.

d. as signifiers of ethnic/national differences – as a focus and symbol
    in ideological discourses used in the construction, reproduction,
    and transformation of ethnic/national categories;
e. as participants in national, economic, political, and military strug-
    gles.

The women's stories in Exodus 1–2 reveal several of these functions of
nationhood and national identity. The beginning of Exodus underscores
the fertile reproductive abilities of the Israelites, which recalls God's
promise to Abraham that his descendants will be more numerous than the
stars above.[71] Their great numbers fill the Egyptians with alarm regarding
the ethnic Other in their land (Exod 1:7), and is the cause of a pogrom
against Israel's newborn sons (Exod 1:15–22). We then read in Exodus
2:1–2 that a man from the house of Levi went and married a woman from
the house of Levi, who conceived and bore him a son. Because women
biologically reproduce members of racial and ethnic groups, control of
women and their sexuality is central to national and ethnic polities. In
order to preserve racial and national boundaries, male-generated laws
and customs define with whom and under what circumstances women
and men can marry and have sexual relations.[72] There are no interracial
marriages between the Israelites and the Egyptians. Moses' father marries
a woman from his own ethnic group, one from the same priestly house
as his. She is the "correct" or "proper" wife who can become the mother
of the national hero. Moses' biological mother needs to be not only of the
same ethnic group, but also from the same priestly family as the father.

The Pharaoh believes that only Hebrew males are a threat to him.
It evidently slips his mind that women also play a crucial role in the
biological reproduction of a people, thus underscoring his unrelieved
stupidity. Resisting Pharaoh's genocidal command to his people (Exod
1:22), Moses' mother, not his father, saves her son by hiding him from
Pharaoh's death squads, putting him in a basket and floating him down
a river. She becomes a signifier of a mother/land protecting her children
in a nationalist struggle. Her unnamed daughter also becomes a symbol
of protection and resistance, as she watches the progress of the basket
down river, and cleverly maneuvers Moses' mother to wetnurse her own
son for Pharaoh's daughter and actually get paid for it (Exod 2:3–9).

[71] Genesis 15:5.
[72] Stoler, *Carnal Knowledge and Imperial Power.*

Because they demarcate national differences among nations, women literally and symbolically designate the "porous frontiers" through which nation, ethnicity, and culture can be penetrated.[73] One horrendous way in which women literally mark the boundaries through which a nation can be penetrated is the systematic rape of enemy women by conquering armies.[74] In Exodus 2, Egyptian sovereignty becomes vulnerable in the person of the royal princess, Pharaoh's daughter. Although many scholars view Pharaoh's daughter positively,[75] she, too, can be comedic foil that emphasizes Egyptian stupidity from a postcolonial perspective. On the one hand, as the means by which the hero of the exodus survives and flourishes in Pharaoh's own court, she inadvertently becomes the agent that pokes fun at her stupid father, the Pharaoh. Through her role as surrogate mother to Moses, the heart (womb?) of the Egyptian empire is "penetrated."

On the other hand, James Ackerman argues that a foolish Egyptian princess stands in contrast to the wise Hebrew midwives. Like her father, she is not named, although the midwives are. Her curt response "Go" to the query of Moses' sister to fetch a Hebrew wetnurse, suggests "a feeling of supreme authority, a brusque manner in dealing with underlings." Her command to Moses' mother, "Take this child and nurse him, and I, even I, will give you your wages" (Exod 2:9) reveals a combination of "haughty condescension," even though at that very moment she is being bamboozled into paying the baby's own mother wages. The story also ridicules the daughter's faulty knowledge of Hebrew. Instead of the passive form, "the one drawn out of the water," she incorrectly names the baby "the one who draws out," which is what he will do in leading Israel out of Egypt.[76]

From a postcolonial perspective, women become a trope of nationalist and ethnic identity, of collusion with empire or of resistance to it.

---

[73] Loomba, *Colonialism/Post-Colonialism*, 159.

[74] Claudia Card, "Rape As a Weapon of War," *Hypatia* 11, no. 4 (1996): 5–18; Pamela Gordon and Harold C. Washington, "Rape As a Military Metaphor in the Hebrew Bible," in *A Feminist Companion to the Latter Prophets* (ed. Athalya Brenner; Sheffield: Sheffield Academic Press, 1995), 308–25.

[75] Whedbee, "Liberation," 140: "Though her father may be a cruel tyrant capable of genocide, she shows the compassion for the helpless that demonstrates the capacity of humans to be humane and sympathetic toward other humans."

[76] James S. Ackerman, "The Literary Context of the Moses Birth Story (Exodus 1–2)," in *Literary Interpretations of Biblical Narratives. Vol. 1* (eds. Kenneth R. R. Gros Louis, James S. Ackerman, and Thayer S. Warshaw; Nashville: Abingdon, 1974), 93.

Hebrew women become a signifier for the fertile Israelite nation, that despite the barbaric measures the Egyptian empire puts upon them, continue to reproduce members of the ethnic group, threatening Egyptian sovereignty. They become agents of resistance that thwart imperial intents and purposes. The wise Hebrew midwives become adept through colonial mimicry in turning Egyptian racist assumptions about their ethnic Other on their head to work on their behalf. On the other hand, the Pharaoh's daughter becomes the embodiment of foolishness, from her father's stupidity to the nation's as a whole. She is the porous boundary that allows the "enemy," the hero of the Exodus, to penetrate Egypt and live to tell the tale.

EXODUS 1–2, 19–20: THE EXODUS IN THE LARGER NATIONAL MYTH

Exodus 1–2 and 19–20 are part of a much larger national narrative recorded in the first two sections of the Hebrew canon (Torah and Prophets), involving the themes of the garden of Eden, paradise lost, the promised land, and the loss of land, to which a postcolonial analysis will be very attentive. The reception history of the Exodus story will expose how later conquerors will appropriate this master narrative selectively to legitimize their seizure of lands and resources that belong to Others. The national myth of ancient Israel describes the formation of a people, in conjunction with a journey motif to and from a desired land. It begins with the first man and woman created *in paradise* who are enjoined by God to "be fruitful, multiply and fill the earth" (Gen 1:28). But because of their sin, they are cast *from paradise* into an arid land, which the man must work by the sweat of his brow. God commands the patriarch Abraham to *journey to Canaan*, promising him that his descendants will be a great nation to whom God will give that land (Gen 12:2, 7). Exodus 1 harkens back to the end of Genesis describing the *exodus from Canaan* by Jacob and his sons *to Egypt*. In Egypt, the promise of many descendants becomes fulfilled, the Israelites "multiplying and growing exceedingly strong, so that the land was filled with them" (Exod 1:7). They become such a threat to Egyptian nationalism that the Egyptians "set taskmasters over them to oppress them with forced labor" (Exod 1:11). After many signs and wonders, the book of Exodus narrates their *exodus from Egypt* and their subsequent formation as a people covenanted to God on Mount Sinai (Exod 19–24). The book of Exodus anticipates the *journey* from the wilderness back *to Canaan*, described as a new paradise: a land of milk and honey. This journey will end disastrously at the conclusion of the Former Prophets (2 Kgs) when Israel is exiled *from paradise*, because of the people's failure to keep God's covenant.

Liberationist readings of the Exodus story, highlighting primarily God's deliverance of the Hebrews from oppression, can be faulted for downplaying or even ignoring the story's primary setting within this larger narrative of Torah and Prophets and its more negative ramifications.[77] Moses does not merely proclaim, "Let my people go," but "Let my people go, so that they may worship me in the wilderness" (Exod 7:16 *et passim*). Israel's liberation from bondage in Egypt (Exod 1–15) is integrally tied to their ultimate servitude to God on Sinai in a covenantal relationship (Exod 19ff). Parallels with Hittite suzerainty treaties between a king and his vassal reinforce the imperial ethos of domination and sub-ordination that lies behind the Sinaitic covenant. In such treaties, the rehearsal of the suzerain's history of favor with his underling was the preamble eliciting a sense of obligation to obey the laws stipulated by the covenant.[78] The story of the exodus from Egypt therefore was just the prologue to the giving of the law in the wilderness of Sinai. Walter Brueggemann even argues that the liberation of the slaves from Egypt is not the main intent of the story at all. Rather, Exodus is about YHWH triumphing over a disobedient vassal, the pharaoh.[79] The story of deliverance thus cannot be considered independent from the giving of the law on Sinai that sealed Israel in a vassal/king relation with God:

You have seen what I did to the Egyptians, and how I bore you on eagles' wings and brought you to myself. Now therefore, if you obey my voice and

---

[77] See the sharp critique of Jon D. Levenson, "Liberation Theology and the Exodus," in *Jews, Christians, and the Theology of the Hebrew Scriptures* (eds. Alice Ogden Bellis, and Joel S. Kaminski; Atlanta: Society of Biblical Literature, 2000), 215–30, and the more temperate assessments by Walter Brueggemann, "Pharaoh As Vassal: A Study of a Political Metaphor," *CBQ* 57 (1995): 27–51; and John J. Collins, "The Exodus and Biblical Theology," in *Jews, Christians, and the Theology of the Hebrew Scriptures* (eds. Alice Ogden Bellis, and Joel S. Kaminski; Atlanta: Society of Biblical Literature, 2000), 245–61.

[78] George E. Mendenhall and Gary A. Herion, "Covenant," *ABD* 1 (1992): 1180–88.

[79] Brueggemann, "Pharaoh as Vassal," 27–51.

keep my covenant, you shall be my treasured possession out of all the peoples. Indeed, the whole earth is mine, but you shall be for me a priestly kingdom and a holy nation. (Exod 19:4–6)

Another integral part of the God/Israel covenant is the fulfillment of God's promise of land to Abraham in Genesis: "To your descendants I give this land, . . . the land of the Kenites, the Kenizzites, the Kadmonites, the Hittites, the Perizzites, the Rephaim, the Amorites, the Canaanites, the Girgashites, and the Jebusites" (Gen 15:18–21). In his revelation to Moses at the burning bush, God will not only free his people from their sufferings under the Egyptians, but also "bring them up out of that land to a good and broad land, a land flowing with milk and honey, to the country of the Canaanites, the Hittites, the Amorites, the Perizzites, the Hivites, and the Jebusites" (Exod 3:8). The straightforward acknowledgment in both these texts that the land is *already* populated calls attention to God as the magisterial regent, sanctioning and sanctifying brutal acts of imperialism. God will "drive out" and "blot out" these indigenous peoples of Canaan, and lays down the covenantal conditions Israel must observe in order to keep the land: "You shall not bow down to their gods, or worship them, or follow their practices, but you shall utterly demolish them and break their pillars in pieces. You shall worship the Lord your God" (Exod 23:23–25). "You shall worship no other god, because the Lord, whose name is Jealous, is a jealous God" (Exod 34:11–14). Tolerating allegiance to no other deity, the imperial God YHWH thus gives the Israelites a religious warrant to conquer indigenous peoples, colonize their lands, and abolish their gods. Exodus, covenant, conquest, and colonization are all of a piece in this national myth of Israel's origins.

As a crucial component of Israel's national history, the Pentateuch describes a continual movement to and from a desired piece of real estate, the land of Canaan. In its canonical formation under Persian auspices, the Pentateuch ends with Moses and the people in the plains of Moab across the Jordan, looking into Canaan. God reiterates his promise of the land to Moses:

"This is the land of which I swore to Abraham, to Isaac, and to Jacob, saying 'I will give it to your descendants': I have let you see it with your eyes, but you shall not cross over there." Then Moses, the servant of the Lord, died there in the land of Moab, at the Lord's command" (Deut 34:4–5).

According to Joseph Blenkinsopp, the death of Moses distinguishes the first five books of the Torah as fundamental and normative, differentiating the Mosaic Age from the narratives that follow in the second division of the Hebrew canon, the Prophets. Moreover, formed and structured under Persian sponsorship as a separate set of canonical texts, the Pentateuch became the civic constitution of the temple community of Yehud.[80] Let us examine the ideological significance of this separation and how it serves Persian imperial interests by exploring the themes of the first book of the canonical section Prophets, viz. the book of Joshua.

Torah and the Former Prophets

Beginning auspiciously from Israel's perspective, the book of Joshua describes the ultimate fulfillment of God's promise of the land to Abraham. Although distinct from the Torah, the book of Joshua is clearly positioned in a close relationship with it. God orders Joshua:

"Only be strong and very courageous, being careful to act in accordance with all the law (*tôrâ*) that my servant Moses commanded you; do not turn from it to the right hand or to the left, so that you may be successful wherever you go. This book of the law (*tôrâ*) shall not depart out of your mouth; you shall meditate on it day and night, so that you may be careful to act in accordance with all that is written in it." (Josh 1:7–8)[81]

The "law" here refers directly back to the first five books of the Hebrew canon, the Torah. Connections between the persons of Joshua and Moses create intertextual parallels between the Exodus/Sinai traditions and the conquest of Canaan. Just as Moses gives the law to the people, Joshua reads the law to the people (Josh 8, 23–24). Just as Moses celebrates Passover before leaving Egypt, Joshua celebrates Passover after entering the Promised Land (Josh 5:10–11). The miraculous crossing of the Sea of Reeds corresponds to the miraculous crossing of the Jordan (Josh 3). The theophany at the burning bush is analogous to the theophany in Joshua 5. As Moses raises his arm with staff in hand before the enemy, Amelek

---

[80] Joseph Blenkinsopp, *The Pentateuch. An Introduction to the First Five Books of the Bible* (New York: Doubleday, 1992), 51.

[81] Note also similar injunctions to meditate on the Torah in Psalm 1 which begins the third section of the Hebrew canon, the Writings.

(Exod 17:8–12), so too does Joshua lift his sword against the inhabitants of Ai (Josh 8: 18–19). The blood of the Passover lamb on the doorposts, protecting the Israelites from the destroyer, finds its counterpart in the scarlet cord outside the window, shielding Rahab and her family from the invading Israelites (Josh 2:18–21).[82]

The glorious traditions of the Exodus/Covenant in the Torah imbue the stories of the conquest at the beginning of the Prophets. The message is very clear: as long as Israel takes care "to act in accordance with all the law (*tôrâ*) that my servant Moses commanded you, . . . you will be successful wherever you go" (Josh 1:7). Success in capturing *and* keeping the land depends conditionally on adherence to Torah.

From the perspective of the indigenous Canaanites,[83] however, God's election of Israel and promise of a land is not their fulfillment but their termination: in being attacked and driven from their homeland, in the confiscation of their property, in the massacre of their women and children, and in their ultimate genocide – all decreed by their invaders' jealous God. Commenting from a "Canaanite" standpoint, Native American scholar, Robert Warrior warns, "As long as people believe in the Yahweh of deliverance, the world will not be safe from Yahweh the conqueror."[84]

Very attuned to matters of conquest and colonization and the motives impelling them, a postcolonial critic poses certain questions at this point: Are the Joshua texts historical? Did these violent acts of conquest really happen? If not, how can they be explained? Scholars have made a case for three different theories regarding the "settlement" of Canaan.[85] The first

---

[82] See the excellent postcolonial analysis of Rahab as a colonized woman in Musa Dube, *Postcolonial Feminist Interpretation of the Bible* (St. Louis, MO: Chalice Press, 2000), 76–80.

[83] One of the earliest writers to critique the exodus story from the Canaanite perspective is the postcolonial theorist Edward W. Said, "Michael Walzer's *Exodus and Revolution*: A Canaanite Reading," in *Blaming the Victims: Spurious Scholarship and the Palestinian Question* (eds. Edward W. Said, and Christopher Hitchens; London and New York: Verso, 1988), 161–78.

[84] Robert Warrior, "Canaanites, Cowboys, and Indians," *USQR* 59, no. 1–2 (2005): 1–8. Repr. from *Christianity and Crisis* 49 (1989). See also the responses in this volume to Warrior's classic essay and Warrior's rejoinder.

[85] Joseph A. Callaway, "The Settlement in Canaan: The Period of the Judges. Revised by J. Maxwell Miller," in *Ancient Israel: A Short History From Abraham to the Roman Destruction of the Temple* (Rev. and Exp. ed.; Washington, DC: Biblical Archaeology Society, 1999) (1988). Online: http://www.basarchive.org/bswbSearch.asp?PubID=BSBKAI&Volume=0&Issue=0&ArticleID=3&UserID=2392&.

adheres closely to the biblical text in that Israel took the land by military conquest. The second theory argues that the "conquest" was more of peaceful infiltration of different nomadic groups that eventually settled in Canaan. The third theory held by most today reflects an internal struggle of different elements of the Canaanite population. In this scenario, there is no conquest of land from an outside invader. Rather, the conflicts arose among the indigenous peoples themselves, and out of those struggles the people of Israel as a distinct ethnic identity came into being. If there was no historical conquest of the indigenous Canaanites from the outside, what purpose did a "conquest" story serve during the compilation of the canon in Yehud during Persian colonization? Who benefited from this story?

On the one hand, such a narrative served the interests of the returning Jewish elite by legitimating their repossession of the lands and status that their descendants lost when they were exiled by the Babylonians. As already noted, Persian support of the returnees created growing class divisions between them and the indigenous populations in Yehud. Certain ideologies buttressed these divisions and the attempts on the part of the immigrants to land grab. The first such ideology has come to be known as the "myth of the empty land": the land was essentially empty, because the "people of Israel" (meaning the returning exiles) had been taken in captivity.[86] Neither Ezra nor Nehemiah exhibit any notion that the exiled elite constituted a small minority and that the major portion of the Jewish population remained in Judah during the Babylonian period.

Related to this myth was the ideological identification of those Jews who remained in the land as the inimical Other. When the problem of intermarriage between the returning elites and the indigenes surfaced,[87] the Jewish natives were stereotypically classified with foreign peoples in Canaan who supposedly fought against Joshua, viz. the Canaanites, the Hittites, the Perizzites, the Jebusites, the Ammonites, the Moabites, the Egyptians, and the Amorites (Ezra 9:1; cf. 6:21). The returnees saw themselves as the true Israel (Ezra 4:1–4; 6:21; 9:2) and envisioned their

---

[86] Hans M. Barstad, *The Myth of the Empty Land: A Study in the History and Archaeology of Judah During the "Exilic" Period* (Symbolae Osloenses 28; Oslo: Scandinavian University Press, 1996); Robert P. Carroll, "The Myth of the Empty Land," *Semeia* 59 (1992): 79–93.

[87] For a complete analysis, see Yee, *Poor Banished Children of Eve*, 143–46.

return from exile and their recovery of the land as a new Exodus and conquest.[88] Although Ezra describes their colonial status as "slaves," he acknowledges the benevolence of the Persian kings, in giving them new life by restoring them to Yehud and helping them rebuild their temple (Ezra 9:9). Drawing an obvious parallel between the returning elite and their Hebrew ancestors before the invasion of Canaan, Ezra proclaims: "The land that you are entering to possess is a land unclean with the pollutions of the peoples of the lands, with their abominations" (Ezra 9:11. Cf. Deut 7:1–4). He enjoins the exiles to separate from "the peoples of the land . . . so that you may be strong and eat the good of the land and leave it for an inheritance to your children forever" (Ezra 9:12; cf. Ezek 36:12). This later reinterpretation of the Exodus/conquest during Persian colonization is filled with irony. The destitute Hebrew slaves suffering the forced labor of the Egyptians in Exodus are transformed into the "slaves" of the Persian Empire, the wealthy elite of Yehud. Co-opting this national myth for their own purposes by making themselves the victims who have been saved from yoke of Babylonian slavery by the Persians, these elite justify their "conquest" of the indigenous Jews of Yehud, taking possession of their lands and exploiting them economically.

On the other hand, the conquest story in Joshua served the interests of the Persian colonizers. According to Blenkinsopp, the canonical creation of the Pentateuch, delimiting the Mosaic age from what follows, can be considered in what it excludes as in what it includes. "Exclusion of the history subsequent to Moses suggests that that history was seen to be for the most part a record of failure."[89] God's promise to Abraham of land, great nation, and blessing (Gen 12:1–3) was utterly contingent upon the people adhering to God's covenant on Sinai and obeying its laws and statutes. In short, observing Torah. The promise of land is dramatically fulfilled in Joshua. However, the rest of the Former Prophets records a dismal history of Israel's continual failure to keep God's commandments. The people's stiff-necked disobedience is chronicled in great detail throughout Israel's tribal period (Judges) and monarchic period (Sam and Kgs). By the end

---

[88] Cf. Ezek 11:14–19; 36:8–12; Isa 41:17–20; 43:14–21; 49:9–12; Jer 32:42–44.
[89] Blenkinsopp, *The Pentateuch*, 51.

of the Former Prophets in 2 Kings, Israel loses the land that it gained victoriously by conquest in the book of Joshua. In its present canonical structure, the Pentateuch sets up the perimeters of Israel's *identity* as a people of Torah. The Former Prophets record Israel's *failure* to live as a people of Torah. Joshua's conquest and colonization of Canaanites at the beginning of this history is reversed at the end. The Israelites are themselves conquered violently by their Babylonian invaders, their land colonized, their sovereign nation destroyed, and they are ignominiously deported to a strange land to serve a foreign king.

Facilitating the empire's mission as pedagogue, Israel's failure to abide by Torah accomplishes several things from a Persian perspective. As an authoritative document of ancient Israelite traditions, the canon "explains" why Israel no longer possesses the land, why it no longer has a king, why it is no longer an autonomous nation, and why it now exists as a colony subservient to a foreign imperial order. "The empire would benefit most from an ideology that emphasizes Yehud's inability to govern itself, to rebel against the imperial power, to expand itself beyond its current borders, or to ally itself effectively with others."[90] The colony's own narratives confirm that it is incapable of administering itself independently. It needs the benevolent protection and custody of the empire. According to Second Isaiah, the Persian king Cyrus will become Israel's messiah, of whom YHWH says: "'He is my shepherd, and he shall carry out all my purpose'; and who says of Jerusalem, 'It shall be rebuilt,' and of the temple, 'Your foundation shall be laid'" (Isa 4:28).

From the perspective of Jewish elite, Israel's failure to obey Torah "explains" why the religious plurality during the time of the monarchy was "wrong," and why the current centralization of worship in the Jerusalem temple and its monotheistic worship of the one God YHWH are "right." In "explaining" why there is no king governing Yehud, the canon shifts the balance of power from the political to the religious. The canon demands the rebuilding of the temple in Jerusalem. It legitimates the authority and orthodoxy of the current priestly circles as ministers in this one temple of the one God, and repudiates any rival priesthoods or supporters. This particular temple bureaucracy served imperial

---

[90] Berquist, "Postcolonial and Imperial Motives," 26.

economic interests as well, since the temple was the central "bank" collecting and distributing the taxes and tributes for the colonial elite at the margins and the empire at the center.

Let us take stock of what we learned about the Exodus/Sinai story. A postcolonial analysis takes us beyond the isolated texts of Exodus 1–2 and 19–20 to its wider literary context in the biblical canon and the broader imperial context of canonical formation. These texts are products of colonial hybridity, serving the interests of the center and the margins, the empire and the colony. Whatever meaning the ancient traditions of "Exodus," "Sinai," and "Conquest" in the other horizons or historical moments, they were given a canonical stamp during the Persian period in colonial Yehud. They were produced through Persian backing by the priestly scribes of Yehud's religious bureaucracy who enjoyed the social and economic benefits of being agents of the empire. In its canonical context, the stories of Israel's deliverance from slavery to be covenanted with YHWH on Sinai and its subsequent conquest of the native peoples are intimately intertwined.

The exodus/conquest story leaves itself wide open to both liberating and oppressive uses because it has yoked two opposing myths together, and the sheer durability of the narrative is such that they have become impossible to disentangle, lending our myths of domination the rhetoric of liberation and giving our myths of liberation the dark side of a fantasy of domination.[91]

Even within the biblical text itself, the ancient Exodus traditions were usurped by the returning exiles, who described their restoration as a new Exodus and their appropriation of the natives' farmlands as a new conquest. It is not surprising therefore that they have been used to legitimate the conquest and colonization of Others throughout the course of history.

The separation of the Torah/Pentateuch, which closes off the Mosaic age from what follows, constitutes the authoritative law to which the Israelites agreed to submit. Yet, the Former Prophets reveal that Israel persistently disobeyed God's covenant, losing the land that God promised

---

[91] Regina M. Schwartz, *The Curse of Cain. The Violent Legacy of Monotheism* (Chicago: University of Chicago Press, 1997), 58.

their ancestor Abraham. The disjunction between Torah and Former Prophets embodies the ideological justification for Yehud's colonization. It "explained" why Israel is no longer a nation ruled by a king and why it now owes its allegiance, rendering a heavy burden of taxes and tribute to a foreign power and its colonial agents.

CONCLUSION

We have learned that the Exodus texts are hybrid, reflecting the competing interests of both the center and margins. Because of these competing interests, the Exodus traditions have been enlisted to serve both the causes of freedom and of tyranny. We unfortunately have many examples of the latter throughout the era of Western colonialism, in places such as the Americas, Africa, Asia, Australia, and even in the rise of the modern state of Israel. The Boers regarded themselves as Israelites as they made their great trek through South Africa, and imposed their beliefs of racial superiority upon the indigenous black population. The Puritans fleeing the persecutions of the British "Pharaoh" saw North America as the land of promise, bringing them into conflict with Native Americans whom they regarded as the Canaanites. Exodus texts have been used on both sides of the debate on African American slavery in the nineteenth-century United States.[92]

From a postcolonial perspective, the Bible can be used to inspire liberation, but also legitimate oppression. This double-sidedness should raise a red flag regarding any reading that enlists the Bible to support its cause. Unfortunately, the Bible has been and continues to be used as a weapon to clobber those who are thought to be inferior, marginal, or different on the basis of race, gender, class, sexual orientation and so forth. An ethics of reading that discerns the applicability of a biblical text for a particular context is incumbent upon the postcolonial critic. Whom does my interpretation help? Whom does it harm? These are the important questions the critic must honestly confront.

---

[92] For a thorough examination of the reception history of Exodus, see Scott M. Langston, *Exodus Through The Centuries* (*Blackwell Bible Commentaries*; Malden, MA: Blackwell, 2006). Also Clifford Longley, *Chosen People: The Big Idea that Shaped England and America* (London: Hodder & Stoughton, 2002).

BIBLIOGRAPHY

For an excellent annotated bibliography of both postcolonial studies and postcolonial biblical criticism, see Stephen D. Moore, *Empire and Apocalypse: Postcolonialism and the New Testament*. Bible in the Modern World 12; Sheffield: Sheffield Phoenix Press, 2006, pp. 124–51.

Postcolonial Studies

Bhabha, Homi K. *The Location of Culture. With a New Preface by the Author*. London and New York: Routledge, 1994.

Lewis, Reina, and Sara Mills, eds. *Feminist Postcolonial Theory: A Reader*. Edinburgh: Edinburgh University Press, 2003.

Loomba, Ania. *Colonialism/Post-Colonialism*. New York: Routledge, 1998.

McLeod, John. *Beginning Postcolonialism*. Manchester and New York: Manchester University Press, 2000.

Moore-Gilbert, Bart. *Postcolonial Theory: Contexts, Practices, Politics*. London and New York: Verso, 1997.

Said, Edward W. *Orientalism. With Afterword*. 1978. Repr. New York: Vintage Books, 1994.

———. *Culture and Imperialism*. New York: Vintage Books, 1993.

Spivak, Gayatri Chakravorty. *A Critique of Postcolonial Reason. Toward a History of the Vanishing Present*. Cambridge, MA: Harvard University Press, 1999.

Young, Robert J. C. *Postcolonialism: An Historical Introduction*. Oxford: Blackwell, 2001.

Postcolonial Biblical Criticism

Boer, Roland. *Last Stop Before Antarctica: The Bible and Postcolonialism in Australia*. 2nd ed. 2001. Repr. Sheffield: Sheffield Academic Press, 2008.

———, ed. *A Vanishing Mediator? The Presence/Absence of the Bible in Postcolonialism*. Semeia 88; Atlanta: Society of Biblical Literature, 2001.

Brett, Mark G. *Genesis: Procreation and the Politics of Identity*. London and New York: Routledge, 2000.

Dube, Musa. *Postcolonial Feminist Interpretation of The Bible*. St. Louis, MO: Chalice Press, 2000.

Kim, Uriah Y. *Decolonizing Josiah: Toward a Postcolonial Reading of the Deuteronomistic History*. The Bible in the Modern World 5; Sheffield: Sheffield Phoenix Press, 2005.

Kwok, Pui-Lan. *Postcolonial Imagination and Feminist Theology*. Louisville, KY: Westminster John Knox, 2005.

McKinlay, Judith E. *Reframing Her: Biblical Women in Postcolonial Focus*. Sheffield: Sheffield Phoenix Press, 2004.

Moore, Stephen D., and Fernando F. Segovia, eds. *Postcolonial Biblical Criticism: Interdisciplinary Intersections*. The Bible and Postcolonialism London and New York: T & T Clark, 2005.

Runions, Erin. *Changing Subjects: Gender, Nation and Future in Micah.* New York: Sheffield Academic Press, 2002.

Segovia, Fernando F. *Decolonizing Biblical Studies: A View From the Margins.* Maryknoll, NY: Orbis, 2000.

Sugirtharajah, R. S. *Asian Biblical Hermeneutics and Postcolonialism.* Maryknoll, NY: Orbis, 1998.

_____. *The Bible and the Third World: Precolonial, Colonial and Postcolonial Encounters.* New York: Cambridge University Press, 2001.

_____. *Postcolonial Criticism and Biblical Interpretation.* New York: Oxford University Press, 2002.

_____, ed. *The Postcolonial Biblical Reader.* Malden, MA: Blackwell, 2006.

Whitelam, Keith W. *The Invention of Ancient Israel: The Silencing of Palestinian History.* London and New York: Routledge, 1996.

Glossary

A list of how some key terms are used in The Study of Exodus:

analytical genre – the generic category that is created for the purpose of technical analysis from the comparison of a target text with similar texts and traditions.

androcentrism – a male-centered perspective.

anthropology – the study of human beings in groups, in foreign societies; cf. "sociology."

antipathy – in literary analysis, the phenomenon by which a reader feels unfavorably disposed toward a character in the narrative; cf. "sympathy."

character groups – in literary analysis, characters who evince such consistency of traits and point of view that they are essentially treated as a single character throughout the narrative (e.g., "the mid-wives").

colonialism – the implanting of settlements on a distant territory almost always as a consequence of conquest and imperialism.

considerate reader – in social-scientific studies, a person who brings to his or her reading of a text a range of scenarios rooted in the social system of the document's writer and presumed audience.

constructive literary method – highlights the artfulness, sophistication, and meaningfulness of biblical literature, often assuming the basic unity, structure, and coherence in the text.

cultural diffusion – a term in genre criticism used to describe a situation in which two texts are similar because the same stream of tradition has influenced them; thus, there is cultural borrowing.

deconstruction – a postmodern interpretive strategy that seeks to demonstrate the nonnormative character of proposed interpretation by unmasking deep internal contradictions and inconsistencies in texts that were often assumed to have a stable meaning.

Deuteronomistic history – the literary theory of Martin Noth that Deuteronomy and the Former Prophets (Joshua, Judges, Samuel, Kings) were composed by an exilic historian and that the book of Deuteronomy, therefore, should be separated from the Tetrateuch (Genesis, Exodus, Leviticus, Numbers).

dialogical literary method – promotes a polyphonic (multivoiced) approach to interpretation, in which the goal is to identify competing voices in the text and to describe how they coexist in the present literary design.

diachronic – a linguistic term that indicates the study of change in language over time. A diachronic reading of Exodus would focus on the history of composition, using the methodologies of source and redaction criticism.

discourse – in literary criticism, the rhetorical component of narrative related to *how* the story is told; cf. "story."

dynamic characters – in literary analysis, characters whose traits or point of view change as the narrative progresses; cf. "static characters."

empathy – the phenomenon by which a reader identifies realistically or idealistically with a character and experiences the story from that character's point of view.

expected reading – in narrative criticism, an interpretation or response to a text that appears to be invited by signals within the text itself; cf. "unexpected reading."

feminist criticism – the discipline of interpreting texts from the perspective of persons informed by feminism.

flat characters – in literary analysis, characters who exhibit consistent traits and a predictable point of view; such characters typically function as personifications of values; cf. "round characters."

form – the structure and element in the discourse of a text, as, for example, whether the text is stated in the first person ("Y"), or in a communal voice ("we").

form criticism – the classification of the form or structure of biblical traditions on the basis of mood, form, and setting.

fragmentary hypothesis – the interpretation of the literary development of the Pentateuch as the combination of legal and narrative fragments without internal continuity.

gender based feminism – interpretation based on the distinction between "sex roles," biological characteristics, and "gender roles," behaviors assigned to each sex through socialization into a particular culture.

genre – a French word meaning "kind," or "type" that is used to classify human discourse.

generic realism – assumes that categories such a myth, legend, and historiography have an existence apart from the writing and interpretation of texts.

generic conceptualism – assumes that humans create generic categories in the process of interpretation.

generic competence – the ability to recognize "types" and "kinds" of discourse and to make adjustments for new and unique combinations.

generic criticism – a complex interpretative exercise that seeks to understand the nature, meaning, and significance of a text by creatively comparing it with similar texts and/or traditions.

hermeneutical circle – a term used to describe paradoxically independent tendencies in interpretation; for example, the "whole" of a text must be understood in terms of its parts, but the parts must also be understood in light of the whole.

hermeneutics of creative actualization – in feminist criticism, a final step in biblical interpretation that utilizes imagination, art, liturgy, and so on, to enable texts to function for those opposed to patriarchal oppression.

hermeneutics of proclamation – in feminist criticism, a goal of interpretation that moves from uncovering androcentric and patriarchal tendencies of texts to a more positive assessment of how texts can be used theologically in contemporary communities of faith.

hermeneutics of remembrance – in feminist criticism, a goal of interpretation that seeks to reconstruct biblical history from a feminist perspective.

hermeneutics of suspicion – in feminist criticism, a stance that presupposes or assumes that biblical texts (and their traditional interpretations) are androcentric and will serve patriarchy; cf. "hermeneutics of proclamation."

hexateuch – the literary theory of many source critics that Joshua, with its account of the conquest of the land, provides the conclusion to the Pentateuch (Genesis, Exodus, Leviticus, Numbers, Deuteronomy).

historical criticism – seeks to interpret texts within their original historical contexts.

hybridity – a term in postcolonial criticism to describe the intermingling of identities between the colonizer and the colonized, which undermines and destabilizes the status quo of the colonizers.

ideological criticism – an umbrella term for numerous disciplines that seek to interpret texts from the perspective of readers who occupy a specific social location and/or evince a particular ideology (e.g., womanist criticism, Marxist criticism, and Jungian criticism).

imperialism – the practice, the theory, and the attitudes of a dominating metropolitan center ruling a distant territory.

imperializing texts – in postcolonial criticism, texts that lend themselves to the legitimation of subordination and domination.

implied author – in narrative criticism, the author of a text as reconstructed from the text itself.

implied reader – in narrative criticism, the reader presupposed by the text, who is to be envisioned as responding to the text with whatever knowledge, understanding, action, or emotion is called for.

interpretative communities – the recognition that readers are influenced, in ways conscious and unconscious, by a complex interaction among diverse and overlapping interpretative communities.

liberation criticism – a method of interpretation that originated in Latin America and is grounded in the experience of oppression as the hermeneutical lens for reading the Exodus as a story of freedom from slavery.

mimicry – a term in postcolonial criticism to describe the colonizer's desire to create a separate class from the colonized population as a recognizable "other" to function as a subject of difference that is almost the same as the colonizer, but not quite.

mood – the internal disposition of an author; whether a text expresses grief or joy.

new criticism – assumes that a given text should be studied on its own terms as an autonomous piece of art or artifact, without focusing on author's intent or the social and political conditions of the era in which the literary work was written.

new documentary hypothesis – the identification of Deuteronomy (D) as an independent work, which eventually led to the theory of four literary sources in the following chronological order: J (Yahwist), E (Elohist), D (Deuteronomy), and P (Priestly).

old documentary hypothesis – the identification of two (an Elohist and a Yahwist) or three (two Elohists and a Yahwist) sources in the Pentateuch based, for the most part, on the study of Genesis.

patriarchy – a social construction based on androcentrism that is often institutionalized as a social-political system that favors the subjugation or oppression of women.

phenomenology – a term in genre criticism to describe a situation in which two texts are similar because of parallel developments in otherwise diverse cultural or social settings.

poetics – traditionally has meant the theory and making of poetry, but the term is also used to describe the theory of literary discourse in general.

point of view – in literary analysis, the norms, values, and general worldview that govern the way a character looks at things and renders judgments on them.

postcolonial criticism – a group of reading strategies either embedded in the text or in the history of interpretation that examines the economic, cultural, and political relations of domination and subordination between nations, races, and cultures with histories of colonial and neocolonial rule.

postcolonial theory – the epistemology, ethics, and politics that addresses matters of identity, gender, race and ethnicity used against a colonized people in service of the colonizer's interests.

postmodern – a form of interpretation that is suspicious or distrusts single explanations of texts that claim rational grounding and objective truth.

reader-centered – emphasizes the social and cultural location of readers as decisive for interpreting biblical texts.

redaction criticism – focuses on the stages, processes, and intention whereby the written sources were combined with each other through editing to give the final form of the text.

repetition of episodes – a criterion in source criticism for recognizing two separate authors sometimes referred to as doublets.

rhetorical criticism – focuses on the structural patterns and literary motifs that accentuate the unique features of individual texts as a complement to form criticism, with its focus on the similarity between texts.

round characters – in literary analysis, characters who exhibit inconsistent traits and a sometimes unpredictable point of view; such characters serve as potentially realistic options for reader empathy; cf. "flat characters."

setting – the life setting (*Sitz im Leben*) in which the text was composed, such as a public liturgy or a private devotional setting.

social institutions – fixed phases of social life, such as kinship, politics, economics, and religion.

social location – the description of any person (e.g., a reader of a narrative, an interpreter of Exodus, an author of Exodus, or a character in a narrative) in terms of features that would be shared with some, but not all, other people (race, gender, age, nationality, social class, etc.).

sociology – the study of human beings in groups, in one's own society; cf. "anthropology."

source criticism – focuses on identifying the earlier written sources of which the present text is comprised, and, if possible, discerning the date and original historical context of each composition.

spatial form devices – literary features in texts that interrupt the usual narrative flow of time with a alternative structure that focuses more on setting (space) and characters.

static characters – in literary analysis, characters whose traits and point of view remain constant throughout the narrative; cf. "dynamic characters."

stereotyping – a term in postcolonial criticism that describes the colonizer's racist stereotypes of the colonized to justify conquest and rule.

story – in literary criticism, the "content" component of narrative (e.g., the events, characters, and setting that make up the plot); cf. "discourse."

structuralism – the application of structural linguistics to the interpretation of biblical texts, in which meaning does not arise from the study of isolated words, but from the recognition of a network of relations and contrasts within a textual language system.

supplementary hypothesis – the interpretation of the literary growth of the Pentateuch as arising from one source that undergoes later additions (supplementations).

sympathy – in literary analysis, the phenomenon by which a reader feels favorably disposed toward a character in the narrative; cf. "antipathy."

synchronic – a linguistic term that indicates the study of language as it exists at a given time. A synchronic reading of Exodus would focus on the text in its present form.

target text – the particular text under study in genre criticism.

text-centered – a method of literary interpretation in which attention is focused "in" the text itself rather than on a reconstructed human author, editor, or historical events "behind" the text.

tradition-historical criticism – the study of the history of oral traditions from their earliest development to their present written form.

traits – in literary analysis, persistent personal qualities that describe a character in a narrative.

womanist criticism – a variety of ideological criticism that seeks to interpret texts from the perspective of African American women.

Name Index

Abbot, H. P., 53
Abelard, 158
Ackerman, J., 221
Advani, R., 195
Ahmad, A., 201
Albertz, R., 73
Alter, R., 18, 32, 86, 96, 116
Alves, R., 136
Amit, Y., 53
Anderson, J. C., 190
Andinach, P., 162
Andrew, M. E., 91
Andrew of St. Victor, 14
Anthias, F., 219
Aquinas, T., 158
Arceo, Don S. Méndez, 135
Aristotle, 22, 133
Ashcroft, B., 199
Assmann, H., 135, 136, 137
Astruc, J., 101
Augustine, 14, 43
Auerbach, E., 17
Ayala, F. Guaman Poma de., 134

Bakhtin, M., 8, 16, 21, 22, 45
Bäntsch, B., 119
Barry, P., 53
Barstad, H. M., 227
Barton, J., 96, 99, 129
Barth, K., 132

Baskin, J. R., 185
Bass, D. C., 190
Beebee, T. O., 94
Bellis, A. Ogden., 184, 190
Ben-Amos, D., 94
Ben Zvi, E., 61, 94
Berlin, A., 53
Berquist, J. L., 204, 211, 213, 214, 215, 229
Bhabba, H., 11, 194, 195, 197, 198, 199,
    200, 201, 202, 211, 214, 215, 218, 232
Bingemer, M. C., 142
Bird, P., 171, 190
Blenkinsopp, J., 225, 228
Blum, E., 67, 68, 109, 110, 114, 120, 123, 124
Boecker, H. J., 76
Boer, R., 201, 204, 207, 232
Boff, Leonardo., 143, 146
Bowker, J., 56
Brekelmans, J. C., 106
Brener, A., 190
Brett, M. G., 204, 232
Brettler, M., 46, 50
Brichto, H. C., 26
Brueggemann, W., 105, 223
Boorer, S., 9, 67, 69, 70, 100, 106, 107, 129
Buber, M., 138
Burns, R., 169, 170, 191

Callaway, J. A., 226
Calvin, J., 14, 56

Camara, Dom H., 135
Card, C., 221
Carlos, Fray., 138
Carr, D., 67, 117
Carroll, R., 53, 227
Castro, Fidel., 154
Césaire, A., 194
Chamorro, G., 145
Chai, P., 204
Childs, B. S., 11, 25, 43, 44, 85, 112, 116,
    119, 122, 123, 127, 129
Chow, R., 202
Chrysostom, 14
Cicero, 22
Clements, R. E., 100, 129
Clifford, R. J., 88
Clines, D. J. A., 191
Coats, G. W., 111
Cody, A., 70
Collins, J. J., 223
Collins, P H., 177, 178, 190
Cone, J., 141
Croatto, S., 145, 146, 161, 162
Cross, F. M., 106, 114
Crüsemann, F., 91
Culler, J., 53

Davies, C., 216
Davies, J. A., 53
Davies, P. R., 211
Day, P. L., 162, 190
Deist, F., 216
DelPlato, J., 203
Derrida, J., 15, 19, 20, 21, 194
Dever, W. G., 209
De Wette, W. M. L., 101
Dick, M. B., 79
Dirlik, A., 202
Dobbs-Alsopp, F. W., 32
Donaldson, L., 165, 190, 202, 204
Dostoevsky, F., 21
Dozeman T. B., 11, 47, 89, 119, 120, 121,
    12, 124, 127, 129

Dube, M. W., 190, 204, 226, 232
Duff, D., 94

Eagleton, T., 194
Eichhorn, J. G., 101
Eliade, M., 65
Emerson, c., 53
Ehrlich, C., 94
Eissfeldt, O., 102
Eskenazi, T., 190
Exum, C., 174, 175, 177, 187, 190, 191, 219

Fanon, F., 194
Fetterley, J., 168
Fewell, D. N., 21, 53
Finkelstein, I., 83
Fish, S., 19
Fleming, D., 81
Fohrer, G., 102
Fokkelman, J. P., 21, 53
Foucault, M., 194
Frankena, R., 74
Frei, H., 56
Frei, P., 211
Fretheim, T. E., 11, 22, 25, 26, 41, 42
Fitzmeyer, J. A., 75
Frerichs, E. S., 209
Frye, N., 17
Fuchs, E., 174, 175, 177, 191
Fuss, W., 106

Gabler, J. P., xi
Garber, F., 59
Gebara, I., 142
Geller, S., 29, 30, 31
George, A. R., 79
Gerome, L. J., 203
Gertz, J., 117
Gilman, S., 203
Gordon, P., 221
Görg, M., 88
Gottwald. N., 139, 152, 162, 209, 210
Grabbe, L., 70

Graf, K. H., 100
Green, B., 22, 53
Greenberg, M., 84
Greenstein, E., 27, 53
Greimas, A. J., 18
Gressmann, H., 67, 103
Griffiths, G., 199
Grimm, Brothers (J. and W.), 57
Guevara, Ernesto (Che)., 154
Gunkel, H., 14, 57, 58, 59, 67, 103, 107
Gunn, D., 21, 53
Gutiérrez, G., 135, 136, 137, 143

Hackett, J., 190
Hallo, W. W., 94
Han, J. H., 204
Harper, W. R., 93
Hauge, M. R., 26, 27
Hayes, J. H., 94, 100, 129
Hempfer, K. W., 59
Herder, J. G., 14
Herion, G. A., 223
Hernández, E. L., 144, 145
Herodotus, 69
Hidalgo, Fr. M., 134
Higginbotham, C. R., 80
Hobbes, T., 100
Holmgren, F., 42
Homer, 14
Horsley, R. A., 162, 211
Houtman, c., 11
Hugh of St. Victor, 14
Hupfeld, H., 100
Hurowitz, V. A., 78
Hyatt, J. P., 111, 115, 129

Iq′, Wuqub′(José Angel Zapeta), 145
Ilgen, C., 100
Irrarázabal, D., 145

Jacoby, R., 195
James, C. R., 194
Jenks, A. W., 105

Jeremias, J., 88
Jerome, 14
Jiménez, Luz., 145
Jobling, D., 162, 201, 216
Johnstone, W., 70
Josephus, 14
Judah Halevi, 14

Kabbani, R., 203
Kim, U. Y., 204, 232
Kipling, R., 198
Knierim, R., 96, 129
Knoppers, G. N., 72
Kratz, R. G., 91
Krishnaswamy, R., 202
Kwok, P. L., 204, 232

Lacan, J., 194
Las Casas, Fray B. de., 133, 134
Laffey, A. L., 182, 190
Langston, S. M., 231
Leder, A. C., 54
Lee, A. C. C., 204
Lesko, L. H., 209
Levenson, J. D., 147, 148, 223
Levinson, B. M., 72, 77
Lévi-Strauss, C., 18
Lewis, B., 84
Lewis, R., 202, 203, 232
Liss, H., 54
Lloyd, A. B., 215
Lohfink, N., 91, 106
Long, E., 203
Longley, C., 231
Longnecker, R. N., 56
Loomba, A., 195, 221, 232
Lowth, R., 14
Luther, M., 14

Macaulay, T., 199, 201
Malinowski, B., 73
Malul, M., 65
Martin, M. W., 86, 87

Marx, K., 154
Marxsen, W., 98
Mattos P. A., 141
McCarthy, D. J., 74
McClintock, A., 194, 202
McKenzie, S. L., 94
McKinlay, J. E., 204, 232
McLeod, J., 197, 232
Meliá, B., 144
Memmi, A., 194
Mendenhall, G. E., 74, 139, 152, 223
Mesters, C., 137, 162
Mettinger, T. N. D., 88
Meyers, C., 12, 170, 177, 182, 183, 187, 190, 191
Meynet, R., 53
Miles, J., 216
Mills, S., 202, 232
Miranda, José P., 136, 137
Moberly, R. W. L., 26
Mohanty, C. T., 202
Molina, Father U., 155
Montesinos, Fray A., 132
Moore, S. D., 196, 204, 205, 232
Moore-Gilbert, B., 194.197, 201, 232
Morelos, Fr. J., 135
Morgenstern, J., 102
Morson, G. S., 53
Mosala, I. J., 219
Moses Ibn Ezra, 14
Mufti, A., 202
Muilenberg, J., 17, 22, 59
Müler, H. P., 73

Narayan, U., 202
Nava, Carmina., 142
Newsom, C., 22
Nicholson, E. W., 100, 105, 106, 121, 122, 123, 124, 129
Niditch, S., 94
Nochlin, L., 204
Noth, M., 104, 107, 108, 111, 115, 119, 123, 125, 129

Olson, D., 8, 52
Origen, 14
Ortner, S., 175, 176
Otto, E., 85

Parry, B., 201
Parpola, S., 90
Parsons, T., 180
Patrick, D., 53
Paul, S. M., 76
Peltre, C., 203
Periera, N. C., 142
Perlitt, L., 106
Pfister, M., 215
Pires, J. M., 141
Pixley, J., 10, 12, 138, 139, 147, 162, 205, 214
Plaskow, J, 167, 190
Plato, 22
Polak, F., 54, 87
Pope John XXIII., 135
Pope John Paul II., 143
Pope Paul VI., 135
Pope Pius XII., 140
Prior, M., 207
Proano, Don L., 136, 144
Propp, W. H., 12, 74, 79, 84, 86, 92, 105, 112, 115, 130

Rad, G. von., 68, 103, 104, 105, 108, 130
Reichl, S., 215
Rendtorff, R., 67, 108, 109, 110, 119, 130
Reuss, E., 100
Richard of St. Victor, 14
Ricouer, P., 62
Robles, R., 144
Rosaldo, M. Z., 175
Rose, C., 216
Rosmarin, A., 94
Roth, M. T., 75, 77
Rudolph, W., 102, 105
Ruiz, Don S., 136, 144
Runions, E., 204, 233

Saadya Gaon, 14
Sakenfeld, K. D., 167, 191, 204
Said, E., 11, 193, 194, 195, 196, 197, 199, 202, 226, 232
Santa Ana, J. de., 135
Sarna, N., 91
Saussure, F. de, 18
Schaper, J., 211
Schleiermacher, F., xi
Schimd, H. H., 107
Schmid, K., 67, 117, 129
Schniedewind, W., 71
Schwantes, M., 139
Schwartz, R. M., 230
Scult, A., 53
Segovia, F. F., 196, 204, 205, 208, 232, 233
Setel, D. O'Donnel., 182, 191
Seuss, Pablo., 144
Shaul, Richard., 135
Sheppard, G. T., 162
Shohat, E., 194, 202
Siebert-Hommes, J., 54, 179, 180, 192
Simon, R., 100
Smart, N., 65
Smend, R., 102
Smith, M., 25, 33, 54, 91
Smith-Christopher, D., 204
Sobrino, Jon., 143
Sommer, B., 48, 49, 50
Sparks, K., 8, 9, 64, 70, 71, 79, 80, 82, 94
Spinoza, B., 57, 100
Spivak, G. C., 11, 194, 195, 202, 232
Sprinkle, J., 52
Stamm, J. J., 91
Stanton, E. C., 163, 190
Steck, O., 96, 99, 130
Stein, M., 215
Steinberg, N., 10, 188, 219
Sternberg, M., 17, 21
Stoler, A. L., 202, 220

Stone, K., 166, 191
Strauss, D., 57
Sugirtharajah, R. S., 195, 204, 207, 233
Sweeney, M. A., 61, 94

Talmon, Sh., 94
Tamez, Elsa., 141, 162, 165, 191
Tamayo, Juan José., 143
Tappy, R. E., 90
Taussig, M. T., 80
Thompson, S., 86
Thucydides, 69
Tiffin, H., 199
Tilly, L. A., 177
Todorov, T., 94
Toorn, K. van der., 73
Tribe, P., 22, 33, 164, 168, 169, 171, 182, 191, 192

Van Seters, J., 68, 69, 77, 97, 107, 108, 109, 110, 114, 115, 120, 122, 124, 128, 130
Vanstiphout, H. L. J., 94
Vaux, R. de., 150
Ventura, T., 142
Vigil, J. M., 143
Volz, P., 102

Walker, A., 165
Walker, C., 79
Warrior, R., 226
Washington, H. C., 221
Watanabe, K., 90
Watson, W., 53
Watts, J., 31
Weber, M., 180
Whedbee, J. W., 215, 221
Weems, R., 165, 182, 183, 191, 192, 218
Wells, B., 77
Weimar, P., 106
Weinfeld, M., 74, 90
Weiss, M., 17
Wellhausen, J. , xi, 100, 102, 103
West, G., 204

Westermann, C., 96, 130

Whitelam, K. W., 204, 233

Williams, D. S., 191

Wilson, R. R., 82

Wolff, H. W., 105, 115

Wright, D. P., 76

Yarchin, W., 57

Yee, G. A., 11, 204, 211, 227

Yegenoglu, M., 202

Young, R. J. C., 194, 232

Young, F., 56

Yuval-Davis, N., 219

Scripture Index

Hebrew Bible

Genesis–Judges 2, 108

Enneateuch (Genesis–Kings), 106, 107, 108

Hexateuch (Genesis–Joshua), 102

Pentateuch (Genesis–Deuteronomy), 4, 9, 31, 66, 67, 72, 79, 90, 95, 97, 98, 106, 107, 110, 213, 230

Tetrateuch (Genesis–Numbers), 105, 106, 107, 108, 109, 110

Genesis 1–Exodus 19, 31

Genesis–Exodus 6, 109

Genesis, 5, 67, 117

  1:1–2:4, 30

  1:1–2:3, 123

  1, 79, 80, 112

  1:4, 30

  1:10, 30

  1:12, 30

  1:18, 30

  1:20, 112

  1:21, 112

  1:25, 30

  1:28, 112, 113, 222

  1:31, 30

  2–11, 104

  2:1–3, 31, 228

  2:2–3, 158

  5, 80

7:11, 120

8:1, 113

9, 112

9:1, 112, 113

9:7, 113

9:15–16, 113

12:1–4, 5

12:1–3, 117

12:2, 222

12:7, 222

13:14–17, 5

15:5, 220

15:18–21, 224

16:1, 85

17:2, 112, 113

17:6, 112, 113

20:8, 115

20:11, 115

22:17, 115

24:10ff, 116

26:16, 117

28:14, 117

29:1ff, 116

45:10, 151

46:8–27, 112

47, 150

50:12–13, 113

50:22–23, 113

50:26, 83, 113

Exodus–Numbers, 110
Exodus
  1–18, 65, 67–72
  1:1–15:21, 5, 223
  1–14, 25, 117
  1–2, 1, 7, 10, 33–45, 66, 69, 81–7, 111–18,
    119, 148–55, 172–84, 200, 213, 214–22
  1, 82, 178
  1:1–7, 7, 146, 156
  1:1–5, 81, 111, 112, 113, 114
  1:1, 111, 115, 150, 173
  1:6–8, 82
  1:6, 111, 114, 115, 116, 118
  1:7, 51, 111, 112, 113, 114, 118, 151, 220, 222
  1:8–2:10, 174
  1:8–14, 7, 149
  1:8–13, 151
  1:8–12, 111, 112, 114, 115, 116
  1:8–10, 173
  1:8–9, 115
  1:8, 111, 112
  1:9–22, 83
  1:9–10, 216
  1:9, 111, 112
  1:10–12, 112
  1:10–11, 112, 114
  1:10, 112, 151
  1:11, 111, 112, 222
  1:12, 111, 112, 115, 217
  1:13–14, 111, 112, 113, 114, 118, 217
  1:14, 151
  1:15–2:10, 7
  1:15–22, 111, 112, 114, 115, 118, 149, 220
  1:15–21, 33, 114, 115
  1:15–16, 173
  1:15, 178, 217
  1:17, 115
  1:18, 218
  1:19, 218
  1:20, 111, 112
  1:21, 34, 38, 39, 115, 155
  1:22–2:22, 34, 35, 37, 37, 40, 42, 44
  1:22–2:10, 35, 45

1:22, 28, 34, 35, 36, 39, 114, 115, 116, 218,
  220
2–5, 6
2, 33, 34, 42, 44, 173, 181, 221
2:1–23a, 111, 114
2:1–22, 114, 116
2:1–15, 85
2:1–10, 25, 116, 153, 179, 218
2:1–2, 36, 220
2:1, 33, 34
2:2–10, 37
2:2–4, 36
2:2, 34, 116, 179
2:3–9, 220
2:3, 34, 36, 169
2:4, 34, 179
2:5–10, 36
2:5, 34, 36, 179
2:6–10, 36
2:6, 37
2:7, 34, 35, 36
2:8, 34, 35
2:9–10, 36
2:9, 34, 221
2:10, 34, 35, 36, 37, 40, 116, 117
2:11–25, 42
2:11–22, 7, 117
2:11–15, 35, 116
2:11–15a, 35, 45, 116
2:11–12, 36
2:11, 37, 39, 41, 116
2:12, 36, 37, 38, 41, 43
2:13–14, 37
2:13, 41
2:14–15, 43
2:14, 36, 37, 40
2:15b-22, 35, 45
2:15–17, 169
2:15, 36, 37, 38, 39, 41
2:16–22, 35, 86
2:16–20, 34
2:16–17, 36
2:16, 34, 36, 178

2:17, 36, 38, 41, 87

2:18, 178, 180

2:19, 36, 37, 39, 41, 87

2:20, 34, 36

2:21–22, 85

2:22, 34, 36, 37, 39, 172

2:23–25, 7, 34, 87, 109

2:23bc–25, 111, 112, 113, 114, 118

2:23a, 116, 118

2:23bc, 113

2:25, 41, 155

3–4, 6

3, 25

3:1, 113, 180

3:6, 115

3:7, 41

3:8, 41, 148, 224

3:9, 41

3:11, 87

3:12, 45

3:17, 148

4:19, 116

4:22–23, 27

4:23, 28

4:24–26, 26, 171, 172

4:31, 41

5–12, 6

5:2, 28

5:21, 41

6:2–8, 113

6:2, 114

6:4–5, 113

6:6, 41

6:9–11, 41

6:20, 179

7–12, 26, 219

7–10, 5

7:14–24, 26

7:16, 223

7:17, 41

7:19, 27

7:25, 41

8:6, 26

9:15, 41

10:5, 26

10:15, 26

11–12, 5, 25

11:6, 148

12, 171

12:2, 120

12:12, 41

12:13, 26, 41

12:21–32, 26

12:29–32, 27

12:29, 28, 41

12:38, 146, 156

13–15, 26

13, 5, 6

13:1, 28

13:3–16, 105, 106

13:3, 148

13:4, 148

13:11–16, 28

13:15, 29

14–15, 45

14, 5, 6, 25, 26

14:8, 148

14:11–12, 41

14:13, 41

14:26–29, 26

14:28, 26

14:30, 41

15, 5, 14, 25, 32, 33, 169

15:1–18, 169

15:1–12, 25

15:1–6, 32

15:1, 32

15:2, 41

15:5, 26, 32

15:7–11, 32

15:12–18, 32

15:10, 26, 32

15:13–18, 25

15:16, 33

15:17, 33

15:20–21, 169, 170

Exodus (*cont.*)

15:22–40:38, 5

15:22–27, 6

15:22, 45

16–40, 25

16–18, 45

16, 6, 25, 29, 30, 31, 80

16:1–35, 169

16:1, 45, 120, 148

16:4, 30

16:19–20, 30

16:22–26, 31

16:22, 31

16:27–29, 30

16:32–36, 30

17:1–7, 6, 169

17:1, 45

17:1a*ba*, 120

17:3, 148

17:7, 45

17:8–12, 226

17:8, 45

18, 6

18:21, 115

19–40, 48

19–24, 6, 65, 67, 72–78, 119, 129, 223

19–20, 1, 7, 10, 45–53, 66, 73, 87–93,
    118–29, 156–9, 184–9, 213, 222–31

19, 10, 47, 50, 75, 88, 89, 129, 186

19:1–8, 7, 47

19:1–8a, 46, 47

19:2–11, 120

19:1–2a, 118, 120, 129

19:1, 45, 48, 121, 156

19:2b–3a, 120, 128

19:2a, 121

19:2b, 119

19:3–6, 106

19:3–4, 75

19:3, 51

19:3a, 48, 119, 122, 125

19:3b–8, 119, 120, 121, 122, 124, 129

19:3b–6a, 105

19:3b–5b*c*, 120, 124

19:3b–4a, 122

19:3ba, 48

19:3bb–6, 48

19:4–6, 224

19:4–5, 121

19:4a, 121, 122

19:5–6, 75

19:5b*b*–6a, 120, 121

19:5, 49, 75, 156

19:5a, 121

19:5b*b*, 121

19:6, 121

19:6a, 122

19:6b–8a, 120, 124

19:7, 47, 88, 121

19:7a*a*, 48

19:7a*b*, 48

19:7b, 48

19:8, 88, 157

19:8a, 48, 121

19:8b–19, 46

19:8b–9a, 120, 124

19:9–25, 123, 125, 128

19:9–19, 7, 120

19:9, 51, 72, 119, 125

19:9a, 49, 121, 125, 126, 128

19:10–19, 122

19:10–15, 125, 184

19:10–13a, 119, 125, 126, 128

19:10–11, 119, 126, 127, 185

19:10a*b*–11a, 120

19:10, 119, 127, 186

19:11–13a, 119

19:11, 125, 127

19:11b, 120, 127

19:12–13, 125, 126

19:12–13a, 127, 128

19:12a*a*, 120, 127

19:12a*b*–13, 120

19:13b–15a, 120

19:13b–14, 119

19:13b, 51, 119, 125, 126, 127, 128

19:14–15, 119, 125, 126, 127, 128

19:14, 125, 186

19:15, 119, 185, 186

19:15b, 120

19:16–17, 119

19:16, 126

19:16a*a*, 119, 120, 125, 126, 127

19:16a, 49

19:16a*bb*, 125, 126

19:16a*b*-17, 119, 120, 125, 128

16:16b, 49, 126

19:17, 125, 126

19:18, 51, 119, 120, 125, 126, 127

19:19, 119, 120, 124, 125, 126, 128

19:20–20:20, 7

19:20–25, 46, 119, 120, 125, 126, 127, 128

19:20, 119, 125, 127

19:21–25, 125

19:21, 119, 125

19:23, 125

19:25, 119, 123

19:24, 51, 72, 125

19:25, 125

Exodus 20–Numbers 36, 31

20, 89, 92, 124, 188

20:1–17, 46, 52, 75, 120, 123, 124, 129, 186

20:1–2, 52

20:2, 148, 157

20:1ff, 122, 123

20:3–11, 52

20:3, 158

20:8–11, 25, 186

20:11, 129

20:12–17, 52

20:12, 159, 186

20:14, 186

20:17, 187

20:18–26, 120

20:18–23, 129

20:18–21, 46, 122, 123, 125, 128

20:18–20, 119, 120

20:18, 115, 125, 126

20:18a, 49

20:18b, 49

20:19–21, 125

20:19, 126

20:20, 115, 126

20:21–23:33, 120

20:21, 125

20:22–23:33, 46

20:22–23:19, 52, 75

20:22–23, 122, 123, 124

20:22b, 122, 124

20:24–26, 78, 122, 129

20:24, 187

21–23, 188

21:1ff, 122

21:2–11, 158

21:20–21, 158

21:28–9, 76

22:16–17, 189

24, 50, 51, 128

24:1–2, 120

24:1, 72

24:3–8, 119, 122

24:3–4a*a*, 120

24:4a*b*-5, 120

24:5, 120

24:6, 120

24:7, 75, 120

24:8, 120

24:9–11, 72, 120

24:9, 72

24:10–11, 50, 51

24:15b–18a, 120

25–40, 7, 65, 67, 78–81

25–31, 6

25:1–7, 78

32–33, 119

32–34, 26, 27, 65, 128

32, 6

32:1, 148

32:4, 148

32:8, 148

Exodus 20–Numbers 36 (*cont.*)
  32:9–14, 105
  32:23, 148
  33:1, 148
  34, 89, 92, 119
  34:1–10, 6
  34:10–28, 26
  34:10–26, 89
  34:10, 92
  34:11–29, 6
  34:11–14, 224
  35–40, 6, 27
  40, 27
  40:1–2 7, 6
  40:34–38, 6
  40:35, 79

Leviticus, 78
  8:34, 120
  15, 185
  15:16–18, 185
  15:29–24, 185
  16:30, 120
  17–26, 77
  19:2, 121
  20:26, 121
  21:8, 121
  22:9, 121
  22:15, 121
  25:43, 112
  25:46, 112

Numbers, 67, 78, 120
  1–4, 71
  8, 71
  16, 71
  12:1–2, 41
  16:12–14, 41
  26:59, 179
  28:9–10, 158

Deuteronomy, 31, 90, 91, 102, 105, 107
  4–5, 49

4, 122
4:3, 121
4:12–13, 49
4:15, 122
4:24, 123
4:32–36, 50
4:36a, 122
4:40, 123
5, 89, 92
5:4–5, 49
5:4, 49
5:5, 49
5:6–21, 123
5:6, 123
5:23, 49
5:33, 123
6:12, 123
6:15, 123
7:1–4, 228
7:6, 121
7:8, 123
8:14, 123
10:4, 89
10:21, 121
11:7, 121
11:9, 123
11:13, 121
12–26, 77
12:1–10, 78
12:11–14, 78
13:5, 123
13:10, 123
14:2, 121
14:21, 121
15:5, 121
17:9, 71
18:1, 71
18:6–7, 71
21:5, 71
22:28–29, 189
23:23–25, 224
26:5b–9, 104
26:19, 121

28:1, 121
29:2, 121
30:18, 123
31:9–13, 31
32, 14
32:11, 121
32:47, 123
34:4–5, 224

Deuteronomistic History, 22
Former Prophets, 9, 213, 229,
   330
Joshua, 225
   1:7–8, 225
   1:7, 226
   2:18–21, 226
   3, 225
   5, 225
   5:10–11, 225
   8, 225
   8:18–19, 226
   23–24, 225
   23:3, 121
   24:19, 123

Judges
   2:8, 111, 112
   2:10, 111, 112
   5, 82
   5:1, 170
   5:4–5, 88
   11, 170
   11:34, 170
   11:37, 170

Ruth, 60
Samuel, 70
1 Samuel
   7, 71
   18:6, 170

2 Samuel 11, 159
Kings, 70

1 Kings
   4:30, 217
   5:13–14, 157
   8:13, 88
   17, 157
   19, 50
   19:12, 50

2 Kings, 105, 229
   14:14, 211
   19, 157
   25:12, 211

Chronicles, 70, 71
1 Chronicles 6:3, 179
Ezra, 151, 227
   3, 212
   4:1–4, 227
   6, 212
   6:21, 227
   9–10, 85
   9:1, 227
   9:2, 227
   9:9, 228
   9:11, 228
   9:12, 228

Nehemiah, 151, 227
   5:1, 212
   5:2–5, 212
   13:1–3, 85

Esther, 22
Job, 32
   1–2, 42, 22
   3–41, 22

Psalms, 32, 58, 59
   1, 225
   8, 59
   18:8–16, 127
   22, 59
   100, 64

Proverbs, 32
Song of Songs, 32
Isaiah
  4:28, 229
  40ff, 121
  41:17–20, 228
  43:14–21, 228
  49:9–12, 228
  61:6, 121

Jeremiah
  31:4, 170
  32:42–44, 228
  39:10, 211

Lamentations, 32, 60
Ezekiel, 71
  11:14–19, 228
  36:8–12, 228
  36:12, 228
  44, 71

Hosea, 92, 93
  4:2, 93
Jonah, 22
Micah, 161
  1:3–4, 88
Nahum
  1:2, 88
  1:3–5, 127

Habakkuk
  3:3–15, 88, 127
Sirach 34:24–27, 133

New Testament
John 18:10–11, 43
Acts 7:23–29, 41, 42
Hebrews 11, 43
  11:24–27, 42

Rabbinic Literature
b. Ber. 11b, 91

Hellenistic Jewish Literature
Josephus, Ant. 2.345–346, 14
Josephus, Ant 4.302–303, 14
Josephus, Ant. 7.305, 14

Greek Literature
Iliad, 14
Odyssey, 14

Ancient Near Eastern Literature
Aramaic Inscription Sefire 1, pt. 4, 75
Autobiography of Kurigalzu, 71
Agum-kakrime Inscription, 71
Bentresh Stela, 71
Code of Hammurabi, 75, 76, 77
  117, 76
  250–51, 76
Cruciform Monument of Manistusu, 71
Enuma Elish, 80
Famine Stela, 71
Gilgamesh and the Land of the Living,
  86
Sargon Birth Legend, 84
Sin of Sargon, 71
Sinuhe, 83